Teaching Music in American Society

Successful professional music teachers must not only be knowledgeable in conducting and performing, but also be socially and culturally aware of students, issues, and events that affect their classrooms. This book provides a comprehensive overview of social and cultural themes directly related to music education, teacher training, and successful teacher characteristics. New topics in the second edition include the impact of Race to the Top, social justice, bullying, alternative schools, the influence of Common Core Standards, and the effects of teacher and school assessments. All topics and material are research-based to provide a foundation and current perspective on each issue.

Steven N. Kelly is a Professor of Music Education in the College of Music at The Florida State University.

Teaching Music in American Society

A Social and Cultural Understanding
of Music Education

Second Edition

Steven N. Kelly

Routledge
Taylor & Francis Group

NEW YORK AND LONDON

Second edition published 2016
by Routledge
711 Third Avenue, New York, NY 10017

and by Routledge
2 Park Square, Milton Park, Abingdon, Oxon, OX14 4RN

Routledge is an imprint of the Taylor & Francis Group, an informa business

© 2011 Taylor & Francis

First edition published by Routledge 2009

Library of Congress Cataloging-in-Publication Data
A catalog record for this book has been requested

ISBN: 978-1-138-92141-2 (hbk)
ISBN: 978-1-138-92144-3 (pbk)
ISBN: 978-1-315-68638-7 (ebk)

Typeset in Goudy
by Apex CoVantage, LLC

MIX
Paper from
responsible sources
FSC® C014174
www.fsc.org

Printed and bound in the United States of America by Sheridan Books, Inc. (a Sheridan Group Company).

Contents

Preface   viii

Acknowledgments   xi

About the Author   xii

1 A Sociological Perspective   1

A Rationale for Sociological Understanding   *1*

Sociology and Education   *3*

Sociology and Music Education   *5*

Sociological Basics   *6*

   Society   6

   Cultures   8

   Multicultural Education   9

Enculturation and Socialization   *10*

   Enculturation and Schools   11

Summary   *12*

Key Items   *13*

Questions for Consideration   *14*

Web Resources   *14*

2 Theoretical Foundations   15

Fundamental Sociological Theories   *15*

   Functionalist Theory   17

   Conflict Theory   18

   Interaction Theory   19

   Objectivism   21

Sociological Theories and Music Education   *22*

Summary   *25*

Key Items   *26*

Questions for Consideration   *26*

Web Resources   *27*

3 The Purposes of Education   28

Public Perceptions, Public Agendas   *29*

Defining "Education"   *30*

The General Purposes of Education in the United States   *32*

   Status Attainment   32

Political Purposes of Education   33
Social Purposes of Education   34
Economic Purposes of Education   35
Music Education's Role in the Purposes of American Education   36
Challenges to Music's Contributions   37
Education and Schooling Instructional Concept Models   38
Music Education's Relation to Schooling and Education   39
High-Stakes Testing and the Changing Role of Education   41
Summary   42
Key Items   43
Questions for Consideration   43
Web Resources   44

4   Music Education's Role in Society   **45**
A Brief Overview of the Foundations Between Music and Our Society   46
Historical Foundations   46
Music's Role in Contemporary Society   51
What Is Music?   52
Why Do We Need Music?   54
Music Education's Role in Society   56
Re-Defining a Music Education Experience   57
Summary   60
Key Items   60
Questions for Consideration   60
Web Resources   61

5   Equality of Education   **62**
An Overview of Educational Models of Equality   62
Common School and Sorting Machine Models   63
Groups Affected by Inequalities   64
Family Influences   65
Gender   66
Race and Ethnicity   67
Students With Disabilities and Diverse Learners   69
Teacher Influence on the Equality of Opportunity   70
Inequality Among Schools   71
Equality of Opportunity in Music Education   74
Family Influences   76
Gender   78
Race and Ethnicity   78
Music Students With Disabilities and Diverse Learners   79
Teacher Influence   80
Music Education Among Different Types of Schools   80
Recent Issues Concerning Educational Equality   82
Summary   84
Key Items   84
Questions for Consideration   85
Web Resources   85

6   **Social Components of Music Learning**   86

Principle Learning Theories   86
   Basic Learning Theory Groups   88
   Jean Piaget: Theory of Cognitive Development   89
   Lev Vygotsky: Sociocultural Theory of Learning   90
   Jerome Bruner: Spiral Curriculum   91
   Benjamin Bloom: Taxonomy of Learning   92
   Erik Erikson: Psychosocial Theory of Development   94
   Howard Gardner: Theory of Multiple Intelligences   96
Intelligence and Musical Ability, Preference, and Taste   97
Summary   100
Key Items   100
Questions for Consideration   101
Web Resources   101

7   **Social Characteristics of Effective Teachers**   102

Student Characteristics   103
Motivating Students to Learn   105
Characteristics of Effective Music Teachers   108
Developing Effective Teacher Characteristics   112
Classroom Characteristics   113
   Classroom Environments   113
   Classroom Organization and Management   115
Summary   116
Key Items   117
Questions for Consideration   117
Web Resources   117

8   **The Teaching Profession**   118

Teaching and Society   118
Teaching as a Profession   120
Challenges to the Teaching Profession   124
Teacher Certification Issues   126
Teacher Accountability   128
Teacher Salaries   129
Working Conditions   131
Common Legal Issues   132
The Rewards of Teaching   135
Summary   137
Key Items   138
Questions for Consideration   138
Web Resources   138

References   141
Index   159

Preface

The purpose of the second edition of *Teaching Music in American Society: A Social and Cultural Understanding of Music Education* is the same as the first edition: to explore social problems and classroom realities encountered by music education teachers in public schools. My ultimate goal is help future and current educators become more aware of the social components of teaching music in American society. My own bias is my belief that teaching involves more than the subject matter of creating and performing music. Teaching music involves an awareness and understanding of how society and cultures interact with schools and individual classrooms. I have encountered few teachers who did not love the act of teaching and making music, but I have met many who are unaware of how politics, policy, parents, business and religious leaders, cultural norms, socioeconomics, gender, and race influence students, schools, expectations, and who, what, and how we teach. It is my desire that this book is a beginning of that awareness and offers some advice as to how to cope with these challenges.

Teaching Music in American Society applies philosophical, social, cultural, and theoretical issues to musical classroom and rehearsal situations encountered daily in a culturally and musically diverse society. The text embraces the basic sociological tenet that everything humans know and are able to do is learned through interactions with other humans and our environment. Its basic hypothesis is that schools are miniature pluralistic societies, reflecting the cultural diversity of the communities they serve. Schools are therefore primary socialization agents, with teachers responsible for knowing and transmitting cultural expectations, knowledge, and skills necessary for students to be successful in these communities. Learning the role of being a music teacher, as well as how music interrelates with the total school environment and the surrounding community, is essential for all teachers to learn in order to function effectively in the education profession.

For whom I am writing . . . .

The second edition of *Teaching Music in American Society* is again written for prospective undergraduate and graduate students, experienced teachers, and other professionals who interact with music students of all levels and abilities. Undergraduate students will be exposed to the diversity of human, educational, and musical interactions they will encounter as professional educators. Graduate students and other experienced teachers seeking to become either supervisors of music student teachers, or future university music teacher educators, will become more aware of the realities, issues, and interactions that preservice teachers need to know in preparing to teach.

Our country is so culturally and musically diverse that I intentionally kept the scope of this project limited to research pertaining to schools in the United States. One difficulty in writing a sociologically based text is that many issues are subjective, controversial, and constantly changing. Consequently, I have tried to present topics from as broad a perspective as I considered reliably possible. This text is not designed to be a philosophical, multicultural, or social theory book. While these important topics are presented in a limited scope, many fine books already in existence present this material in greater detail and should be read by those seeking more in-depth information.

How This Book Is Organized

Teaching Music in American Society is not a method book. Rather it is a music teacher-training book about the realities and issues involved with teaching. A major emphasis is understanding that music curricula and learning are not isolated from the general school curriculum and must relate to the total school environment. General education issues are consequently initially presented for each topic, followed by their relationship to music education.

The book begins by introducing basic sociological information and terminology in Chapter 1, and then proceeds into philosophical and theoretical foundations relating to the prospective music teacher in Chapter 2. An important addition to this edition is the web resources presented at the conclusion of each chapter. While cited references within each chapter are available at the end of the book, the web resources are intended to provide additional information which the reader may pursue. Chapter 3 presents the basic purposes of education in American society and music's contribution and connection to these aims. The effects of political issues and policies such as the government initiatives of No Child Left Behind and Race to the Top, the effects of state mandated testing on music education, and the curricular issues of STEM/STEAM are among the topics discussed. Illustrating the connection of music in society to music in our schools is the intent of Chapter 4. A brief historical overview is presented, illustrating how school music experiences have historically reflected the values and needs of the United States society. An important point is made that teachers need to be aware of the multi-musical characteristics of their students and making school music relative to out-of-school music experiences. Chapter 5 presents the inequalities in all of education, including music education. Differences in schools through various layers of discrimination, stereotypes, subjective assessments, and school choice are discussed. The issues relating to social justice, the achievement gap, and the Common Core Initiative are included in this edition. Chapters 6 and 7 address the social components in developing effective teacher characteristics. Major learning theories, society's perceptions of music ability and its effect on musical preference are presented. Specific characteristics such as eye contact, dress, pacing, and student interactions are presented. The book concludes with a chapter on professionalism. The basics of becoming a teacher are presented, from initial certification to salary structures, and legal concerns are addressed. Included in this edition are changes in certification, tenure, and social media, and challenges to labeling teaching as a profession are discussed.

New To This Edition

- Updated material including information on changes in cultural diversity and the new *National Core Arts Standards*, social justice, and bullying;
- Theoretical information concerning Objectivism and Ayn Rand, and updated materials on music education theory;
- An expansion of information affecting the teacher profession, including student and teacher assessments and evaluations, school reform, changes in tenure and salary structures, certification issues, and challenges to the concept of teaching as a profession;

- Updates on curricular issues such as STEM and STEAM, the Common Core Initiative, and music's relationship with the achievement gap;
- An expansion of legal issues relating to the use of social media and the private lives of teachers;
- Web Resources at the end of each chapter to supplement the cited references.

To the Reader

I hope you will find that the book offers few definitive answers. The science of sociology offers few absolute answers due to the ever-changing nature of human thought and behavior. One intention is to stimulate the reader to realize issues that may not have yet been thoroughly considered. Many inexperienced preservice students often believe teaching music involves only conducting performing ensembles with little consideration of the multitude of responsibilities and issues involved in functioning as a professional educator. It is hoped that you will critically and creatively develop your own means for addressing and coping with the material presented, thus adapting information to your unique perspectives and classroom situations. Throughout each chapter questions are presented which have no correct or incorrect answer, yet they deserve consideration in a broad cultural context since few preservice teachers know what type of social and musical culture in which they will be teaching.

This book has a companion website, www.routledge.com/cw/kelly, that serves both teachers and students. Professors will see a set of PowerPoint slides to assist in classroom instruction.

Students should find these slides helpful as chapter outlines for review and assessment. There will be additional links to other sites for further study and information. Students will also find quizzes that will help them quickly test their knowledge, with answers graded and provided online.

Acknowledgments

As I stated before, no single person is never completely responsible for a scholarly project. This second edition is no exception. I am deeply indebted to the scholars and researchers whose studies provided the basis for this book. I am astonished by the diversity of interests, methods, findings, and overall quality. I personally know many of the researchers mentioned in this edition, and I am proud to have them as friends and colleagues. Thank you to everyone that used the first edition of this text in your classrooms. Your feedback was motivational and vital in the development of the second edition. I am also extremely grateful to the professionals at Routledge Press for their encouragement in the development of the edition. Thank you to the reviewers whose critiques and analysis improved the scope, detail, and accuracy of this edition. Frankly, this book would not have been possible without the many fine undergraduate and graduate students in the College of Music at Florida State University. I am so grateful to the outstanding music educators in the state of Florida. Thank you so much for your perspectives and critical feedback regarding K-12 music education realities. I also cannot thank my colleagues in music education at Florida State University enough for their encouragement and input into this material. I will be forever indebted to my wife Beth and daughter Marin for their understanding and patience for when I could not always be there during this process. Finally, thanks again to Cliff Madsen for his continued support and guidance. On a daily basis, Cliff demonstrates that when you understand the social world, everything else comes easy.

Steven N. Kelly

About the Author

Steven N. Kelly is a professor of music education in the College of Music at Florida State University in Tallahassee, Florida. He received his bachelor's and master's degrees in music from the University of North Carolina at Greensboro and his Ph.D. in music education from the University of Kansas.

Prior to his appointment at FSU, Dr. Kelly taught in the Virginia public schools, and on the faculties at Brevard College (NC) and the University of Nebraska at Omaha. He is an active clinician, adjudicator, consultant, and guest conductor across the United States. Dr. Kelly has served on the review board for the *Journal of Research on Music Education* and as a guest reviewer for the *Psychology of Music* journal and the *International Journal of Music Education*. He currently serves on the editorial boards of the *Journal of Band Research*, *Research Perspectives in Music Education*, the *Desert Skies Symposium on Research in Music Education*, and the *Suncoast Music Education Research Symposium*. He is also the Editor-in-Chief of the *Florida Music Director*.

At FSU, Dr. Kelly teaches undergraduate and graduate music education classes, conducts the University Concert Band, and coordinates in the music education internship program. He has been a recipient of the University Undergraduate Teaching Award and is the director of the FSU Summer Music Camps, one of the country's oldest and largest summer music camps.

Chapter 1

A Sociological Perspective

The school is a social world because human beings live in it.

—Willard Waller

Preparing to become a music teacher requires command of a diversity of knowledge and skills. As a teacher or future teacher, you may ask, "How does sociology contribute to becoming a teacher?" Many music education students want to study methodology, applied music, or other courses they perceive as providing information that is more practical and applicable to rehearsals and classrooms. However, sociology is practical and directly applicable to music education. An awareness of basic sociological material enables teachers to understand different perspectives and experiences encountered every day involving parents, administrators, community members, race, political agendas, religion, and gender. While it is important to learn "tricks of the trade," a sociological perspective helps music teachers recognize the array of experiences affecting inter-relationships between students, school environments, communities, and home environments (Kelly, 2002). A basic awareness of sociological information enables teachers to better discriminate between facts and bias within the complex world of teaching. Thus, a sociological understanding becomes very practical and applicable to the success of all music teachers.

Chapter 1 presents basic sociological information and concepts and their applications to music education. Much of the material will be re-introduced in different contexts throughout other chapters. The initial material begins with ideas concerning foundations, roles, benefits, and relationships, reflecting what teachers may believe. The material provides a rationale for understanding sociological issues within classrooms from which a philosophical perspective can be formed. A teacher's philosophical beliefs affect instruction with regards to how and what information is presented, and who will be the recipient.

A Rationale for Sociological Understanding

A sociological analysis provides educators with a deeper understanding and awareness of the purposes of education and interactions within educational settings. These benefits contribute to informed decision-making and change in education institutions. Examining social foundations enables teachers to have a broader perspective about themselves, the world in which they teach, and how they "fit" into that world. Many social factors influence what, who, and how individuals teach, and subsequently affect their philosophical beliefs. For example, many music education majors initially view themselves as performers, not educators (Froehlich, 2007; Froehlich & L'Roy, 1985; L'Roy, 1983; Madsen & Kelly; 2002; Roberts, 1991, 2000). How might this initial perspective influence the teaching philosophy? Can music educators effectively be both performers and teachers?

Furthermore, teachers increasingly need an awareness of how political and social issues interrelate with education. For instance, what effects do policies such as Race to the Top, the Individuals with Disabilities Education Act, or state mandated testing have on music participation and curricular development? How do social issues such as school violence, teenage pregnancy, or religious freedom influence school music curricula and the role music may have in addressing these issues? Other cultural information influencing teachers includes knowledge of a student's age, socioeconomic status, students with disabilities, and the effects of immigration on education institutions. These issues not only influence the delivery of instruction, but they also affect non-instructional aspects of teaching (Woodford, 2005). For example, policies such as student dress codes or fees for participating in music can have immediate effects on how students react to or the extent they participate in music classes.

The need for teachers to have a sociological understanding is supported in most state departments of education across the United States. Because sociology deals with human interactions, it is not surprising that many state teacher certification exams contain a strong sociological emphasis (Henry, 2005; Spring, 2006). Teacher certification exams often require knowledge of cultural diversity, such as the effects of racial or gender expectations, the influence of stereotypes on learning, and the effects of socioeconomic status on school dropout rates, graduation rates, ethics, and academic achievement (Spring, 2006). Classroom issues such as creating a safe learning environment, motivating students, and assessing student performance influenced by social factors are included on teacher certification exams. Additional topics frequently include social factors that may influence a teacher's attitude, appropriate dress, and proper student/teacher interactions (Lortie, 2002; Waller, 1965).

In demonstrating a broader national prospective, the need for understanding sociological aspects is reflected in both the original *National Standards for Arts Education* (Music Educators National Conference, 1994) and the newly revised standards known as the *National Core Arts Standards* (National Association for Music Education, 2014a). The original music standards reflected social issues by stating, "those who construct arts curricula should attend to issues of ethnicity, national custom, tradition, religion, and gender. . ." (p. 14). Content Standard Nine specifically called for an "understanding of music in relation to history and culture" (pp. 29, 45, 63). The newly revised standards, introduced in 2014, are based on national common core curricula. In promoting the arts as connectors, the new standards state, "Understanding artwork provides insights into individuals' own and others' cultures and societies, while also providing opportunities to access, express, and integrate meaning across a variety of content areas" (National Association for Music Educators, 2014b, p. 10). Furthermore, the new standards acknowledge the social aspects of music education by stating in Anchor Standards #11 that music education should be able to "relate artistic ideas and works with societal, cultural, and historical context to deepen understanding" (National Association for Music Educators, 2014a).

Fundamentally, sociology in music education investigates the interaction of music, people, and culture in an educational setting. The interactions of musical and social components can be seen throughout history. The foundations may be discovered in ancient Greek civilizations, where the social aspects of education gained through developing the mind, body, and soul were valued and considered essential (Grout & Palisca, 1988). Music instruction was included in the original seven liberal arts, in which knowledge was essential for an individual to be educated in order to contribute to society. Music was cherished for its ability to develop the human soul and prepare citizens for higher good within society. Plato (1995) believed music helped to civilize humans and was essential to their success in society. Plato placed great importance on music training to maintain critical cultural values and develop moral behavior. More recently, U.S. President Ronald Regan stated, "The arts and humanities teach us who we are and what we can be. They lie at the very core of the culture of which we are a part" (Mark, 2008, p. 72.).

An increased interest in a sociological awareness within music education was cited by McCarthy (2002), who stated that a better understanding and application of sociological skills in education, and specifically music education, has arisen. McCarthy provided five reasons for this growth: (1) the move by schools toward a more inclusive curriculum reflecting students' social, cultural, and musical diversity; (2) an increasing awareness of music education's relationship to music overall reflecting the diversity of cultural values and meanings within society; (3) a growing theoretical perspective of how social constructivism and critical theory are providing new insight into music teaching and learning; (4) an increasing tolerance for diversity and the perceived need for incorporating a variety of perspectives beyond traditional processes and products involved in music instruction; and (5) a growing commitment within the music education research community to advance a sociocultural agenda to better understand social and cultural influences in music education settings.

Despite calls for a sociological awareness, music teachers may not realize the influence of this perspective on teaching. Few music teacher-training programs offer insight into social issues that affect teachers such as: (a) students with different cultural backgrounds than their own, (b) music students listen to and participate in that symbolizes cultural values different from the teacher's, and (c) student, community, and educational attitudes, dress, and languages considered normal by students, yet very unfamiliar to the teacher. Much of what is taught and experienced in music classrooms reflects the community the school serves, its holidays, celebrations and ceremonies, moral and civic values, and cultural understandings. These social interactions can affect educational expectations and experiences. By including a sociological perspective in teacher-training curricula, music teachers can better implement instructional and musical approaches that interrelate school music with community music experiences, thus making the study of music more meaningful and relevant.

Sociological Benefits for Music Educators

- Explain the relationship of music to different cultural points of view
- Make better connections from music in the schools to music in society
- Help teachers understand and relate to students from different backgrounds
- Assist teachers in developing instructional and rehearsal strategies to become more effective
- Help to connect school music programs to school and community expectations
- Help teachers better understand their role in educational processes

---

Sociology and Education

It is difficult to imagine a society without some system of education. Not surprisingly, sociologists are interested in school environments and individuals within education. They are especially concerned with the interactions of people within educational structures (Ballantine & Spade, 2012). Teaching is a human behavior involving human interactions that affect education experiences in many venues, including music classrooms, hallways, during lunch period, at school football games or dances, and on school busses. Understanding the diversity of interactions requires knowledge of cultural variance, including an awareness of a student's family background, musical interests, expectations, and previous music experiences.

Sociologists are less interested in how to teach than in what and why we teach. They are interested in learning experiences of all types because of education's relation to life in general. An understanding of social and cultural influences has always been important to understanding teaching and learning processes (McCarthy, 2002). Education is frequently considered a formal process involving individuals attending structured schools. However, education is a constantly evolving entity reflecting the perpetual change in society. Subsequently, education is a lifelong process achieved formally and informally in many different manners and places. Our education begins the day we are born and ends the day we die. Experiences between birth and death make

Photo Figure 1 World music ensembles are excellent opportunities for teaching cultural norms.

each of us as diverse as the situations and people we encounter throughout our lives. Because of our diversity, humans have the capacity to learn all the time in any setting and in multiple manners (Gollnick & Chinn, 2002; Valsiner, 1989). Our parents, or parental figures are our first teachers, our home environment our first school. Siblings and peers are our first classmates. We learn by watching others and listening, interacting with the world around us.

Sociologists view formal education as the social institution that guides a society's transmission of knowledge to its members. From a social perspective, education may center on skill development, helping students to engage and function successfully in society. For example, as children learn roles in their social world, they also become aware of how different their world can be from other children's worlds. Education helps children confront differences and effectively cope with diverse cultural expectations such as gender roles, age, religion, geographic differences, language, and other cultural views (Gollnick & Chinn, 2002; Swift, 1976).

Globally, education is a vital part of every society, including industrial and non-industrial communities, rural and urban settings, and literate and non-literate cultures. Behaviors involved in teaching and learning are social phenomena influenced by various societal expectations. Consequently, education serves different purposes, depending on social and cultural standards and expectations. Despite this, it essentially serves the same function in all societies: transmitting a wide range of cultural knowledge and skills in order to be successful.

Sociology and Music Education

Music education also involves human interactions influenced by a variety of ever-changing cultural variables. Learning music reflects a social perspective, involving the development and interactions of cognitive, psychomotor, and affective social skills. Concepts of music instruction vary greatly in our society, as music is learned both informally and formally. While many may think learning occurs through formal lessons, our first music lessons begin informally, in home environments. As our first teachers, parents introduce us to music, and our homes are frequently our first performance stages. We learn our first musical values, including our sense of musical preference and ability, through our homes and families (Gordon, 1971; LeBlanc, 1982). These informal experiences frequently influence us to pursue (or not to pursue) music in a more traditional formal school setting.

Having a social perspective enables music educators to recognize they face the same challenges educators in other subjects confront, including:

student poverty	at-risk behaviors
immigration	budget/funding
accountability	school violence
racism	discrimination
inequality	passivity
achievement	assessment

Music educators ask the same questions as colleagues in other academic areas, including:

1. What are the implications of required testing and accountability of students and teachers?
2. What types of teachers and classroom environments provide the best learning experiences?
3. What are the effects of teacher expectancy on student achievement?
4. What effect is technology having on social development?
5. Should schools be responsible for the selection, training, and placement of individuals in society?

6. To what extent do schools have the responsibility for the socialization of students into society?
7. How can schools overcome cultural expectations and standards while providing equal educational opportunities for all students?
8. Why is there seemingly constant tension between what society expects education to accomplish and what educators deem necessary to teach?

As in education, the role of music education is perpetually changing, reflecting evolving cultural standards and expectations, including music within societies. Like general education, music education's essential purpose is to transmit a variety of cultural skills and knowledge for individuals to be successful in society. Perhaps music education's primary goal is to enable students to function musically in a very musically diverse world.

Sociological Basics

Teaching is a social process reflective of the most basic sociological principles. To appreciate a social perspective, it is important for teachers to begin with basic sociological principles and foundations. The study of sociology may be defined as the systematic study of human behavior: its origins, organization, institutions, and the general development of human society (Macionis, 1997). As part of the social sciences (like music education), sociology is an interdisciplinary field containing aspects of other studies, such as psychology, biology, anthropology, history, and philosophy. These fields contribute to a better understanding of human beings by seeking answers to questions involving the development and influences of topics such as self-identity, self-concept, racial interactions, religion, socioeconomic status, marriage and divorce, the media and technology, gender, ethnicity, education, and musical experiences (Valsiner, 1989).

Sociologists study human interactions in wherever they are found, including neighborhood streets, workplaces, prisons, shopping malls, homes, churches, recreational activities, concert halls, and schools (Macionis, 1997). They are curious about how social order is derived from ordinary human behaviors. This curiosity presents a great challenge, as human beings are very unpredictable due to their constantly changing behavior, which is influenced by a variety of factors. For example, the time of day can influence students' attention and behavior, which may be different in the morning than just before lunch. Behavior may change again just after lunch and again minutes before the end of the school day. Therefore, learning can be influenced by different periods during the day, and activities within that day. Other social factors influencing students include the amount of sleep received, whether they have practiced or completed homework, if they have had breakfast, if they have had a disagreement with a friend or other teacher, or the excitement of an upcoming sport or musical activity.

Sociology attempts to address the challenge of multiple influences by approaching human behavior from a broad context. It tries to explain human societies less by universal rules than by contextual parameters highlighted by the uniqueness of each society and its cultures (Macionis, 1997; Valsiner, 1989). The considerable variety of unique social and cultural characteristics affecting humans has made sociology an inexact science with few absolute answers. As a result, sociological researchers look for trends and objective generalizations while gathering data from a large variety of sources. Sociological research contributes a wealth of information to educators by providing a broad base of information, both instructional and non-instructional, from which decisions can be made.

Society

Sociologists study human societies. A society may be defined as a community of people having common traditions, behaviors, values, beliefs, and interests (Macionis, 1997). The word *common* is key. Every society is complex in that it is comprised of many different institutions, structures, and individuals, yet commonalities exist (Fulcher & Scott, 2011). The United States is a society that, while reflecting diverse characteristics, is comprised of common traits. Our commonalities include a love of democracy and freedom, an understanding of governmental structure and laws, a belief in capitalism and the opportunity to make oneself financially better, and an understanding of American symbols such as the flag, the "Pledge of Allegiance," and music such as *America* ("*My Country, 'Tis of Thee*"), *America the Beautiful*, and the *Star-Spangled Banner*. These symbols represent common characteristics many individuals consider to be "American." However, symbols of America can be interpreted very differently. Individuals from Miami may perceive symbols of America differently than citizens in Kansas City or Seattle. Consequently, traditional symbols are not the sole representations of "American," as many diverse groups of people comprise our society.

Cultural variability in our country fascinates sociologists, yet challenges many individuals in our society. Sociologists state that there is no universally accepted definition of a society (Macionis, 1997). A society is as unique and diverse as its members, and this characteristic is very apparent in American society. For example: "What is an American?" There are many responses to this question but no absolute resolution. Historically, the United States has been comprised of native Indians, but also of immigrants from around the world. Individuals came and assimilated their traditions, behaviors, dress, language, and other life aspects to live their, or someone else's, concept of what it is to be a citizen of the United States. One unified culture was viewed as necessary for national strength. This approach is known as the melting pot, where individuals would meld together their behaviors, values, attitudes, even language, music, and dress to form a single view of America (Goodenough, 1987).

However, around the late 1950s, a change in how many individuals viewed our society began to occur. The growing number of different groups altered how our society was viewed (Gollnick & Chinn, 2002; Goodenough, 1987). Though immigrants continued to come to the United States, they desired to maintain their native traditions, values, dress, language, and music. Still, these individuals wanted to be United States citizens. They valued the American lifestyle, its characteristics and behaviors; however, they wanted to maintain their native customs. This concept became known as a pluralistic society (Goodenough, 1987). Pluralism recognizes the acceptance of differences among various groups, while incorporating traditional American values. Our pluralistic society embraced diversity, even expanding characteristic behaviors and values considered "American" by many individuals in our country (Banks & Banks, 2001; Oakes & Lipton, 1999).

However, embracing diversity has not always been met with approval. For example, according to the U.S. Census (2013), international migration to the United States is projected to surpass natural increase sometime between 2027 and 2038. This demographic shift is resulting in the end of the historical role of White Americans in our society as other racial populations increase (Ross & Bell, 2014). According to the Council on Foreign Relations (Lee, 2013), this perceived loss of power has caused great concern and unrest in many parts of the country. In 2014, one school district in Minnesota attempted to redraw school zoning lines to create more diversity with the district's schools. The redistricting bid resulted in tremendous anger and resentment among the community, forcing many school board members to resign (Toppo & Overberg, 2014).

Characteristics of society's diversity will become even more evident in school classrooms as students not only reflect differences in race, gender, ethnicity, social class, language, ability, religion, and age, but also in attitudes, motivation, desire, self-concept and self-esteem, physical, cognitive, and emotional development, and music interests. For example, Dillon (2006) reported that the number of students of color in U.S. public schools grew from 22 to 43 percent in the 30-year period from 1973 to 2004. A more recent report indicated that schools in the United States were preparing to teach up to 50,000 new migrant students 2014 alone (Lee, 2014). With so many different groups of people, resulting in a variety of views of what constitutes United States society, debates over values, ideas, language, behaviors, dress, and even music has caused great divisions among our population. These debates have had a tremendous effect on American education, because our society views schools as the principle source of training in the American way of life (Banks, 2001). Thus, a dichotomy and debate exists between pluralism and the melting pot that often places schools in the middle regarding which societal concept of the United States should be taught and which groups within our country should be represented.

Cultures

Diversity usually centers on different groups of people who share some form of behavior, trait, or thought. Different groups of people within a society are known as cultures (Erickson, 2001) and may be thought of as subsets of society. A culture is a group of people who share a way of life (Gollnick & Chinn, 2002). Everyone has a culture and is a member of at least one cultural group. A person's culture determines how the individual perceives, believes, evaluates, and behaves in society, explaining why all societies have diverse thinking and behaviors. Thus, a sociological view of life, including music, is that "beauty is in the eyes of the beholder." What is considered "good" can only be evaluated to the extent that the properties are familiar and understood in that particular culture. Subsequently, culture determines many of our behaviors and expectations.

Like societies, cultures include common characteristics, such as beliefs, values, behavior, and materials possessions that interact with each other. Cultures are created by humans and are not genetic; rather they are learned through interactions with other members of that culture (Macionis, 1997). Through culture, humans learn language, accepted ways of dressing, religion, family life, economics, and even music. Since humans create their culture, these characteristics are constantly changing to reflect shifting ideas and needs. Thus, culture contributes to the pluralistic concept of our society through its diverse interactions (Gollnick & Chinn, 2002).

Our society is comprised of numerous cultural groups, some similar, some very different, and yet all contributing to a concept of America. An individual is often a member of multiple cultural groups. For example, an individual can be an African-American Catholic adolescent, with a middle class socioeconomic status, playing tuba in the public school band. Each group represents has its own norms, which are cultural expectations and attitudes, including behaviors, dress, language, jargon, beliefs, and musical interests. Norms help determine how people within a culture think and behave (Fulcher & Scott, 2011). Individuals adapt to their desired cultural norms in order to be accepted and successful with others within that culture. Behavioral norms are actions or events known as folkways (Macionis, 1997). Folkways are behaviors not required, but expected by a group. In music, orchestra members standing as the concertmaster or conductor walks onto stage is an example of a folkway. As people move from one cultural group to another, an individual's norms change to reflect the expected characteristics. For example, college students respond differently to a lecture style class than to an ensemble, and differently to a private lesson setting than with friends at the end of the day. Thus, humans are accepted and can successfully function within multiple cultural settings. As we move from one culture to another, we become proficient at behaving, speaking, and thinking differently to meet the expected norms of each group. People who do not meet cultural norms are considered abnormal and countercultural (Banks & Banks, 2001; Valsiner, 1989). They have difficulty interacting with members of an existing culture and must search for a group that shares their cultural ideals.

Societies are usually comprised of many cultures and are therefore known as multicultural societies (Goodenough, 1987). A multicultural society is a society encompassing many various ways of life that blend (and sometimes clash) together in ordinary life. Due to the diversity of its population, the United States (and most other countries as well) is considered a multicultural society (Goodenough, 1987). Multiculturalism is not confined to differences based on race, ethnicity, or geographic location. Like any culture, multiculturalism includes race and ethnicity, but also other common factors such as interests, abilities, traditions, language, religion, family life, occupation, economics, and music. Consequently, multiculturalism is a normal human experience, and indeed is represented in every American classroom. It is an indicator that individuals are different because they participate in more than one culture. Thus, all humans are in a sense multicultural. Multiculturalism is present in music. Different cultural groups have different musical expectations and standards. Sounds defined by one group as "good" music may be considered noise by another. Consequently, our society is not only multicultural; we are multi-musical by way of our multiculturalism.

Sociological Basics

Sociology—the systematic study of human behavior through the study of human societies

Society—a community of people having common traditions, behaviors, values, beliefs, and interests; no universal definition of society as they are as unique as are their members

Melting pot society—individuals meld together behaviors, values, attitudes, even language, music, and dress to form a single view of America

Pluralistic society—acceptance of differences among various groups, while incorporating traditional American values as well; embraces diversity

Culture—a group of people who share a way of life, including beliefs, traditions, values, and possessions

- Subset of society
- Constantly changing
- Created by humans
- Music is an important part of any culture

Multicultural society—a society encompassing many various ways of life that blend (and sometimes clash) together in ordinary life

---

Multicultural Education

The multicultural nature of our society is reflected in the population diversity of schools and the development of multicultural education. Multicultural education is a strategy that uses students' cultural backgrounds as the basis for classroom instruction and curriculum (Banks & Banks, 2001). Achieving a true multicultural experience in American schools is no easy task. A multicultural educational approach supports and extends the concepts of culture, diversity, and equality of opportunity for all students. Incorporating diversity throughout the learning process is a requirement. Multicultural education seeks to achieve four primary goals: (a) build acceptance of other cultures, (b) eliminate discrimination, (c) teach different cultural perspectives, and (d) teach students to view their world from differing frames of references (Gollnick & Chin, 2002).

Multicultural education extends to music teaching and opportunities for students. In a 21st-century music class, every teacher will encounter multiculturalism that differs to some extent from their own cultural background (McKoy, 2013). Considering the role of students' cultures will result in a more culturally responsive classroom (Abril, 2013). Traditionally, teaching music has been based on a Western European art music perspective. As American society has taken on a more pluralistic composition, social attitudes have sought to include a diversity of cultural perspectives that include ethnicity, race, gender, religion, sexual orientation, special needs, and age, among other cultural groups (Campbell, 2004; Fung, 1995; Kelly & VanWeelden, 2004). New attitudes toward a more diversified music experience have led to the inclusion of rock and roll ensembles, world music ensembles, steel drum bands, gospel choirs, music by women composers, mariachi bands, midi ensembles, and fiddle groups, among the innovative curricula being offered to students (Bakan, 2012; Kelly & VanWeelden, 2004). It is not surprising that some research suggests that more diverse school music curricula help students connect school music to music outside of the classroom (Hoffman, 2012; Kelly-McHale, 2013; Kuntz, 2011; Shaw, 2012).

Multicultural education, including multicultural music education, is controversial in our country. Many citizens believe schools should teach only "American" values, frequently reflecting a narrow personal perception of these ideals (Banks & Banks, 2001; Olsen, 1997). One national poll found that 90 percent of American adults endorsed the teaching of diversity in public schools (National Conference for Community and Justice, 1994). Yet social discrimination toward all cultural groups and in many forms appears to remain an issue of debate (National Conference for Community and Justice, 2008, 2011). For example, the issues of social justice for all groups of people and the elimination of acts of bullying have increased in prominence within American schools.

Frequently, the debate surrounding multicultural education is affected by: (a) concern that non-citizens do not pay taxes to support schools, and (b) the fact that many individuals do not speak English, which is the primary language used in this country (Cartledge, 1996; Olsen, 1997). Critics (reflecting a more melting pot perspective) argue schools should focus on American values, traditions, and behaviors, which they believe best represent our country (Oakes & Lipton, 1999). Berstein (1971) argued that schools should present specific curricular activities specifically designed for different social classes in order to prepare students for predetermined roles in society. Proponents (reflecting a more pluralistic perspective) contend multicultural education creates a broader experience for all students, which contributes to a better understanding and tolerance of other cultures both within the United States and outside our country. Multicultural education proponents seek to teach students to view the world from differing cultural frames of reference with the goal of helping students from all cultural backgrounds succeed (Banks, 2001; Oakes & Lipton, 1999).

Enculturation and Socialization

For teachers, the sociological perspective offers a unique approach toward teaching and learning. A basic tenet of sociological research is that everything humans know and are able to do is learned through observing and interacting with other humans (Macionis, 1997; Valsiner, 1989). Interactions provide knowledge regarding language, feelings, attitudes, biological functions, and even perceptions of music ability. Unlike other living species whose behavior is biologically set, sociologists believe humans rely on social experiences to learn the nuances of their culture in order to survive (Geertz, 1965; Hughes, Sharrock, & Martin, 2003). Thus, knowledge and skills are not genetically determined, but learned through the process of enculturation.

Enculturation is the process of acquiring characteristics of a particular culture (Oakes & Lipton, 1999). It is society's way of teaching necessary skills and behaviors. Through enculturation, individuals become aware of the cultural norms and expectations that impact their lives. Socialization is the part of the enculturation process that involves learning how to be members of a society. Socialization is the process of experiences and interactions through which individuals learn patterns of accepted behaviors and attitudes from other humans (Hughes, Sharrock, & Martin, 2003; Macionis, 1997). It is the act of learning social norms. Stated otherwise, socialization is

Photo Figure 2 Socialization is an important component of classroom experiences.

learning expectations associated with a particular culture in order to be accepted and function effectively. Through socialization, we learn our expected roles, such as mother, father, teacher, banker, student, child, and musician. Indeed, one study demonstrated how students can be enculturated into the expectations of musicians, thus teaching individuals how to behave and think within a musical culture (Vat-Chromy, 2010).

Because cultural characteristics are learned through interactions, enculturation and socialization begin at birth. Due to socialization, humans become products of their culture (Hughes, Sharrock, & Martin, 2003). Our initial "teachers" or socialization agents include parents, parental figures, siblings, teachers, peers, and the media. These "teachers" demonstrate acceptable forms of behavior, dress, religion, and values according to the patterns and symbols of the culture in which we are raised. Through interactions, we learn cultural norms. Community holidays and celebrations, languages, food, arts, socioeconomics, and religious views are all reflected in schools. Sharing customs and behaviors binds like-minded people together as an identifiable group. As our environmental conditions, information, and resources change, we adapt to the situation.

Enculturation and Schools

In Western societies, next to the family, schools are often considered the most important socializing agents (Ballantine, 2001; Feinberg & Soltis, 1998). According to the National Center for Education Statistics (2014a), there were approximately 98,817 elementary and secondary public schools housing 49.5 million students in the United States during the 2011–2012 school year. The number of enrolled students in public schools is expected to increase to over 52 million by 2024. Within all schools, students are enculturated into the society and culture expectations.

With such large numbers, it is easy to understand that schools in the United States are microcosms of many different cultural groups (Feinberg & Soltis, 1998).

Schools are not autonomous, isolated entities free to chart their own course. Public schools reflect the larger society they serve and are subject to community influences from citizens, businesses, government, traditions, and laws. A reciprocal relationship exists between schools and community groups where each influences and reflects the socialization of the other. Students bring community knowledge, views, norms, and folkways into schools. In turn, students return to their communities with new knowledge and experiences from schools.

Learning through Sociology

Basic tenet of sociology—that everything humans know and are able to do is learned through observing and interacting with other humans

Enculturation—the process of teaching and acquiring characteristics of a particular culture

Socialization—the process of experiences and interactions through which individuals learn patterns of accepted behaviors and attitudes from other humans; part of enculturation

- How humans learn expected cultural expectations
- Begins at birth
- Through socialization, humans become products of their culture
- In Western societies, next to the family, schools are often considered the most important socializing agents

---

Can the impact of schools overcome the influence of students' enculturation? An individual's cultural background can have tremendous effect on school success (Gollnick & Chinn, 2002; Oakes & Lipton, 1999). Society's expectations of what and how information should be taught do not always align with what schools perceive as the needs of the group and individual student. Because of the variety of cultural diversity in United States, its schools are inherently pluralistic. Due to vast cultural differences, universal rules frequently fail. Diverse students learn in multiple ways, at varying times, and have assorted expectations, behaviors, attitudes, and values, resulting in potentials unique to each individual. Students from diverse populations come from a variety of home environments with different views of what is defined as education and success. Hence, schools often find it difficult to effectively manage the multitude of ideas considered part of a normal education. Consequently, schools frequently have difficulty in overcoming cultural backgrounds such as family influences, religious beliefs, political views, and gender stereotypes. For example, diversity issues relating to genres of religious music performed during holidays are a challenge in music education.

Summary

Sociologists recognize that music is an important part of any culture (Etzkorn, 1989). An awareness of sociological basics and creating a social perspective can help music teachers understand how communal forces influence classrooms (Froehlich, 2007). Because of social diversity, it is easy to understand that every school is a miniature society comprised of many different cultures all having commonalities reflective of the school in general. Cultural diversity requires successful teachers to understand the power of enculturation and socialization. Much of what and how students learn is a result of human interactions in the hallways, lunchrooms, on school buses, and during school-sponsored activities such as dances or football games. Interactions from these processes lead to an awareness that humans learn by actively doing. Due to differences in students, there are no absolute answers and no universal rules to what teaching approach works best. A social perspective helps teachers realize that schools reflect a broad student diversity, requiring a pluralistic teaching approach rather than a single education model. This perspective demands multiple teaching approaches due to the variety of learning styles.

Teachers in the 21st century must be aware of ever-changing societal forces within school dynamics. The American society is constantly changing. Trends demonstrate that we are becoming more diverse ethnically, racially, socioeconomically, religiously, and musically. We tend to live in different cities than our parents, come from more single parent families, and work more hours each week than other industrial countries (National Center for Education Statistics, 1999). All of these factors contribute to an increasingly diverse and constantly changing society. Schools in the United States are required to manage an increasingly diverse student population reflective of population trends across America. An implication of classroom diversity is that, for many students, schools will be their only exposure to cultures different from their own. This multicultural experience helps break down stereotypes and foster acceptance of different lifestyles.

Music and music education are certainly affected by cultural diversity. Our multicultural, multi-musical society is saturated with music representing all facets of society and its diverse cultures. Music students bring this diversity to schools. Music classes reflect the diversity of the general school student population (Kelly & Heath, in press). Music is often viewed as a primary tool in bringing different factions of society together, and yet is so individually valued. Music is a symbol of our different cultures that serves to unify us as a group, while still preserving our individuality. Simply stated, we participate in music in ways as diverse as our cultural norms require. A sociological perspective can provide music teachers with a broader cultural knowledge base to enhance the presentation of skills and information, thus making music experienced in schools more relevant to music outside of schools.

Being aware of the wide variety of sociological factors influencing society is a challenge for teachers. Understanding their role as socialization agents requires teachers to view student behaviors from different cultural perspectives. The noted anthropologist Clifford Geertz (1965) said to understand human diversity we must understand the diversity of human cultures. Thus, from a social perspective, it is important that effective teachers learn the culture of their students, the schools, and the community the school serves. Teachers must recognize that each student brings a different background of social, musical, and academic experiences into every class. To meet this demand, effective music teachers understand their role in an active, dynamic classroom full of social interactions, each a learning experience in itself.

Key Items

Sociology	Culture	Society
Melting Pot Society	Pluralistic Society	Norms
Socialization	Folkway	Enculturation
Multiculturalism	Education	Diversity
Social Justice	National Core Arts Standards	

Questions for Consideration

1. Why have sociological issues become more prevalent in schools? How can music curricula be more reflective of cultural and musical diversity?
2. According to the sociological perspective, everything that humans know is learned. If music is not a genetic endowment, why is it part of every known culture?
3. How do schools resemble a multicultural society? What characteristics of music classes may define them as a culture with a school society?
4. If society embraces the concept of cultural diversity, should schools expect every student to achieve at the same level?
5. To what extent should music teachers impose their cultural values on the music their students listen to and participate in?
6. How do educators handle situations where the values learned in school conflict with values learned at home?
7. Do schools reflect the product of society or does society reflect the product of schools?

Web Resources

Changing Population Demographics

U.S. Census Bureau: http://www.census.gov/

National Core Arts Standards

http://www.nationalartsstandards.org/
http://www.nationalartsstandards.org/sites/default/files/NCCAS%20%20Conceptual%20
Framework_2.pdf

Social Justice & Bullying

National Conference for Community and Justice: http://www.nccj.org/

Sociology

American Sociological Association: http://www.asanet.org/about/sociology.cfm
International Sociological Association:
http://www.isa-sociology.org/

Chapter 2

Theoretical Foundations

What cannot be understood cannot be managed intelligently.

—John Dewey

To begin understanding how educational processes work or do not work, it is helpful to have knowledge of social theories. Theories provide frameworks, which help explain and predict patterns and practices between individuals and social systems (Ballantine & Spade, 2012). Theories help us to think differently and are the basis for many cultural perspectives. There are many different perspectives regarding education and music education in our society. Varying social perspectives represent all facets, from individuals to businesses, from academia to religion. It becomes easy to understand how the diversity of views can overwhelm any teacher. Yet in a pluralistic society, teachers are expected to effectively work within a multitude of ideas, each grounded in a philosophical basis.

Chapter 2 will present basic philosophical and theoretical views associated with sociology and how these perspectives influence music education. Understanding differing perspectives helps music teachers expand their social awareness of students' backgrounds. An awareness of different perspectives further provides music teachers with an understanding of what different cultural groups want education to accomplish. Frequently, society and education are at odds due to differences in perspectives. For example, different perspectives provide a variety of answers to some of the most basic education questions, related to:

1. What should be taught in a school curriculum?
2. Who should have access to information?
3. Should all students have equal access to information?
4. How should this information be used?

Fundamental Sociological Theories

A theory is a belief or perspective explaining how and why specific facts, actions, behaviors, and attitudes are related (Ballantine, 2001; Hughes, Sharrock, & Martin, 2003). Theories are structured explanations or arguments applied to real-life situations (Ballantine & Spade, 2012) and help educators understand not only words, but also contexts. Subsequently, theories are useful in examining and coping with educational issues and problems by serving as a basis for educational approaches.

Theories are neither true nor false; they are credible based on logic and information that has some degree of validity. Furthermore, no theoretical perspective has an absolute answer. Consequently, more than a single theory is usually required to understand educational phenomena. The value of theories is in their use in organizing and understanding events and behaviors. Theoretical social perspectives are frequently based on historical comparisons, political authority, economic issues, laws, religious beliefs, and the extent of growth in individualism, as well as societal ethics and values. Theoretical ideas have contributed to the debate regarding the role of music in American society, and the place and stature of music in our schools. An understanding of different theoretical perspectives enables music teachers to become more aware of the complexity of teaching, and music's place and function in schools.

Theories often lead to the formation of theoretical paradigms, which are basic images or ideas of society that guide sociological thinking (Ballantine, 2001). Theories and paradigms define and help conceptualize beliefs, behaviors, and relationships. Early social theories were ground in myths or religious beliefs (Fulcher & Scott, 2011). Because many early societies were viewed as a collection of individuals, early social theories had an individualistic perspective. To understand an individual, only the individual was considered, without regard to events and others around that person. However, as the world became more industrialized, resulting in more people living in smaller areas (e.g., cities/towns), the influence of others, along with environmental surroundings, became more evident (Fulcher & Scott, 2011). Consequently, to understand an individual, it was helpful to understand the group and events in which that individual participated.

Over time, there have been many competing theories attempting to explain the roles, functions, and relationships of education and society. Historically, three principle theoretical views have formed the basis of many sociological attempts to explain the relation of modern society to education: functionalist theory, conflict theory, and interaction theory. However, in the mid-1900s, a new philosophical theory, objectivism, was introduced and quickly became influential in American society. Because each theory views society and education differently, they often form the foundation of educational debates, thought, and methodology in our country.

Photo Figure 3 Teaching and performing music can involve multiple theoretical perspectives.

Functionalist Theory

Functionalist theory, or functionalism, assumes society and its institutions are comprised of interdependent parts, working together in predictable ways to enable society to function efficiently (Durkheim, 1893; Hughes, Sharrock, & Martin, 2003). All parts of society complement each other through shared values that create a social balance (Ballantine & Spade, 2012). The well-being of the group is the center of focus. By working together, and assuming an equilibrium model, each part promotes solidarity and stability in society. Our lives are influenced by the resulting social structure or stable patterns of behavior. Every societal component plays an important unique role and yet is interdependent with the others. Thus, all parts of a society are interrelated, integrated, and necessary for society to work or function properly (Durkheim, 1893).

The French sociologist Emile Durkheim (1858–1917) advocated functionalism. Durkheim was the first to promote science as a basis for making sociological decisions (Fulcher & Scott, 2011; Hughes, Sharrock, & Martin, 2003). Rooted in the French political and social upheaval from 1870 to 1895, Durkheim (1893) believed changes in social institutions and quality of life occurred through political reform and scientific advances. He was the first to suggest that to understand an individual one must not look at the individual, but rather at the society or group in which that individual is a member. Durkheim believed society was greater than its individuals and that society's components had tremendous power to shape and influence human behavior. He believed individualism and self-interest threatened the cohesion of social institutions and undermined the authoritative nature of group life. As a result, individual autonomy came at the expense of the good of the collective forces. Consequently, Durkheim was an advocate of moral education, due to his concern with increasing individualism. He advocated that society's different components comprise a collective conscience that affects individual thought and behavior for the good of the whole.

Functionalist Theory Basics

- Society is comprised of interdependent parts
- Society is greater than its individuals and has tremendous power to shape and influence human behavior
- Education's primary function is to socialize and integrate individuals into a larger society
- Schools should transmit knowledge and behaviors necessary to maintain order in society, including moral knowledge and attitudes
- Society and education have a reciprocal relationship reflecting each other's needs

---

Education is a vital component in the functionalist process. Functionalism assumes the more educated an individual, the more productive and valuable to society that person becomes. Functionalists perceive schools as the most efficient institution for controlling the values and behaviors needed to benefit society. Creating a moral code is vital to establishing common values. Functionalists view schools as vital tools that enculturate students into the larger economic, political, and social institutions that sustain society's continuation and survival (Ballantine, 2001). As such, functionalism uses education to facilitate stability as individuals work together to create a functioning social system (Ballantine & Spade, 2012).

Durkheim (1893: 28) stated, "Education is the influence exercised by adult generations on those that are not yet ready for social life." Hence, a primary function of schools is to transmit knowledge and behaviors necessary to maintain order in society. For society to prosper it must train members to be productive and perform required roles. Another function of schools is to develop, sort, and select individuals by ability to fill hierarchical positions. Through schooling, individuals discover what they do best in order to contribute to society. As society's attitudes and values evolve, education is modified to reflect altering cultural norms and needs. Consequently, society and education have a reciprocal relationship reflecting each other's needs.

Conflict Theory

Conflict theory is characterized by a dichotomy between conflict and domination, and oppression. Centering on the perceived destructive aspects of industrial capitalism, conflict theory is based on every component of society operating in concert with society's economic system (Hughes, Sharrock, & Martin, 2003). A degree of alienation and identifying power relationships are key components. In contrast to the harmonic aspects of functionalism, conflict theory assumes a constant tension due to all societal parts being created by competing interests of individuals and groups (Morrison, 1995). This belief results in an unequal distribution of status and wealth that constantly shifts among groups. Once tension becomes too strong, change occurs by force.

Conflict theory's premise is based on the writings of Karl Marx (1818–1883) and Max Weber (1861–1920). The idea of social class, where one group controls the other through alienation, is at the heart of Marx's beliefs (Marx & Engels, 1845). Conflict theory assumes a person's societal status identifies his/her position in a group or class. Class is a category of people with a specific position in the division of labor (Fulcher & Scott, 2011). Marx was concerned about the inequality between classes. He was outraged by his belief that poor social conditions resulted from exploited workers within a class system based on capitalism. He speculated how, in a society so rich, there could be so many that were so poor. This thinking led to Marx's idea of social conflict (Marx & Engels, 1845). Marx stated society contained competing groups, the "haves" and the "have-nots," who were in a constant state of class struggle and tension over the distribution of wealth and power. Through manipulation, the "haves" used their position to hold society together in a self-beneficial manner. However, conflict theory recognizes that change is inevitable and out of constant conflict, change occurs. Like Durkheim, Marx believed advances in scientific knowledge would provide opportunities for social improvement (Marx & Engels, 1845; Morrison, 1995). Still, Marx recognized social change would not come easy or quickly. Through class consciousness, workers, united in opposition to capitalism, would rise up en masse to overthrow the existing power group. The struggle for power would determine the structure and function of various organizations and the hierarchy within society.

Max Weber, a German sociologist, shared many of Marx's views regarding social conflict and widespread social alienation. He perceived an increase in the division of labor and bureaucracy, resulting in an oppressive routine, rising secularism, and an increased loss of individual freedom. However, where Marx had faith humans could change society through scientific growth, Weber was less optimistic that science could affect real change in human conditions (Weber, 1918). Weber was concerned about the dehumanization of society while believing that humans could shape society and improve human conditions. Thus, social actions would lead to better awareness, understanding, and change (Fulcher & Scott, 2011).

Conflict Theory Basics

- There is constant tension because of inequalities in society due to all societal parts being created by competing interests of individuals and groups
- Change is inevitable and out of constant conflict change occurs
- Societies differ primarily in terms of how their members think about the world
- Education has a dual character in society: used to promote meritocratic processes or as closure process to keep outsiders from obtaining access
- Schools are product-orientated and exist to serve the dominant group by providing for the social reproduction of the economic and political status quo

According to the conflict theory, schools exist to serve the dominant group by providing social reproduction of the economic and political status quo (Ballantine, 2001). Schools reproduce the attitudes and dispositions required for the continuation of the existing group in power. Accordingly, the primary purpose of schools is to teach a particular cultural status, representing the dominant social group perspective. Skills and knowledge are taught when the learner needs them and not when the curriculum mandates it. Education is product-orientated and is applied to get results and attain goals. Consequently, the existing power group uses education to maintain its dominance by determining what, when, and how information is taught in schools.

Both Marx and Weber placed a strong emphasis on values (Marx & Engels, 1845; Weber, 1918). They believed education systems perpetuate existing class structures through social reproduction of existing social characteristics and expectations. Social reproduction, the intentional reproduction of existing social status, was attained through tracking and ability grouping (thus contributing to different social classes). Leaders of the power group selected individuals who were best qualified for jobs at different levels of the social hierarchy. Consequently, the dominant group's power was maintained through controlled access to information and resources.

Interaction Theory

Unlike the functional and conflict theories that focus on group interactions, interaction theory focuses on individual interactions. Also known as constructivism, interaction theory recognizes the power of the environment to shape behavior and explains how humans can construct personalities and perceptions based on interactions with other individuals and their surroundings (Hughes, Sharrock, & Martin, 2003). Knowledge is not discovered, but created through social exchanges. Thus, human actions and thoughts are socially determined. Consequently, perceptions, thoughts, and concepts of truth become individualized and unique to the individual rather than an external source (Schwandt, 1998).

Interaction theory focuses on the development of the human self through social interactions in both school and society. The view envisions society as an ongoing process resulting in a product of everyday interactions through which the development of self is inherently a social product (Mead, 1934). Interactions enable individuals to create or construct their own perspective on how they will function in society. Social reality is not an absolute; individuals create their own unique relative meanings of the world around them based on how they want to exist within it (Berger & Luckmann, 1966). Society is a shared, constantly evolving reality constructed by its members as they interact with each other. Through this process, humans define their identities toward each other. Because humans define themselves, their perceptions of reality vary and constantly change (Cook, 1993). The use of cultural symbols (such as language or music) is important, as they help make reality unique to each person. Symbols help define and understand reality (Ballantine & Spade, 2012). The musical gestures of a conductor are examples of a "language" that is a unique symbol of an individual or culture constructed to make sense of a particular communication behavior.

Interactive theory is based on the writings of American philosopher and sociologist George Mead (1863–1931). Mead (1934) believed society was in constant change based on constant human change. His approach was known as social behaviorism. At the center of this approach was the human self, a dimension of human personality composed of an individual's self-awareness and self-image. Mead emphasized the importance of an individual's capacity to project themselves into the position of other people, to see things as others see them, and to take the role of the other. The development of an individual's self amounts to learning the role of another individual. According to Mead, the self emerges from social experiences with other humans. Human interactions result in an exchange of symbols that aid in making sense of our culture. To understand how other humans view us, we must imagine how another person may perceive us. Our actions are often guided by how others respond to and perceive us. Hence, the capacity to view ourselves through others is essential to developing, or constructing, our sense of self-image.

A colleague of Mead's, Charles Cooley (1902), expanded interactive theory by stating that, in social life, other people represent the mirror or looking glass image in which we perceive ourselves. Cooley coined the term "Looking-Glass Self" to designate the image people have of themselves based on how they believe others perceive them. Consequently, individuals act as they imagine others will act in response to their own envisioned actions. Thus, how we perceive ourselves as musical individuals depends on how we think others view our musicianship. According to Cooley, there are three dimensions to developing our self-image: (a) one's perception of how one appears to others; (b) one's perceptions of their judgment about him/her; (c) one's reactions to those perceptions. An application of the Looking-Glass Self with preservice music teachers is transitioning from a performer enculturation to a teacher persona. To construct their self-image as a teacher, they place themselves in teacher situations where interactions with students provides feedback from which the individual perceives what behaviors are necessary for being viewed as a teacher.

Interaction Theory Basics

- Recognizes the power of the environment to shape behavior and explains how humans construct personalities based on interactions with other individuals and their surroundings
- Society is in constant change based on constant human change
- Social reality is not an absolute for all individuals; individuals create their own unique relative meanings of the world around them based on how they want to exist within it
- The capacity to view ourselves through others is essential to developing our sense of self-image
- Education is based on the power of socialization to shape an individual's development of how they perceive themselves and interact with others

---

Education based on interaction theory reflects the interaction of humans. The role of schools is to create situations where interactions are common. Thus, classrooms that are student-centered are more effective than teacher-centered approaches. The power of socialization becomes evident through the ability of groups such as family members, peers, and teachers to shape an individual's development of how they perceive themselves and interact with others. Mead based many of his thoughts on the works of American education philosopher John Dewey. Like Dewey (1900), the interactive theory assumes all humans, especially children, have an active desire to learn based on a natural curiosity and motivation (Ballantine, 2001). Learning is most effective when individuals learn at their own pace, dependent on the interaction of a broad base of knowledge gained in school, connected with the "real life processes" in the world outside of school (Dewey, 1900). Previous knowledge is important, however, new knowledge gaining meaning requires an immediate awareness of the world around the individual.

A positive learning environment occurs when students are able to construct their own reality that fits their personal needs. Meaning arises from an awareness of an individual's own activities in relation to past knowledge. An individual creates a basis of new meaning from resolving conflict between past and present knowledge. Thus, the interactive theory (like Dewey) embraces teaching as a process over product approach that can enable skills and knowledge to be flexible as situations and demands change. Such flexibility empowers individuals with intelligence to create new knowledge, apply this knowledge, and adapt to changing situations.

Objectivism

Objectivism originated through the personal philosophy of Russian-born author Ayn Rand, who came to the United States in 1926. Her experiences with American society led her to believe that American democracy was the model of what a free nation could be. First expressed in Rand's fictional books *The Fountainhead* (Rand, 2005) and *Atlas Shrugged* (Rand, 1996), objectivism is a philosophy that has as its basic premise that reality is that which exists. Facts are facts independent of any consciousness and emotion. Human values and knowledge are objective and determined by reality. Emotions cannot alter facts. Realty cannot be changed, but must be dealt with (Ayn Rand Institute, 2014; Peikof, 1993).

According to Rand (1996, 2005), objectivism has three axioms: existence, consciousness, and identity. Existence is self-evident in all other knowledge and is identifiable as it is what it is. Consciousness is perceiving the existence of something specific. Existence cannot be a thought because an individual's mind cannot create reality; rather the mind is a tool to help discover, or become conscious, of what is real. Identity is action. The manner in which reality acts is caused by the object's identity. Consciousness possesses identity and must be validated.

Like interaction theory, objectivism places importance on the individual, not the group (like conflict and functionalist theories). An important tenet of objectivism is that individuals have the moral responsibility to pursue individual happiness and rational self-interest. Consequently, respect for individual rights is necessary and embodied within a laissez-faire capitalistic system free of government influences. Within this approach, government has only one responsibility and that is to protect the rights of individuals. However, objectivism acknowledges that humans are prone to making mistakes and do not always immediately understand the implications of their knowledge or actions (Ayn Rand Institute, 2014; Peikof, 1993).

The role of education, according to objectivism, is to help humans learn how to reason, how to think conceptually, and how to define, form, and apply principles. According to objectivism, all knowledge is based on perceptions. Perceptions are real. Feelings are not sources of knowledge because they are subjective. An awareness and understanding of the facts within a topic is necessary to being capable of determining a course of action. Determining a course of reason, free of emotion, faith, or authoritative guide is essential. Subsequently, individuals must think individually. Individuals must choose their actions, values, and goals and are responsible for those behaviors. Through individual thought, self-interest can be determined and lead to happiness. Thus, humans are responsible to themselves as individuals. Being responsible for yourself leads to true freedom (Ayn Rand Institute, 2014; Peikof, 1993).

Sociological Theories and Music Education

While the formal study of sociology of music education is relatively new, there have been many theories regarding the role and function of music education in American society. Many views have contained a strong social element and have extended to how music should be taught and experienced. For example, Lowell Mason was perhaps the first proponent of music being valuable to everyone and all humans having some degree of musical ability (Pemberton, 1985). Later, progressive educators led by John Dewey and James Mursell viewed music as a tool to improve an individual's quality of life (Kelly, 2012). For example, Mursell (1934, 1943, 1948) sought to connect school music to out-of-school experiences while believing music was a lifelong influential activity. This perspective was later emphasized in Vision 2020: The Housewright Symposium on Music Education (Madsen, 2000).

An early advocate of a social agenda for music education was John Mueller (1958), who was a professor of sociology at Indiana University and believed the nature of musical taste was essentially a social phenomenon. Mueller's theoretical perspective was based on aesthetics and individual standards of beauty and feeling. He believed that music was a form of human behavior influenced by social elements unique to individual cultures. According to Mueller, musical preference is not individualistic or solely confined to the influences of musical factors. Rather, taste and preference reflected norms and expectation of different social groups. Thus, music's beauty and feeling was a result of its interactions with society.

From an educational perspective, Mueller believed that education was a formal procedure for passing down information among generations. Within education, he believed the arts played an important role by teaching students about the nature of human feeling. However, Mueller (1958) believed that arts education was often unsociable because it often failed to connect human nature to musical sounds. Mueller stated, "In its extreme form, music does not adapt itself to man, but man adapts himself to music" (p. 95). Education was responsible for connecting human nature to musical sounds in a manner that students continued to participate in musical activities beyond formal schooling.

From 1958 through the 1990s, the concept of aesthetic education was the primary theoretical basis for music's position in American schools. Drawing on the works of Dewey, Mursell, David Berlyne, and Suzanne Langer, among others, Abraham Schwadron, Charles Leonhard, and Bennett Reimer became leaders for an aesthetic perspective. Aesthetic education's focus evolved to center on music's formal elements rather than any referential meaning related to the musical experience. For example, musical meaning and beauty was gleaned from the structure of a musical piece, or from the tonal elements constructed by the composer. Unique individual reactions to experiences were considered important. Consequently, a major goal of aesthetic education was for an individual to be free and able to make unique decisions and thus think for oneself.

For Schwadron (1967), musical meaning was a psychological product of orientation. Schwadron used the concept of relativism to assert that personal values in music are relative to and conditioned by cultural groups and historical periods. Bennett Reimer, however, argued that the primary purpose of music education was to develop the capacity for aesthetic knowledge through experiencing music. Music should be valued for its own sake, and its effect is unique to each individual. Reimer considered music autonomous, so extra-musical ideas should be irrelevant to the experience. Therefore, music education should place a strong emphasis on quality music with allowances for individual meaning in situations that focus on music's intrinsic ideals (Reimer, 2003).

A somewhat opposite view of the aesthetic perspective is the utilitarian position that music instruction should serve some function or use that frequently pertains to nonmusical aspects of a musical experience. The utilitarian position grew out of society's fear that education does not effectively train citizens in skills needed for current business and military situations. For music, and reflective of the functionalist theory, the general aim of the utilitarian approach is to train students through music to become capable, useful members of society. For example, music instruction can be used to teach values and other subjects such as math or science. Music is viewed as a tool to affect emotions, improve intelligence, and socialize students.

More recently, new perspectives regarding the sociological theories of education have emerged. These ideas argue that alternative approaches to education are needed due to changing educational roles. One of the most common perspectives is known as critical theory. Critical theory evolved around 1923 from German social theorists with diverse backgrounds in philosophy, social theory, and social science (Calhoun, 1995). Known as the Frankfurt School, this group perceived society, despite scientific and technological progress, as becoming dysfunctional and problematic. Ironically, as a social theory, critical theory rarely comes to any agreement. In fact, no adequate single answer can exist primarily because it is not possible to construct an agreement due to the diversity of views represented in society. Disagreement is the essence of critical theory, because it seeks to view traditional beliefs and behaviors in many different ways due to cultural diversity.

Self-analysis is important to critical theorists. The group's aim is to analyze components of society and develop new concepts of how to resolve issues in nontraditional manners. Critical theorists seek to understand the motivations that underlie human action and thought (Calhoun, 1995). Subsequently, an individual's interpretation within a situation must be taken into consideration regarding motives and goals. To mindlessly accept a situation or authority is unacceptable and leads to social inequalities. Acceptance of the status quo empowers only a small dominant

Photo Figure 4 Experiencing music for its own unique value is a focus of aesthetic theory.

group, often at the expense of other groups or individuals. If individuals expect knowledge and truth to be revealed by the various authorities and institutions of rationalism and empiricism, they abdicate or deny their personal responsibility for constituting the knowledge, truth, and values upon which they act (Regelski, 2007).

Theodor Adorno (Callaghan, 2007) was a leading proponent of critical theory relating to music. Adorno was a philosopher and sociologist interested in the place and function of music in society. A trained pianist and composer, Adorno was a member of the Frankfurt Group and rejected the concept of aesthetics as the theoretical basis for music enjoyment, referring to the view as inadequate for individual relevancy. Rather, Adorno speculated that the effect of music was determined by the listener's reaction within situational context. To Adorno, society was filled with distracters, which affected musical meaning. Distracters associated with music that resulted in inattention and standardized reactions negatively influenced the musical experience. Adorno favored classical music because it was more free of distracters so the listener could focus on matters of musical performance and the resulting individual reactions.

According to Adorno, the media contributed to artificial values in music and was considered a distracter to music. This was especially true of radio and television's influence on popular music. Adorno characterized popular music as anti-intellectual and manipulative. Consequently, popular music was perceived as anti-social and part of the manipulation of the media in influencing an individual's musical preference. Essentially, Adorno (1976) believed that whenever music was used for commercial purposes it ceased to be art music because it lost its authenticity. Adorno termed this music "consumer music." Even when serious art music was used for commercial means, it ceased to be art music and became devalued. Thus, Adorno called for music education to promote more serious classical genres of music that promote intellectualism, individual thought and behavior, and resistance to conformity.

More contemporary critical theorists in music education are concerned with teaching and curricular approaches that fail to provide stimuli or opportunities for individual thought and creativity (Regelski, 2007). Approaches that prompt students to follow the proper procedures without question are viewed as single-minded devotion. The result is a product that is irrelevant, non-transferable, and lacking in any educational value. Teaching is not a matter of right or wrong answers, or how-to methodologies. Rejection of the status quo is the goal. The act of teaching involves facilitating situations so that students are encouraged to question existing situations and structures, so the formulation of new perspectives and creations can occur. Through this process, students take ownership of new information and experiences, thus creating relevancy that transfers to out-of-school situations.

Critical theorists worry that experiencing music has become too structured and opposite to a child's natural interest in music. They reject scientific quantification of music research and methods as stifling natural process. They believe that music education, as traditionally taught, minimizes a student's ability to experience music rather than empowering the student to make musical decisions for his/her self. Simply telling students what to do or how to perform makes the music experience one-dimensional. Students need to think, to be analytical, explorative, and creative. Students need to be empowered to participate in a musical experience of their choice. Subsequently, a "true" or valid music experience can be performing music, discussing music, listening to music, thinking about music, or any behavior or idea concerning music. Only in this manner can the experience be rewarding and meaningful, thus leading to lifetime participation in music.

Among the leading contemporary critical theorists in music education are Estelle Jorgensen, David Elliott, and Thomas Regelski. Regelski, whose writings are concerned with aspects of music education practice, asserts that the practice of music is both social and politically influenced. Along with another proponent of critical theory within music education, Terry Gates,

Regelski formed the MayDay Group to promote discussion of the purposes and practices of music education. Among the issues concerning Regelski (2007) is his belief that a lack of relevancy has weakened music's position in the school curriculum. Students fail to continue their participation in music after graduating from high school because no connection to music beyond formal school environments is made. Consequently, failing to transfer school music experiences into adulthood leads to a lack of support from the general public, whose school music experience was irrelevant to any music participation outside of the formal school environment.

Estelle Jorgensen is a music philosopher who frequently takes the position of justifying music education based on social issues. Professor Jorgensen (2003) has been critical of music education's slow transformation in meeting contemporary challenges. Maintaining that commonalities among different musics are not universal, she advocates a pluralistic perspective (Jorgensen, 2006) where there is no single correct manner to participate in music. Participation can be through formal and informal means and experienced in all aspects of life. Accordingly, music education needs a diversity of perspectives that embrace common human aspects involved in music. She persists that music education fails to connect to social issues and events in which students are participating, thus becoming irrelevant.

Since the late 1990s, David Elliott's philosophy of music praxes may have become the most influential theory concerning the nature and role of music education in the United States. According to Elliott and Silverman (2014), music education should be comprised of interrelationships of music, education, and people. Unlike Bennett Reimer's assertion that music itself is the primary focus of music education, Elliott's concept of music education involves interactions with humans at the center of all experiences.

Elliott and Silverman (2014) argue that music involves both processes and products. Music is a global phenomenon that is practiced in as many diverse manners as are culturally deemed. Consequently, music education should reflect global diversity and be practiced as such. As society and cultures change, so does music and how humans interact with music. Elliott disputes the aesthetic perspective because of (1) its sole reliance on intrinsic qualities to define a quality music experience, and (2) its passive approach to music participation. According to Elliott (1995), music participation should be active, purposeful, thoughtful, and embedded within the context in which it is occurring. Therefore, to understand music requires awareness of the relationships between music and the events, people, and cultures in which music occurs. Elliott states music is an intentional human activity involving four dimensions: (a) people that do music (musicers), (b) musical doings (musicing), (c) musical something done (performances, audible music achievements), and (d) the context in which doers do what they do (performance venues, audiences). Through these dimensions Elliott emphasizes that music is a diverse human practice encompassing many different styles, activities, practices, and functions. Elliott (1995) and later Elliott and Silverman (2014) adopt and promote the concept of a praxial philosophy to explain music, not as a universal or absolute art, but rather as phenomena that is unique to individuals and cultural contexts. This position has had tremendous influence on redefining the role and purpose of contemporary music education.

Summary

Theoretical perspectives form the basis of how music education functions in our society. They help explain the forces that shape our musical world and how individuals function as musicians, teachers, and students. Students and educators often dismiss theory as being out of touch with the practical nature of classroom activities, but the opposite is actually true. Music teachers can certainly exist without a theoretical understanding. However, an awareness of theoretical perspectives helps teachers understand fundamental issues that influence teaching every day.

Consequently, music teachers with an understanding of theory are better able to adapt and apply knowledge to changing social and educational situations. Theoretical understanding provides a practical basis for much of what is done and accomplished in music class, including the following:

1. The basis for decision-making and actions,
2. A sense of direction and purpose for the music curriculum, especially in relation to the overall school curriculum,
3. A basis for consistency in process and product involving music instruction and how it relates to music throughout American society.

Many theoretical concepts regarding contemporary education reflect strong disagreement concerning the processes and products associated with education. Thus, there continues a need for further discussion regarding the relationship of music education to American society. Continued discussion and analysis can provide concepts useful in the recognition and understanding of new issues, processes, and social developments affecting music education's relationship to society as a whole.

Much debate exists within our society regarding the diversity of musical values held by different social groups. The debate is reflective of the melting pot and pluralistic deliberations and is an example of the relationship between music in society and music education in our schools. The different theoretical models associated with music are reflective of the debates within music education, debates which are necessary if music education is to grow and become more relevant to American society. Acceptance of the status quo leads to complacency, resulting in a cessation of growth and relevancy. Our approach is frequently less concerned with learning about music, and more concerned with learning through music. Debates often reflect the perspective regarding music and its interaction with society and schools. For example, what should be the role and value of music contests? Should popular music be taught within the school curriculum? To what extent should music be valued for its extrinsic qualities? Perhaps the outcome in these debates is that music education is a means to an end, that end being the practice and participation in some form of music by our students.

Key Items

Theory	Conflict Theory	Functional Theory
Interaction Theory	Objectivism	Emile Durkheim
Social Conflict	Max Weber	Karl Marx
Ayn Rand	Paradigm	Constructivism
Social Behavioralism	Looking Glass Self	Charles Cooley
George Mead	Critical Theory	Theodor Adorno
Thomas Regelski	John Mueller	Bennett Reimer
Aesthetic Education	David Elliott	Estelle Jorgensen

Questions for Consideration

1. What are the pros and cons of the functionalist, conflict, and interactive theories?
2. How might the concept of Looking-Glass Self be used to develop teacher behaviors?
3. How might the music classroom be structured so students can construct their own music experiences?
4. What are components of American society and its schools that critical theorists might reject as status quo?

5. How do children exhibit Dewey's feeling that they have a natural desire to learn? How might music educators take advantage of this perception?

6. How does the aesthetic approach to music education uniquely justify music inclusion into the school curriculum? How does the aesthetic approach differ from the utilitarian approach to music education?

7. How might Adorno's position on the commercialism of music affect the types of music experienced in schools?

8. How do the philosophies of David Elliott and Bennett Reimer reflect each other, yet differ? How does each philosophy influence how teachers teach, who they teach, and why they teach?

Web Resources

Theories

Ayn Rand Institute https://www.aynrand.org/
Frankfurt School: https://www.marxists.org/reference/archive/adorno/
MayDay Group: http://www.maydaygroup.org/

Chapter 3

The Purposes of Education

If I were not a physicist, I would probably be a musician. I often think in music. I live my daydreams in music. I see my life in terms of music.

—Albert Einstein

Why have schools? What is the purpose of education? These questions, while seemingly simple to answer, are quite complex because of our diverse society and the number of groups interested in educational processes and products. Some information and teaching approaches can be threatening to one cultural group while affirming another group's beliefs or expectations. Chapter 3 looks at the role and purposes of education in the United States and music education's relationship to those purposes. The overall premise is that music education cannot be viewed as an isolated subject within school curricula. Music education must clearly demonstrate, musically and nonmusically, how it contributes to the total education of each student.

A 2014 Gallup Poll shows that Americans value education (Gallup, 2014). Yet schools are frequently criticized regarding their role and how to implement curricula to meet different cultural constituents. For example, a Phi Delta Kappa poll in 2014 found that a majority of Americans (58 percent) believes that the curriculum in their community schools needed to change (Bushaw & Calderon, 2014). This example illustrates the challenge of presenting information to a pluralistic society as different constituents view the role and purpose of schools differently.

The role and purpose of education has been debated since the very beginning of American society. Schools in the United States have historically played a major role in the process of developing a common society among our many different cultures (Thayer & Levit, 1966). However, achieving commonalities is challenging, due to social divisions including cultures: (a) representing a different facet of society, (b) having different theoretical views, and (c) having traditionally been directly or indirectly involved in what and how information is taught. Furthermore, since the inception of federal education initiatives such as No Child Left Behind and Race to the Top, public education has been in a constant upheaval as educators, politicians, businesses, and religious and parent groups have sought to determine not just what is taught, but how well information should be taught, to whom, and how teaching and learning are assessed.

Division within our society has led to frequent confusion, contradictory beliefs, and debates concerning the function of American schools. Views range from academic information and social values to patriotic goals, including music within school curricula. Conflict and debate concerning education's purpose is extensive and ongoing, frequently surrounding questions that include:

1. To what extent should elected officials, businesses, or religious leaders determine the subject matter and values taught in schools?
2. Should schools teach only academic courses?

3. Should the subject matter concentrate only on what are considered core academic courses, such as mathematics, reading, and writing?
4. Are schools responsible for teaching morals, religious information, or political values?
5. Do schools teach from a pluralistic perspective or from a single melting pot concept of American culture?
6. Should schools teach social and health skills such as pregnancy prevention or reducing alcohol consumption?
7. How much actual determination should teachers have in controlling subject matter and classroom activities?
8. How should learning and teacher effectiveness be assessed and who is accountable for educating citizens?

Public Perceptions, Public Agendas

When considering education's purpose, perhaps a starting point is recognizing that public schools exist to serve public goals. Thus, education systems do not operate in a vacuum and cannot ignore the cultural groups within society. Individuals and groups including politicians, parents, businesses, the military, religious leaders, and educators are among the interested groups that provide input in determining public goals. Each group has a different view of what and how education should be addressed. For example, in 1999, Florida became the first state to require public high schools to teach marriage and relationship skills (Spring, 2002). Lawmakers hoped such information would reduce the increasing divorce rate. Other states such as Georgia and Kansas tried to de-emphasize the teaching of evolution in high school science curricula, opting to place a stronger focus on creationism or "intelligent design" to explain the beginnings of the Earth and humans (Hanna, 2005; Zernike, 2002). This curricular change was due to a growing religious faction who put political pressure on lawmakers to place moral and ethical instruction within a religious context based on their Christian perspectives. Other states deliberate education issues relating to driver education, stopping the spread of AIDS, reducing crime and poverty, increasing patriotism, saving the environment, and building cultural tolerance, all while ensuring students learn traditional academic courses and pass state achievement tests.

Adding to schools' challenges are public perceptions of what occurs within classrooms. It seems everyone has a concept of what schools should be. This concept is usually based on an individual's past experience in schools. Subsequently, parents can become confused about the nature of contemporary schools because they may not see their children developing the same skills and information they worked on in school. Furthermore, as teaching approaches change, students may not learn material in the same manner as their parents. Due to these new and unfamiliar factors, the public may question many facets of education regarding the relevancy and need of information presented in the classroom.

The questioning of education often leads to calls for schools to teach skills and information deemed necessary to existing situations and needs, not realizing the necessity for preparing students for the future. One basis for this concern is a report that at least 70 percent of U.S. jobs now require specialized knowledge and skills (U.S. Department of Labor, 2012). However, economic forecasts suggest that the nature of work in our country will continue to change. For example, the most in-demand jobs in 2010 did not exist in 2004 (Gunderson, Jones, & Scanland, 2004). Consequently, schools must prepare student for jobs that do not yet exist, using technologies and skills that have not been invented (Darling-Hammond, 2010).

Historically, when a problem has occurred in our country, society has at some point looked to public schools to help solve the challenge (Spring, 2006). This has led to American public schools having multiple roles that require flexibility as society changes. The need for diverse knowledge explains why public schools are accountable to so many segments of our society, from parents to businesses and politicians to educational agencies (Spring, 1988). This same diversity explains why education is difficult to characterize with a single purpose.

Music education is not exempt from multiple public views of its purpose. One could easily question the need for music education. If music is so prevalent in our society, why should we worry about where it comes from? Won't music always be there? If music in society is questioned, it seems reasonable to debate the need and purpose of music education in our schools. Should music programs focus on large ensemble performance or have an expanded curriculum to include non-performance opportunities such as music theory, composition, or the recording arts? Can performing opportunities be expanded to include small ensembles such as quintets, salsa bands, or steel drum ensembles? Should the goal of music programs be to achieve a superior rating, or provide opportunities for individuals to experience music in ways unique to them? Can achieving a superior rating and providing individualized music experiences co-exist? Furthermore, some individuals believe music programs should contribute to solving social problems such as school dropouts, drug and alcohol abuse, and gang violence.

Public views influence answers regarding music education's purpose. Many individuals believe schools should place more emphasis on basic skills (reading, writing, mathematics), believing courses such as music are "frill" classes intended to be a curricular enhancement rather than a necessity. Indeed, many music educators have difficulties clearly addressing the need and purpose of music education in schools (Madsen & Kuhn, 1994). Yet being able to answer "why" music is important is vital to understanding music's place in school curricula and its contributions to individual development.

Defining "Education"

What is meant by the term "education?" In every society children must be taught behavior and attitude expectations, as well as skills to prosper within the specific social order. Consequently, education may be defined as a social institution that guides a society's transmission of knowledge to its members (Ballantine, 2001). Howard Gardner (1993) stated education should enhance understanding—understanding of the world, and understanding of oneself and one's own experiences. Achieving a goal of broad understanding requires acknowledging education as a lifelong process, occurring in many forms, and serving multiple purposes. Education may be viewed as a principle source for human progress and an agent of change, enabling individuals to meet the needs of an ever-changing world (Ballantine, 2001; Thayer & Levit, 1966). Accepting such a broad perspective requires education to provide students with opportunities to develop abilities in order to participate intelligently as mature members of society. However, enabling individuals to be successful in a constantly changing world requires education to be as diverse as the different members of society.

Concepts of Education

1. Education—a social institution that guides a society's transmission of knowledge to its members
2. Education should enhance understanding—understanding of the world, and of oneself and one's own experiences
3. Education—a principle source for human progress and an agent of change enabling individuals to meet the needs of an ever-changing world
4. Education is achieved through both informal and formal means

A social perspective of education embraces diversity as a requirement for accomplished learning. Sociologists are interested in learning because of education's relation to life (Macionis, 1997, Spring, 2006). From a social view, an educational process is diverse because learning occurs through formal and informal means. Formally, a school's stated curriculum establishes academic skills and information that students will learn in classes, activities, and textbooks. However, within every school exists a hidden curriculum. Intentionally or unintentionally, the hidden curriculum informally teaches acceptable values and morals. Students learn through activities and processes which occur naturally and regularly in schools and which, while part of a curriculum, are education experiences which are frequently not formally assessed. Social interactions, competitions, hallway exchanges, lunchroom conversations, sporting events, and music trips are common examples of hidden curricula from which students learn.

In the United States, three different institutions have traditionally been active in education: families, religious organizations, and schools (Thayer & Levit, 1966). At times, each institution has defined education in different manners, yet has melded skills together in a coherent whole. However, traditional sources of learning and information have changed (Spring, 2006). Contemporary families are anything but traditional. Many families are now two (or single) parent working families and almost half of the marriages in the United States end in divorce (Center for Disease Control and Prevention, 2011). While many Americans claim to be religious, countless families do not regularly participate in structured religious activities, and increasingly diverse religious views challenge the traditional stereotype of American families (U.S. Census, 2012). Furthermore, a 2014 Pew Research Poll found the majority (72 percent) of American citizens believed religion was losing its influence on our society.

Schools are frequently viewed as "catch-all" institutions asked to teach skills traditionally learned at home or through religious venues. The concept and definition of "education" has changed as the American public's perceptions of schools have altered. Accordingly, society views one role of schools as being the primary institution to educate children in skills and knowledge necessary to function successfully (Thayer & Levit, 1966). Yet, because of so many different social groups, there are multiple views of what should be taught in order to be successful. Defining education requires determining what is needed for success. Yet success is subjective, resulting in the definition of education being slanted toward personal needs or goals. This paradoxical position frequently results in schools being criticized for presenting information that is contrary to family or social perceptions of what is useful or correct (Spring, 1988, 2006).

With numerous views regarding education's definition and role, schools often wrestle with issues of tradition versus progress. Schools are frequently expected to pass down "traditional" cultural heritage such as American history, basic mathematics, English grammar, reading, and writing skills. One might also expect information to include folk songs and patriotic songs in music class. However, as information changes, schools must also blend new knowledge with existing knowledge. The public is frequently unaware of how quickly new information is developed and disseminated. For example, one study estimated that in the three-year period from 1999 to 2002, the amount of new information produced nearly equaled the amount previously produced in the entire history of world! Furthermore, the amount of new technical information nearly doubles every two years (Varian & Lyman, 2003). New approaches and information in science, computer technology, and communications presented via the Internet and social media are examples of rapidly changing information and how we can become aware of it in contemporary society. Adding a class in MIDI, a guitar ensemble, steel pans, or a music composition course are examples of how the music curriculum can be altered to reflect contemporary interests and relevancy. Whatever the curricula focus, blending new and traditional information can be a challenge for music educators as they seek to educate their students.

Photo Figure 5 A diverse curriculum can blend traditional music experiences with new trends and opportunities.

The General Purposes of Education in the United States

Status Attainment

Defining education involves addressing two questions that dominate discussions concerning the purpose of American schools: (1) What should be taught in the public schools? and (2) Who should have a voice in what is taught? Both questions reflect conflict and debate between personal and public goals for education in the United States. Answering each question places education in the middle of the conflict regarding preparing students with either traditional or more progressive knowledge. Answers to both questions often reflect the theoretical views of functionalism, conflict theory, objectivism, and interaction theory (Chapter 2). Consequently, debate over what concept is best for students can be intense and often emotional. Because society is a constantly changing cultural phenomenon, educational debates are rarely conclusive, often generating more questions than answers.

From a sociological perspective, one influential interest in the purpose of education concerns the concept of status attainment. Reflective of the conflict theory, Weber (2000) argued that education could either hurt or hinder an individual's position in society. Schools do not merely train but also sort individuals by granting access to resources and desirable occupations to some while limiting opportunities for others. Sociologists such as Bernstein (1971) and Bourdieu (2000) argue that school curricula are selected and presented in manners that maintain power structures in society. Consequently, a person's status in society is affected by the type, amount, and quality of educational experiences received. Status is thus a reflection of the fact that the quantity and quality of an individual's education positively correlates with the amount of income received (U.S. Department of Labor, 2014).

The concept of status attainment through education has led to processes regarding human, cultural, and social capital (Arum & Beattie, 2000). By investing in human capital, businesses would seek to improve schools and provide education that would improve employee skills and thus increasing profits (Schultz, 2000). In the early 1970s, Pierre Bourdieu expanded the status attainment concept to include cultural capital. Bourdieu (2000) believed individuals were stratified based on different levels of cultural understanding. According to Bowles and Gintis (1976), cultural understanding was often exhibited through personality traits and self-presentation. For example, individuals from privileged backgrounds were trained from birth to possess specific cultural dispositions, attitudes, and styles. Bourdieu (2000) believed individuals whose behavior reflected more cultural accumulation received better educational training and opportunities. Differences in cultural capital, therefore, led to divisions in educational achievement and occupational status. In the 1980s, James Coleman (Coleman & Hoffer, 2000) developed the concept of social capital. This concept was based on the belief that focusing on human and cultural capital diminished social relationships. Coleman believed schools that developed relationships between students and communities formulated a stronger bond that enforced common norms leading to better achievement.

The concept and perception of status directly influences American public schools, as they are charged with the process of enculturating students in the behaviors, heritage, values, and roles of our society (Thayer & Levit, 1966). The classroom teacher is the individual primarily responsible for enculturation through the transmission of culture norms. The cultural transmission process often involves selecting, guiding, training, and placing individuals into specific roles. There is some debate as to whether this process actually promotes freedom of choice or reflects a sorting machine model of education. In some respects, socialization restricts individuals, limiting them to only the experiences encountered. However, debate between personal and public views over the purpose of education is frequently reflected in three broad general purposes of education: political, social, and economic.

Political Purposes of Education

It is important that American citizens share the same political values and obedience to established laws. We live in a democracy where freedom and equal rights are valued. Schools are ideal "societies" for fostering democratic ideals that acculturate our citizens into the American way of life. The socialization process within schools is a powerful means of political control that begins with the student/teacher relationship. Therefore, the goal of the political purposes of education is to instruct and train future citizens in political values and obedience to laws of the United States (Spring, 2006). This process requires knowledge and understanding of various political structures in society, from local and state policies and political systems to national-level policies and structures. The process often involves selecting and training future political leaders and the promotion of pride in the American lifestyle.

Schools accomplish political goals through the presentation of a variety of information and activities. Students learn to obey school rules and accept consequences for not following those rules. The student body elects class officers and establishes a hierarchy among its leadership. A sense of citizenship is instilled through the display of school codes and colors that promote pride, spirit, service, and loyalty to the school. Students stand and recite the Pledge of Allegiance and sing the National Anthem before the start of school-sponsored athletic events. Historical people, events, and works of literature that form the foundations of our country are taught in classes. In recent years, many schools have implemented community service requirements to instill a sense of citizenship and promote community responsibility.

A challenge with the political purposes of American education is obtaining a consensus of what constitutes political values in the United States. Achieving a consensus of what should be taught regarding the political structures in our country can be very controversial. In a democratic pluralistic society, should public schools teach a specific political doctrine? Even past events have been interpreted differently based on cultural perceptions. For example, some religious groups are opposed to reciting the Pledge of Allegiance, believing it involves the worship of a graven image. Schools can be criticized for teaching a too liberal or too conservative approach concerning values or personal biases. Defining a single view of what an "American" citizen is in our diverse society is even more problematic. Furthermore, developing a concept of good citizenship is very subjective. For example, should every citizen vote, or is it okay to not vote as a sign of protest? Is it proper to criticize the government over an issue that you do not believe in, despite this action being viewed as unpatriotic? Each question represents varying interpretations of how good citizenship may be defined.

Social Purposes of Education

The American educator Horace Mann believed public schools were key to social improvement in our society (Hinsdale, 2010). Indeed, for many Americans, schools are symbols of hope in achieving a good society. Many individuals believe the school's primary purpose is the socialization of students to follow rules, successfully interact with each other, and interact in group activities. However, many also believe schools should be involved in teaching moral values and dealing with social issues such as AIDS, alcoholism, a growing divorce rate, spousal abuse, and unwanted pregnancies. Thus, the social purpose of education is to teach the moral and social skills of our society (Spring, 2006).

Once again, schools strive to accomplish the social purpose of education through a variety of methods. Students are taught to be neat and clean in appearance, wash their hands, and brush their teeth. Many schools have dress and behavior codes in an attempt to instill certain community values. Dances, sporting events, and other social gatherings promote positive interactions with other students who may be similar or dissimilar, such as students with disabilities, students with different gender orientations, or students from different racial, ethnic, or socioeconomic backgrounds. In preparation for future interactions and family roles, students frequently take classes that deal with social issues such as marriage and family life, health education, racial and cultural differences, and diverse religious viewpoints.

Social concerns such as divorce rates, political agendas, and religious participation have placed increased responsibility for teaching social skills and solving social problems on public schools. Consider the issue of obesity. In 2001, the United States surgeon general reported teenage obesity was a growing problem, leading to future health problems in society as the generation becomes more elderly (U.S. Department of Health and Human Services, 2001). This information led many states to consider legislation requiring physical education classes to help students manage increasing weight problems (Paige, 2004). Additionally, in 2010, the federal government passed the Healthy Hunger-Free Kids Act, which sought to establish a nationwide core child nutrition requirements for public school lunch programs (U.S. Department of Agriculture, 2010). The major advocate for the program was First Lady Michelle Obama, who promoted a wellness lifestyle that included physical fitness and better nutrition. In response to school violence, many school districts have begun offering instruction and activities focusing on character education, including bullying, hazing, ethics, and matters frequently associated with social justice. A primary emphasis on such instruction began with the 2001 No Child Left Behind education act and was later adopted by the Race to the Top education program in 2009. Both programs called for schools to teach character education in an attempt to mold students into the "proper" American citizen (No Child Left Behind Act, 2001; U.S. Department of Education, 2009). Both legislations called on educators to train students to be caring, respectful, responsible, and trustworthy. Furthermore, some religious groups believe schools should implement religious instruction reflective of their specific views, including prayer before classes and the teaching of creationism, not as a religious view but as a viable alternative scientific theory to existing evolution theories.

Different issues and views have contributed to the basic problem facing the social purpose of education: What social values and morals do schools teach? In a culturally diverse society, is there a single viewpoint that should be represented? Gaining a consensus of moral values is an even greater challenge than gaining a consensus on political values. Dealing with social issues such as teenage sexuality, birth control, and substance abuse is often very controversial and frequently places schools in the middle of public debate and criticism. Yet schools are often expected to serve as a social bridge between society's different components.

Economic Purposes of Education

Our American society is based on a capitalist philosophy where wealth and income are valued and viewed as a source of pride and power. Indeed, many citizens in the United States equate the amount of money a person has to the amount of status held by that individual. Reflecting this view, American schools are often charged with maintaining national wealth and advancing the national economy. Investing in education has long been considered necessary to improving the quality of workers and consequently increasing the level of wealth in a community. Hence, the economic purpose of education is to train individuals to be successful workers in business (Spring, 2006). Compounding this challenge is the recognition that in the 21st century American workers will be competing in a global economy. Many individuals believe schools should be run like businesses. Consequently, economic education must link schooling to interests of both national business communities and international markets.

Following other purposes of education, schools prepare students for economic challenges through a variety of methods. School rules such as being on time, completing and turning in work by a specific deadline, and learning the roles of student and teacher, which reflect the worker/boss relationship, are ways that informally and formally prepare students for future business experiences. The curriculum reflects business skills perceived as necessary with a focus on reading, writing and mathematics, computer technology, and foreign language. Some schools require students to declare an "academic major" focusing on specific experiences and skills deemed necessary toward developing a future vocation or college major (Florida Department of Education, 2006b). Businesses frequently get directly involved in schools by making financial donations and adopt-a-school programs. Such involvement can give businesses more influence over what is taught in the curriculum.

Again, conflict arises over what should be taught. Do schools teach skills immediately needed in existing jobs or give students a process preparing them for lifelong learning as information, products, and skills requirement change? Many states have high-stakes testing aimed at requiring students to demonstrate skills deemed necessary by local communities, including businesses. Failing to pass these tests can result in students not graduating and a reduction in state funding for schools. Many argue that focusing on narrow economic training results in sorting and tracking future workers into roles as business leaders and workers, eliminating real equality and freedom of choice. Such an approach may ignore a broader curriculum that engages students in learning to adapt to constant changes in technology and work requirements.

Music Education's Role in the Purposes of American Education

Why do American schools need music education? Music education is often difficult to rationalize. Can music contribute to improving abilities in subject areas such as math or reading? Can the study of music be justified for its own unique contributions? Should students be required to participate in music to help reduce the student dropout rate or to help stimulate individuals with learning challenges? These are among many questions regarding music education's role in American schools. Music education often assumes that music study is not only valuable but also necessary to every individual (Woodford, 2005). Still, questions concerning the need and purpose of music in schools are asked, even by many in our profession.

Music education is frequently criticized for being out of touch with the average American by failing to present experiences reflective of the variety of musical opportunities available in our society (Madsen, 2000, Woodford, 2005). For example, as classically trained musicians, most music teachers have traditionally believed that music instruction focused on (1) preparing musicians for making and participating in music throughout their lives; (2) repertoire based on classical European traditions; and (3) creating audience interest in traditional European music education (Froehlich, 2007). Yet, while there are students interested in traditional instruction, many students participate in music not for musical reasons but for social reasons often included in music activities (Adderly, Kennedy, & Berz, 2003).

Music education must communicate musical and social values experienced in their classrooms to public entities such as school administrators, politicians, community and business leaders, the media, parents, and students (Madsen, 2000; Mark, 1996). Individuals, often with limited musical knowledge, need a clear understanding of music education's value in an intellectual, political, and economical process, as well as a social, personal, and musical perspective. Such understanding necessitates making school music connect with individual lives outside of school. Consequently, expressing the value of school music must often be expressed in ways that are less musical, and more utilitarian. How do experiences in a music class transfer to life experiences?

It is imperative that music educators keep music as a focus of instruction and value while embracing the three primary overall purposes of education (Mark, 1996). Through music, American values, traditions, skills, and knowledge in social, political, and economic interests can be addressed. It is ironic that many activities occurring in music education already provide such skills. Performing patriotic songs, teaching the value of teamwork, and developing leadership skills are just three examples. Yet music education is frequently its own worst enemy by focusing on a narrow curricular aspect that relies too heavily on performance as its sole basis for existence. Increased emphasis needs to be placed on skills learned through music participation, their contributions to our total welfare, and their value to public interests.

In our society, schools are social agencies where students learn society's standards and expectations. Music education addresses the social purpose of education by using music to teach social roles and values that contribute to cultural identity and continuation (Adderly, Kennedy, & Berz, 2003). Music education contributes to socialization by providing opportunities to experience the human relationship to music. While music can be an individual experience, public school music often focuses on group interaction. Teaching the value of teamwork to achieve a quality performance is a goal requiring the demonstration of values such as respect, cooperation, caring, and trust: all values prescribed by the federal and state education standards (U.S. Department of Education, 2009). However, music performances also require additional social skills such as dedication and proper attitude toward other individuals working in the group.

Economically, music education addresses skills, knowledge, and values required and sought after in American businesses. Successful music activities require students to be punctual, attend required rehearsals and performances, be organized and prepared, respond to and follow directions, take criticism, communicate with others, think individually as well as a group, and even dress appropriately to represent the organization. Teamwork is again a goal, as students must work together to develop and complete projects. Achieving such standards requires students to discriminate between different levels of accomplishment by distinguishing between poor, good, and excellent. This requirement compels students to understand dedication and concentration skills. All of these goals result in achieving pride in one's work.

Music education also addresses the political purposes of education in diverse ways. The concept of democracy is not a new idea in music education (Woodford, 2005). Many music programs contain a leadership structure resembling our country's political organization. Programs elect an ensemble president, vice-president, treasurer, and secretary to represent the needs of the ensemble members. Through this structure issues are presented, discussed, and voted on, giving individuals a voice in the ensemble. Additionally, other forms of leadership are frequently implemented with the inclusion of section leaders, soloists, and student conductors. National pride and heritage is presented through rehearsal and performance of patriotic songs and folk songs. Concerts are produced for school and community venues, each with a purposeful or non-purposeful goal of instilling pride, loyalty, and a sense of patriotism.

Challenges to Music's Contributions

With the primary purposes of education frequently addressed, why is music education still challenged to demonstrate its value? Perhaps one reason is communication. Music educators are trained and enculturated to be musicians and teachers. This process rarely involves developing skills in advocacy. The National Association for Music Education (2014c), or NAfME, the world's largest arts organization, advocates the value of music education to a broad segment of the population. However, educators often miss the total contribution that music provides. Music itself is a valuable experience that teaches a variety of skills and knowledge. However, *through* music, students also learn other skills and knowledge directly related to the overall purposes of education. Consequently, music education can contribute to a total education.

The basis of advocacy is social through interactions. Music teachers should never miss opportunities to demonstrate how information and skills, learned through participation in music, can influence an individual throughout life. These opportunities are everywhere: at meetings, in the hallways, on concert programs, in newspapers, through the Internet, and over email. Like general education, learning music's value requires active experience through music participation. Music educators should welcome administrators, non-music-teaching colleagues, parents, and even local politicians into their classrooms to observe and directly participate in the array of skills learned through music.

A second reason for the American public's inability to realize music education's value may reflect how music education is approached by some music educators themselves. Public school music instruction in the United States has historically focused on large group instruction and public performances (Labuta & Smith, 1997). The general public, school administrators, and even students and teachers expect school ensemble classes to perform, and often perform frequently. As a result, many music programs do not, and often cannot, take opportunities to teach the diversity of skills and experiences required to successfully meet the primary education purposes. Time becomes an issue, as time is required to make transfers and connections to multiple life experiences. Yet research has shown that taking up to ten minutes from a performance rehearsal to teach non-performance information does not negatively affect an ensemble's performance, and may actually improve the performance (Goolsby, 1997; Kelly, 1997b; Madsen & Duke, 1993). Additionally, research has shown that music educators often falsely assume that students learn skills solely through the act of performing (Blocher, Greenwood, & Shellahamer,

1997). It is important that music teachers, school colleagues, and the public realize that music by itself is not music education. An effective advocacy effort must present a complete musical experience. Changes in music instruction must ensure that skills and information necessary to meet public education expectations are presented.

Education and Schooling Instructional Concept Models

Until recently, many people believed an educated person could do anything. Horace Mann (often referred to as the "Father of American Education") stated, "Education, beyond all other devices of human origin, is the great equalizer of the conditions of man—the balance wheel of the social machinery" (Thayer & Levit, 1966). The educational philosopher John Dewey (1900) stated, "An educated person is the person who has the power to go on and get more education" (p.9). Both statements reflect how schools have historically been expected to increase opportunities for a better life, provide for equal opportunity, and identify individuals most qualified for various positions in society.

However, contemporary public views have narrowed, as people commonly believe education is directly linked to occupation and financial success more than overall intellectual, social, and emotional development (Zuckerman, 2011). This emphasis is highlighted by the national promotion of the curricular program known as STEM (Science, Technology, Engineering, and Mathematics) that seeks to increase the number of students studying these fields and promote job growth (U.S. Department of Education 2014b). Arts advocates have responded to STEM by insisting on the contributions of the arts in economic growth, thus adding the letter "A" to form STEAM: Science, Technology, Engineering, Arts, and Mathematics (STEAM, 2010).

To better comprehend education's multiple roles it is helpful to understand the two contrasting instructional concept models of education and schooling. Both concepts reflect process versus product as goals for instruction and reflect different social classroom interactions. It is important to remember both concepts exist and are effective in providing essential knowledge and skills, and therefore neither is better than the other. However, both concepts are very different in the manner they provide knowledge and expected outcomes. Thus, both are viewed differently and are at the center of controversy regarding what is considered an "educated" citizen in our country.

The instructional concept model of *schooling* provides specific specialized information and training. The approach to outcomes is product-centered, meaning the end result is more important than the manner or process used in achieving the goal. An emphasis on providing skills and information for perceived current societal needs frequently exists in product-centered schooling approaches. Many successful institutions such as technical schools or high school vocational curricula are designed for students seeking to immediately enter the work force after graduating from high school and provide precise knowledge and skills necessary for specific vocations. Additionally, students, parents, and various agencies desiring only presentation of information covered on the test is an example of schooling. The recent focus on competency-based instruction and the resulting standardized testing has led to claims that teachers teach only material covered on the test. Music education that focuses solely on performance or a conservatory approach to instruction is an example of a schooling approach to music instruction.

The instructional concept model of *education* provides a broad base of knowledge and more generalized training. Rather than presenting specific information for precise situations, the educational instructional approach requires students to assimilate knowledge from many sources for the correct answer. Consequently, the education concept is process-centered, meaning that understanding the manner or method used to achieve the results is more important than the end product. Many liberal arts college curricula (including most education programs) reflect the education approach to instruction. Music programs providing experiences in addition to large performing ensembles, such as composition, world music, and relating music experiences to other information, frequently reflect the educational approach.

Instructional Concepts

Schooling	* Specific specialized information and training
	* Product-centered
Education	* A broad base of knowledge and more generalized training
	* Process-centered

Societal conflicts between the education and schooling instructional concepts have historically existed. Various factions of society have different views of what future citizens need to know and be able to do to function effectively within their culture. However, at times even these factions conflict with each other. For example, businesses want people who know how to follow specific directions while at the same time understand and learn trends in business cycles in order to develop new ideas and strategies to keep their business running effectively. Parents want children who know the same information they learned, yet want their children to gain computer knowledge for the future, all the while being prepared for a job that achieves the American dream of doing better than their parents. These examples demonstrate how both instructional processes work independently and yet interdependently within society. When functioning correctly, both approaches are effective at balancing each other. When one approach is viewed as more important than the other, schools can get caught in the middle, resulting in criticism that they are not providing necessary skills and knowledge to future citizens.

Music Education's Relation to Schooling and Education

Music education is not immune from the schooling and education instructional approaches, as both have shaped music education. Both concepts represent differing theoretical views and the social interactions within each perspective. Historically, the utilitarian and aesthetic perspectives of music education have conflicted by representing schooling and education approaches respectively. However, Elliot's later praxial approach (Elliott & Silverman, 2014) essentially combines both schooling and educational aspects, as both qualities are considered valid music experiences that should be represented in school music curricula.

The clearest example of either instructional approach can be seen in a music program's approach to performance. If the instructional focus is on the concert, and the instructor believes students learn purely from performance, this is an example of the schooling instructional approach. The example is product-centered in that the focus is on the music and the actual event. During, before, and after school, hours are spent rehearsing to learn notes and rhythms, and playing together as an ensemble to produce a high quality final performance. At the end of the performance, the whole process starts over again. Frequently, students spend long hours rehearsing the same notes and rhythm to play together as an ensemble. Transfer of information from the previous performance is minimal. The drill teaching approach, in which students are taught only the material being performed for the sole purpose of a specific concert, is part of the schooling instruction. Yet this approach is quick and efficient at producing many performances in a relatively short period of time. Furthermore, presenting numerous concerts may please administrators who may view music programs as curricular tools to promote the school, or meet community expectations of performing at public events.

Whereas the schooling approach focuses on learning the music, the educational approach focuses on using the music to learn how to perform. The idea is process-based, meaning that if

Photo Figure 6 Performing music involves a balance of process and product.

students are taught to sing or play their instruments correctly, they can perform any music presented to them, at any time. Transfer of skills is essential and a focus of instruction. This approach is the basis of teaching students to be independent musicians, so when they leave the director-led music room, they will be able to continue to participate in music in their homes, churches, or any other parts of their culture. The educational approach does not de-emphasize performance, nor does it produce a lower performance quality. If students are taught to think independently they can be more musical. Less rehearsal time outside of class may be needed because in-school rehearsals are more efficient. Directors can spend less time talking about music and more time performing music. Yet this approach requires more time than the schooling approach. Students need time to thoroughly learn their craft. Music educators will need to think more frequently from a "teacher" perspective than a "conductor" view. The result may be the presentation of fewer concerts, which may not meet the approval of some school administrators and community expectations.

Like education in general, the best instructional approach to music education combines both schooling and educational approaches. The effective music educator understands the program and requirements needed to prepare students for both immediate and long-term success. Careful planning based on a sound philosophy and program goals can provide students with the knowledge and skills to perform high quality concerts quickly, while allowing time for students to explore and learn proper skills that enable them to develop musical independence. Music educators employing both approaches realize there are periods in a school year during which more time can be devoted to one approach than the other. The beginning of the school year is an excellent point in the semester to focus on the process of music-making, using the music as a "textbook" to teach performance concepts that will be used in later performances. The weeks before a performance require shifting to a more schooling approach, focusing on specific skills required by the music to be performed. After the performance is over, a return to the educational approach can re-emphasize performance concepts necessary for all music, not just music for the next concert.

High-Stakes Testing and the Changing Role of Education

Recently, school districts have implemented an expansion of the schooling model that creates a greater emphasis on product-based education. The multiple uses of standardized tests, known as high-stakes testing, is changing the role of education by placing a stronger emphasis on some curricular subjects, deemed by various groups as more necessary and important than other subjects (Spring, 2014, Ravitch, 2010). Courses receiving more emphasis, known as core courses, typically include English, reading, writing, and mathematics. The impact of core courses is highlighted when students are tested using state- and federal government-mandated standardized tests in core subjects. The test results are used to grade not only student learning, but also teacher effectiveness and overall school quality (see Chapters 5 and 8 for more information).

Critics of high-stakes testing state that data from tests have been used by school districts in ways that were never intended by the education mandates (Figlio, 2006). High-stakes tests begin in elementary school to determine if individuals are to be promoted from one grade to another each year and continue through high school, where they are ultimately used as a graduation requirement (No Child Left Behind Act, 2001; U.S. Department of Education, 2009). Consequently, the test is the basis for graduating, receiving a diploma, admissions to college, even assessing job skills or showing proof of qualifications for jobs. Thus, much of what an individual can or cannot do is not based on what is accomplished in the classroom, but on the score received on the annual test.

Data from the results frequently influence individual school funding, school staffing, teacher salaries, and parent school choice decisions. Consequently, the impact of high-stakes testing and on the role of education appears to be causing a shift further away from a process education model, toward a greater prominence of a product-driven schooling model.

Various components of society have always been interested in what schools are teaching and how well information is taught. Initiatives such as compulsory school laws and teacher certification standards are examples of both state and federal involvement in local school curricula. However, in the 1980s and 1990s, state governors began to respond to constituents' concerns of school quality (Hallinan, 1990). Concerns included teacher quality, facilities, safety, curricular content, and the degree of student achievement. The concerns evolved into a school reform movement which called for statewide testing of public school students. Thus, high-stakes testing as a concept appears to have begun in 2002 with the federal government initiative No Child Left Behind (NCLB), which required annual testing of core subjects. NCLB expanded school reform to include mandated benchmarks for each grade level and subject. Later, further expansion included assessments of teacher effectiveness and teacher-training standards (Spring, 2014).

The growing emphasis on standardized high-stakes tests at all levels of government is further evidence that the American school system is increasingly test-driven (Hallinan, 1990; Marzano, 2003; Ravitch, 2010). For example, Khadaroo (2014) reported that students commonly take at least one standardized test each month (frequently more each month) and take more district tests than state tests. Every aspect of each school, from the administration to counseling to curricular and instructional approaches, is reflected in the test data. No Child Left Behind created a national education policy that was continued and further expanded by Race to the Top (U.S. Department of Education, 2009) where the results of high-stakes testing has led to scores on multiple tests being the end goal of education. Furthermore, despite the Tenth Amendment to the U.S. Constitution, which gives states and local communities power to determine educational objectives, No Child Left Behind was the first time that the federal government became directly involved in mandating local curricular decisions. Consequently, most states currently require standardized testing to assess academic standards, student achievement of standards, and teacher quality (Spring, 2014).

The possible beginning of an apparent backlash to the amount and emphasis on school testing could be seen in 2014 (Khadaroo, 2014). As reports and research data showed little correlation between high-stakes testing and college or vocational success (Ravitch, 2010; Spring, 2006), the American public began to become more dissatisfied with high-stakes testing. Data from one poll conducted by the Friedman Foundation for Educational Choice showed that 44 percent of school parents reported the amount of time schools spent on testing was too high (DiPerna, 2014). Only 22 percent of school parents in this poll reported the amount of testing time was too low. Yet the poll's results showed that 59 percent of the American public believed that students should be held accountable for learning through standardized testing.

However, opinion concerning how standardized testing should be used to assess teachers appears mixed. A 2014 Phi Delta Kappa/Gallup poll found that only 38 percent of U.S. citizens favored using student performances on standardized test scores to evaluate teachers (Bushaw & Calderon, 2014). Yet another poll showed that 59 percent of Americans favored using standardized testing to hold teachers accountable for classroom experiences (DiPerna, 2014)

Summary

It appears that the purpose of education is to do more than simply provide training and skills. Traditionally, American society has tended to be complacent about education, honoring it, perhaps, more widely than any other culture, but also taking it for granted (Labuta & Smith, 1997; Thayer & Levit, 1966). However, history has shown that citizens of the United States have always had faith in education. Historically, schools have shared a growing involvement in the development of American civilization (Thayer & Levit, 1966; Spring, 2006). Consequently, throughout history virtually every aspect of our society has been suggested for inclusion in school curricula. When our society has faced a problem, it has looked to schools to provide a solution. This includes questioning the roles and functions in the formal and informal means of education. From teaching basic reading and writing to complex technical and professional skills to teaching how to cope with social problems, schools often are caught between the need to teach freedom of thought, and conforming to traditions and public views. There is little consensus regarding the place of schools in our society. Thus, the role and purpose of schools will constantly be negotiated and reconsidered, depending on the interest and power of various components of society.

Controversy may continue to be part of American education as the United States faces increased issues over growing diversity and its role in a global society. Schools in the United States have always played a major role in the process of developing a common culture among our country's diversity (Spring, 2006). From a sociological view, schools accomplish a common culture by expanding a child's world to include people from different social backgrounds. Consequently, children learn by confronting and interacting with diversity. New social interactions result in becoming aware of new ideas, behaviors, dress, gender roles, language, religion, and music. However, while many families want their children to learn, they do not necessarily want them exposed to ideas that contradict their family values. Controversy over what should be taught contributes to debate over how schools should accomplish their responsibilities.

The role and function of school music instruction goes beyond the mere performance of notes and rhythms. Few would argue that a primary purpose of music education is to encourage students to perform, listen, and respond to music. Perspectives that are more contemporary call for an expansion of this purpose to include discrimination skills, knowledge to transfer and create new music, and to participate in music in a mode that meets individual interest and satisfaction. However, the status of any music education program reflects society's views regarding music as a whole. This includes a perspective of music's role and function in the education of each student.

Such perspective appears to increasingly call on the arts, including music, to contribute to non-musical experiences such as STEAM.

However, a belief that music education is only for those with talent and only for "classical" music often influences society's view. This elitist perception conveys the notion that music is only for a select few in our society. Interestingly, two nationwide polls found that adults in the United States strongly believe in the value of music. A 2003 Gallup poll found 95 percent of Americans believe music is a key component in a child's well-rounded education. Furthermore, three-quarters of individuals polled indicated music education should be mandated in the schools. In 2009, the National Association of Music Merchants (NAMM) found that despite challenges to school music programs, more people are participating in music that ever. Furthermore, the NAMM poll showed individuals believe that a wide array of benefits result from music participation. Perhaps the task for music educators is to communicate a meaningful basis of shared values with the general overall purposes of American education, which is flexible as society's needs change. Put another way, music education must demonstrate its value to society so schools will ensure music opportunities for *all* students.

Music has always been an interaction of human experiences. Yet music's role in human life does not, by itself, justify its place in the formal school curriculum. In fact, music may be learned best through informal means, outside of school. Music educators must recognize that music can be learned in many different ways and venues. Thus, the process and product of learning music becomes personal and more meaningful. A sense of ownership and belonging develops that motivates students to continue musical interests outside school walls. A connection is made between music experienced in schools and music experienced outside of schools, through which the role and purpose of music instruction can be realized.

Key Items

Instructional Concepts	Process and Product	Status Attainment
Human Capital	Cultural Capital	Social Capital
Primary Purposes of Education	Horace Mann	John Dewey
Informal and Formal Learning	STEM/STEAM	High Stakes Testing

Questions for Consideration

1. Is music education for the few or the masses? How does the general American public view the purpose of music education?
2. How might music educators defend the inclusion of music into the school curriculum to school board members and superintendents?
3. In a democratic society such as the United States, should public schools teach a specific political doctrine?
4. To what extent do music teachers serve as parental models for students? Does teaching non-musical skills preclude teaching musical skills?
5. Can you explain how music education contributes to the socialization of an American citizen? Would the recognition of a more diverse society affect music education's role in the enculturation process?
6. Should students be required to participate in music to help reduce the dropout rate or to help stimulate individuals with learning challenges?
7. How can music education better connect music experiences in formal music education classes to music experienced informally outside of schools?
8. If society is so concerned with what and how students are taught, why isn't the teaching profession more valued and teachers better paid?

Web Resources

John Dewey

John Dewey Society: http://www.johndeweysociety.org/

Phi Delta Kappa International

Home Page: http://pdkintl.org/

Purposes of Education

Association for Supervisions and Curriculum Development: http://www.ascd.org/Default.aspx

STEM/STEAM

Edutopia: STEM to STEAM: Art in K-12 Is Key to Building a Strong Economy: http://www.edutopia.org/blog/stem-to-steam-strengthens-economy-john-maeda
STEM Education Coalition: http://www.stemedcoalition.org/
Science, Technology, Engineering and Math: Education for Global Leadership: http://www.ed.gov/stem

Chapter 4

Music Education's Role in Society

There is probably no other human cultural activity which is so all-pervasive and which reaches into, shapes, and often controls so much human behavior.

—Bruno Nettl

Chapter 4 explores the reciprocal relationship of music in society to music in schools. As shown in both the Tanglewood and the Vision 2020: The Housewright Symposium on the Future of Music Education conferences, school music is greatly affected by all genres of music in society. Additionally, music in society is influenced by music in schools. The relationship is reciprocal. However, music education is frequently criticized for not relating to music in which groups outside of schools participate. Consequently, citizens do not always understand, or are not always aware of, the role or function of music, and particularly music education, in their lives. They often fail to connect school music experiences to experiences in their daily lives, thus not realizing the need for music instruction for all students. Chapter 4's premise is that by becoming more aware of music's power and role in society, educators can more fully connect school music experiences to music in their communities. Consequently, school music becomes more meaningful beyond the school environment.

The reciprocal relationship between schools and society also exists between music and music education. Music is not music education. Participating in music does not dictate that learning is occurring, therefore, rehearsing is not necessarily teaching. The same can be said of music's relation to society. Simply hearing music does not necessarily mean an individual is listening to the music. Yet music's influence on human behavior, even subconsciously, can be evident.

Music is an important component of a thriving society and thus can be found in virtually every aspect of our country. Because music is so pervasive does not mean that people are aware of or understand its value and power. Indeed, society, including many music educators, may not fully understand music's potential power over human behavior and thought, and we do not always understand music education's potential influence on our students. Paul Haack (1997) acknowledged music's pervasiveness and power, stating that music is an uncontrolled substance, a multi-billion-dollar industry, and a potent social entity. Haack understood the power music has over individual behaviors and thoughts, and challenged music educators to provide skills and knowledge that that broaden individual awareness. Through awareness, individuals can be empowered to make their own musical choices regarding music they participate in and how they want to participate. When people are able to make their own decisions, no other cultural variable (e.g., the media or recording industry) decides individual music values.

To fully understand music's power, professional music educators must understand that the full extent of a music experience includes both in-school music and out-of-school music. Relevancy is an issue. Like music, music education cannot be understood unless it is examined with regards to the social processes and contexts in which it occurs. A better cultural understanding of the relationship between music, music education, and our society may bridge the gap between academic music expectations and social music interactions. Consequently, music educators need to prepare students for the musical world outside of their rehearsals by enabling them to make musical decisions for themselves. Deciding the best approach to enable students to make decisions requires teachers to be aware of the past and present events, people, and issues that shaped the development of music education and impact our profession's future.

A Brief Overview of the Foundations Between Music and Our Society

To understand that teachers are links between the past, present, and future requires knowledge of music education's historical foundations in the United States. To understand history helps avoid its mistakes, while repeating its successes. Frequently, experiences present-day music educators encounter can be traced to previous events and issues that established the foundations of current expectations and standards. Furthermore, music educators need to understand that current events, expectations, and standards will influence future benchmarks. Hopefully, by understanding issues that affected our profession's past, music educators can deal more effectively with current issues and prepare for future challenges. History informs us that as society has valued music, music education has remained strong in our schools. Yet school music has suffered as its value to society has dwindled. The reciprocal relation of society to education, and music to music education, remains evident. The following is a brief outline of the many different events, issues, and people that helped shape present day music education. The reader is encouraged to investigate our historic foundations further by referring to the cited references at the end of this chapter.

Historical Foundations

Historically, society has placed great expectations on teachers. The development of the professional educator has occurred in concert with cultural standards and expectations. During the Colonial period and through 1840, teaching was a part-time job dominated by men (Labuta & Smith, 1997). Because schools were in session for only about three months each year, most teachers supplemented their income with additional jobs. Since teaching was considered part of the "sacred order of society," additional jobs were usually held within the town clergy, ranging from leading the church choir to digging graves. In the mid-19th century, teaching became a full-time profession. To meet the existing job demand, policymakers theorized that hiring women could achieve the task of nurturing the increasing number of students. Administrators, who were mostly male, believed women were more readily available for teaching jobs and would work for lower salaries. In the 20th century, schools began to teach more math and science classes as the school curriculum began to expand. School officials believed males had more knowledge of these "advanced" subjects and were thus better suited to teach these topics. This belief resulted in the teaching force becoming more balanced between men and women than at any other time in history (Lortie, 2002; Serow, Castelli, & Castelli, 2000; Thayer & Levit, 1966).

Similar to all education in society, music education has historically reflected the events and people of the times and cultural contexts in which it operates. As society has encountered a problem or need, it has historically turned to education to provide a solution. Music education, by contributing to the overall purposes of education, must also contribute to solutions to societal challenges. Many of society's challenges have shaped what has been taught, and frequently how it has been taught, both in and out of the music classroom. Thus, the reciprocal relationship between schools and society, including society and music education, can be traced to the very beginnings of our country. Consequently, much of what music education experiences today has in some form been experienced by music educators throughout American history.

Due to the population of Colonial America originating primarily from European countries, the beginnings of the country's approach to education were based on European models that emphasized religion, civic skills, and responsibilities (Labuta & Smith, 1997). Many educational approaches were determined by socioeconomic factors; the extent to which a person received an education was frequently determined by the value a particular region placed on education. For example, in the southern colonies education was not considered a necessity for all individuals. Affluent southern families could afford private tutors while less prosperous individuals received no formal education unless it was through religious venues. In this way, individuals with money retained knowledge and power over those with less money and less knowledge. However, in other parts of the country, education was viewed differently. In the middle and northern colonies, education was valued more as a necessity for all individuals because of the belief that education could improve the quality of life.

American music education has its foundations in the earliest colonies of what was to become the United States. Music was highly valued by our earliest societies. Our earliest formal music instruction can be traced back to religious venues and attempts to improve congregational singing, but throughout the colonies, there was no uniform approach to music education. Consequently, few people knew how to sing with any musical approach. However, individuals in early colonies valued music because it provided relief to the harsh conditions they frequently endured. Music instruction was generally presented informally, in rote form. The most "formal" music education was usually received through various churches (Birge, 1966; Keene, 1987).

The *Bay Psalm Book*, printed in 1752, is an example of early formal music instruction provided by churches. This crudely printed book contained no actual music notation, but rather words of well-known songs used in congregational singing. The *Bay Psalm Book* was significant to music education because it was one of the earliest examples of our society turning to an educational venue to solve a problem. By all accounts, music was valued, to some extent, by all cultures in our young society. Individuals participated in music socially through secular music, but participation primarily occurred during religious meetings. By most historic accounts, the singing was not very good and music illiteracy was rampant. The *Bay Psalm Book* provided the basis to help individuals learn words to songs, thereby improving singing (Birge, 1966; Keene, 1987). Thus, the *Bay Psalm Book*, a music book, may be one of the earliest instructional textbooks in our country and illustrates the value of music in early American society (Keene, 1987).

As the musical abilities of individuals improved, participation in music activities increased. Music in our growing society continued to be highly valued. Singing societies, where people would come together to enjoy each other's company as well as sing songs, were formed in many communities. These societies evolved into singing schools to further improve singing in the communities (Keene, 1987). Instructional approaches in these schools evolved from teaching by rote to teaching notation. Singing schools existed as the primary means by which individuals learned to read music until music was later adopted into public schools (Birge, 1966). Thus, though privately run, singing schools were among the first formal schools in many communities.

The popularity of singing schools made them not only educationally viable, but also socially important. They were as popular for their role in bringing individuals in together for socializing and bonding as they were for the music instruction presented (Keene, 1987). Singing schools were taught by singing-school masters who, while mostly self-taught, became the first formal school music educators in our country (Birge, 1966). Singing-school masters were the first professional music teachers who taught the basic rudiments of music and are credited for laying the foundations for future music educators. Furthermore, the growth of singing schools represented a break from music education taught primarily through religious venues. They also continued to be an example of the value that music played in society. The popularity of the schools grew to such an extent that they frequently became the center of social and musical life in communities (Birge, 1966).

As our country grew, so did the need for a more formal means of providing education to a broader segment of the population. Education became viewed as a necessity for all citizens. However, there was much division among societal members regarding what should be taught. European attitudes and philosophies were still influencing educational thought, and related to meeting the needs of a changing society. Religious groups were still very influential on educational processes, yet religious groups were divided regarding the value of learning, its subsequent knowledge, and the processes involved in developing instructional objectives and methods (Labuta & Smith, 1997). Increasingly, schools focused on meeting immediate societal concerns. A more organized approach to formal education emerged with the development of the common school developed from federal funds.

Common schools were state-controlled (previous schools were mostly privately run) and taught a common body of skills and information to students from all cultural backgrounds (Spring, 1990). Known as the "father of the common school," Horace Mann (1796–1859) promoted schools that were free of influences by outside organizations (Tyack & Hansot, 1982). He considered education as the "great equalizer" among different cultural groups in our country (Cremin, 1957). Mann believed that all social groups should have equal access to education and be taught the same basic skills and knowledge that focused on nonsectarian moral instruction.

The call for moral instruction led the common school movement to search for individuals believed to be best qualified for teaching virtues. Many leaders (including many women) felt females were more qualified for this duty than males. This decision was based on the religious belief that women were ordained by God as the gender best suited for shaping moral character. Furthermore, it was also felt by many societal leaders that teaching was an occupation that prepared single women for motherhood (Labuta & Smith, 1997; Lortie, 2002). Additionally, because men were considered the principal financial providers for the family, community leaders did not believe female teachers needed to be paid as much as their male counterparts (Lortie, 2002). Thus, the foundation was laid for teaching being perceived as a low-paying profession and an occupation more suited for females than males.

The changing structure of music education followed the development of general educational concepts by broadening musical offerings and becoming more formally structured. The development of the common school greatly affected music education. The broader curriculum provided by common schools enabled more individuals to be exposed to music instruction, but there were stark contrasts in educational thought and opportunities between the north and south. People in the southern United States regarded education as a luxury and privilege for the wealthy. Organized public schools were virtually nonexistent in the south, making music instruction only available either through private means or informally, usually by rote. Northern communities were far more progressive. Education in the north, while still affected by class status, was considered more important for all children to receive. Music instruction reflected these general attitudes. Individuals in the north had access to diverse musical instructional opportunities, while music instruction in the south was available only to those with wealth (Keene, 1987).

While music instruction was available in the north, it was only through private instruction, not formally offered in the schools. Many believed music instruction was only for individuals perceived to have musical talent. One man took exception to the attitude that music was only for the talented few. Lowell Mason (1792–1872) believed anyone could learn music. His instructional approach was based on the Pestalozzian theory that learning was a natural human behavior; therefore, anyone could learn any subject (Birge, 1966). Mason, who was living in Boston at the time, petitioned the school board to have music included in the public school curriculum.

His request was initially denied until he offered to teach music for free, for one year. Furthermore, Mason requested to teach music at the Hawes School, considered a school for poor-performing lower-class students. This request was accepted. After one year, Mason and his students performed a public concert on the footsteps of the Boston school board. By all accounts the performance was wonderful and generated so much public enthusiasm that the school board, in 1838, implemented music instruction into the public school curriculum and Mason was hired, with pay, to teach (Birge, 1966; Keene, 1987; Pemberton, 1985). The recommendation to include music in the school curriculum was based on Mason's demonstration that music could benefit children intellectually, morally, and physically (Mark, 1996; Pemberton, 1985).

Lowell Mason's hiring represents the first time that public funds were used to support music instruction (Mark, 1996). From a national perspective, since Boston was considered the cultural center of the United States, the implementation of music into the public school curriculum started a nationwide acceptance of music into the public schools. Thus, Lowell Mason is considered the "father of American music education."

Lessons from Lowell Mason for Contemporary Music Educators

1. Everyone has music ability
2. The power of the individual teacher to make a difference
3. The ability of community action to keep music in schools
4. Schools and communities must work together for music to be at its greatest influence

---

In the early 1900s, a great debate occurred among musicians regarding how to best teach music. Music specialists were being trained by music supervisors to teach in the schools. However, there was still a shortage of trained music teachers, resulting in most music instruction being taught by the classroom teacher. Concerns about the teacher shortage and instructional issues led to a meeting in 1910 of 30 music supervisors from around the country. The meeting, which occurred in Keokuk, Iowa, was to become the first ever meeting of the Music Supervisors National Conference, later renamed the Music Educators National Conference (Birge, 1966; Labuta & Smith, 1997) and now known as NAfME—the National Association for Music Education.

The beginning of the 20th century came to be known as the Progressive Era. The period has often been considered as the "Golden Age of Music Education." This period was marked by a general belief that society could be managed by scientific organizations. Schools were viewed as a means for perpetuating prosperity and as sources to resolve social problems (Labuta & Smith, 1997). There was great faith in individual capability; anyone could achieve if enough effort and training was available. High schools first appeared and participation in their curricula was based on the perception of a student's natural ability. This was the first example of the sorting machine educational model. Junior high schools began as a means for providing more advanced training for younger students who were not yet ready for more advanced training in high schools. Schools began to successfully use music offerings to attract students. Music curricula expanded to include opportunities in both performance and non-performance classes, including music appreciation. Never before had there been so much interest in and enthusiasm for school music. The public's interest was so great that families would huddle around the newly invented radio to listen to music appreciation contests between different schools or communities (Birge, 1966; Keene, 1987). Due to the diversity of musical offerings, it was not unusual for entire school populations to be enrolled in some sort of music class.

Further influencing pubic interest in school music were professional bands, such as those directed by Patrick S. Gilmore and John Philip Sousa, that toured the country in the late 1800s and early 1900s (Fennell, n.d.). These ensembles performed in cities and towns of all sizes throughout the United States, playing at the highest musical levels, connecting average citizens to music, and inspiring desire to participate in such ensembles. These bands, along with an increasing number of professional orchestras, increased the public's calls for schools to provide music instruction (Birge, 1966). The number and scope of music classes continued to grow to unprecedented levels and included performing ensembles in band, strings, and vocal music.

Much of the popular role music played in education came to a quick halt in the late 1950s when Russia launched a small satellite named Sputnik into space (Mark, 1996). Americans had believed they were technologically superior to other parts of the world. However, the launching of Sputnik demonstrated that other countries also had advanced technology. Furthermore, this technology could be used to launch nuclear weapons against the United States. This was a shock to Americans and brought immense fear, resulting in the federal government becoming directly involved in educational issues (Mark, 1996). Many schools revised their curricula to include a stronger focus on mathematics and science, considered crucial to improving technological advancements (Labuta & Smith, 1997). This curricular revision could be viewed as the first back-to-basics movement in American education. Classes such as music that were considered anti-intellectual, or not relevant to national security, disappeared from course offerings.

Many leaders in society became concerned about the emphasis placed on instruction perceived as academic or intellectually advanced (Mark, 1996). Several national meetings were held to discuss more non-academic experiences being re-implemented into school curricula. Perhaps the most meaningful meeting was the Tanglewood Symposium in Boston in 1967. This was one of the first meetings to include a wide diversity of cultural groups from society, including scientists, psychologists, sociologists, corporate leaders, government officials, and music teachers (Mark, 1996). The meeting's primary objective was to assess and define the role and function of music in schools and other areas of American culture. Music educators attending the meeting called for music education to better reflect societal changes by broadening the scope of the school music experience (Choate, 1968). Two resulting documents were the Tanglewood Declaration and the Goals and Objectives (GO) Project. One of the leaders of the Tanglewood Symposium was Wiley Housewright. Housewright was concerned about the lack of relevancy in students' musical experiences in school and their music experiences outside of school. Housewright's work and vision led to the concept of the Tanglewood Declaration and the GO Project. Both concepts identified all forms of music, including popular music, music of the "youth," and folk music, as well as classically oriented music, as legitimate forms of music deserving the attention of music education and inclusion in school curricula (Choate, 1968; Mark, 1996). Thus, the Tanglewood Symposium provided an impetus to expand school music curricula so as to entice students back into the music classroom, and was integral in connecting society's music to music in schools.

Despite the Tanglewood Symposium's strong recommendations, varying degrees of success marked the expansion of school music curricula over the next 30 years. (Labuta & Smith, 1997; Mark, 1996). Social issues often affected the music education profession. These issues frequently related to school and community financial insecurities, increases in school populations, a concern for teacher and educational quality, a growing debate over the inclusion of religion and moral education throughout the school curriculum, and increasing calls for a stronger emphasis on core classes considered necessary to the country's economic and military power (Mark, 1996). Music education responded to constant concerns for its inclusion into school curricula by holding a follow-up meeting to the Tanglewood Symposium. In 1999, Vision 2020: The Housewright Symposium on the Future of Music Education convened over 300 music educators from across the nation. The meeting had similar goals to its Tanglewood predecessor. Participants attempted to assess and define the role of music education in the 21st century while providing guidance regarding what actions music education needed to take to remain a viable curricular offering (Madsen, 2000). While there was considerable discussion concerning the future direction and focus of music education, no true consensus was achieved. Consequently, music education entered the 21st century still searching for a stronger presence within a constantly changing educational and social environment.

Education in the 21st century has seen further concerns for school reforms, student learning, and teacher quality. Calls for accountability regarding how students learn and what teachers teach have led to increased use of standardized testing, state education standards, and national standards that became known as the Common Core Initiative. Testing pre-determined educational benchmarks, at both the state and national levels, was used to assess the amount of student progress, as well as to determine the instructional effectiveness of teachers (Spring, 2014). The emphasis on testing became so great that many teachers claimed they must teach to the test at the exclusion of teaching to individual student needs. The emphasis became so strong that in some school districts widespread cheating by both students and teachers became an issue (Toppo, Amos, Gillum, & Upton, 2011).

Similar to the 1960s and 1970s, the inclusion of music education in school curricula remained in question (Abril & Bannermann, 2013; Abril & Gault, 2008). Music was not exempt from standardized testing. Yet evidence that including art and music in schools benefits student learning while improving dropout rates has grown (Kelly, 2009; Kelly & Heath, in press; Kinney, 2008). Evidence suggests that diversifying music curricula can enhance the overall experience and possibly improve the number of students enrolling in music classes (Green, 2008; Isbell, 2007). Consequently, music remains valued by society, and thus in our schools as well.

Music's Role in Contemporary Society

Music education's role in our country's history illustrates music's wide appeal and use within various cultures in society. Music continues to serve many basic roles while remaining multidimensional in its value to and use by our citizens. Music brings us together in times of need or great excitement by serving as a symbol of democracy and freedom, and is an outlet to entertain and remind us of many different facets of our lives. Participation in music is also multidimensional as music is both passively and actively valued and enjoyed in many ways, including listening, dancing, studying, reading about, and performing. Consequently, music serves many roles and, based on data from the Gallup Organization (2003a), appears to be valued among the vast majority of members in society. Gallup's study, which illustrates music's wide appeal and use, was conducted for the National Association of Music Merchants and found that 90% of Americans value music. Additional results, obtained by surveying American homeowners ($N = 1,005$) across the country, indicated:

- 97% of those surveyed agreed that playing a musical instrument provided a sense of accomplishment and was a good means of expression.
- 80% believed playing a musical instrument made them smarter.
- 93% believed playing an instrument helped children to make friends.

Music's value is frequently reflected in how it makes us feel, think, and behave. Music makes us happy, helps us to grieve, scares us, and makes us angry. Additionally, music helps us to relax, concentrate, be creative, and even increases our heart rate. Individuals use music as a means of bonding together, as a symbol of unity, or as an indicator of defiance or rebellion (Radocy &

Photo Figure 7 Defining sounds as music is culturally based.

Boyle, 2003). Thus, it may be concluded the appeal and use of music within our society, and indeed across the entire world, is as diverse as we are human.

How we value music is also reflected in the many ways that we use and experience music. Conceivably, music's value cannot be fully understood unless music is examined in relation to its social processes and contexts. In addition to the concert hall, music is experienced in a wide range of venues, including recreation activities, businesses, the military, sports, advertising, our religions, supermarkets and shopping malls, the media, and medicine, among many others. We work and exercise to music, study to music, eat to music, wake up and go to sleep to music. Even decisions regarding what clothes we will wear are frequently influenced by music. These many uses illustrate the multidimensional value that music holds within society. However, despite its apparent value, its appeal, and our wide variety of participation, we are not always aware of music as a perpetual and cohesive force in our society. One explanation could be a lack of understanding or awareness of music's many roles in our lives.

What Is Music?

A basic starting point for understanding music's immense role in society is understanding the definition of music. What is music? Can any sound be a musical sound? What is the difference in sounds thought of as noise, and sounds considered musical? Individuals regularly make judgmental assessments of what is or what is not music. However, such assessments are usually preference-based and subject to many human variables (Radocy & Boyle, 2003).

Theories on the origins of music state that music began as an imitation of nature sounds and children's babbling, or from imitating human emotional sounds such as signal calling or cries (Nettl, 1956; Wallin, Merker, & Brown, 2000). Other theories associate music's origins with rhythm and language development (Nettl, 1956; Wallin, Merker, & Brown, 2000). The many theories regarding the origins of music help to define music as more than written symbols on a piece of paper. Perhaps one fundamental definition is that music is sounds and silences, sometimes organized, sometime unorganized, involving various pitches, volume, and timbres occurring within some sort of rhythm context (Radocy & Boyle, 2003). However, even this broad definition may not account for all of the cultural diversity affecting what sounds represent music.

Perhaps one place to start in the debate over what sounds are musical is to accept the position that there is no one single answer to defining music. As already stated, music is a social phenomenon that is as varied as the humans that create and use it. Therefore, Radocy and Boyle (2003) summarize:

> Virtually everyone is drawn to music of some kind and, despite our cultural differences, almost every individual understands what music is, or at least what his/her culture defines as music. (p. 19)

Consequently, from a sociological view, what sounds constitutes music is essentially defined by cultural norms (Nettl, 1956; Wallin, Merker, & Brown, 2000). Through enculturation we learn the musical norms and folkways for our particular culture (Macionis, 1997). Through this process we learn that sounds alone do not constitute musical sounds. Even sounds produced by musical instruments do not necessarily constitute musical sounds. Human intent is necessary, and thus music becomes a human creation (Radocy & Boyle, 2003). Cultural norms and expectations shape what are deemed musical sounds, as opposed to simply sounds or noise.

An awareness of diverse cultural norms explains why what sounds constitutes musical sounds varies so much around the world, even within the United States. As we change cultures, the meaning of what sounds are intended to be musical sounds within that culture change. Without cultural or human intent, sounds are simply sounds, without meaning or value. They are not musical sounds because humans living in the culture in which the sounds exist do not recognize them as music. Subsequently, music appears to be a perceptual phenomenon for which sounds must be structured in a manner that people understand them as musical sounds. Thus, it may be summarized that sounds are recognized as music when they:

1. Are created or combined by humans
2. Are recognized as music by some group of people
3. Serve some human function (Radocy & Boyle, 2003)

Put simply, humans create music, thus making it a social phenomenon. Sounds are ultimately defined as musical sounds if people are willing to accept them as music and humans intend the sounds to be musical.

What is music?

- Music is sounds and silences, sometimes organized, sometime unorganized, involving various pitches, volume, and timbres occurring within some sort of rhythm context?
- Music is a social phenomenon defined by cultural norms, requiring human creation and intent?
- Music appears to be a perceptual phenomenon for which sounds must be structured in a manner that people understand them as musical sounds?
- Sounds are ultimately defined as musical sounds if people are willing to accept them as music?

Because musical sounds are determined by human intentions, society and its various cultures have considerable influence on the music and musical behaviors of its members. Enculturation teaches that the same cultural norms that constitute musical sounds also affect our music behaviors. This includes not only how we participate, but also the extent of our participation. Similarly, like the wide variety of musical sounds, music behaviors vary greatly from culture to culture and are influenced by standards and expectations. In the United States, there are many ways to participate in music, each unique to its culture and each a valid way to enjoy music.

Because music is so greatly influenced by human standards, it is easy to conclude that music behavior is a human behavior (Merriam, 1964). Anthropologists report that evidence of musical behavior has been found in the earliest findings of human existence (Nettl, 1956). As music has been passed down through the ages, it has continuously been associated with human activity, even as humans have evolved. In contemporary society, music continues to be pervasive and prominent in many human activities and events. It is both personal and interpersonal, enjoyed individually and in groups. While it is enjoyed individually, humans usually intend music to be shared with some other form of human presence (Kaplan, 1990; Small, 1997). The ever-presence of music in virtually all aspects of today's society makes it an immense force that influences many human behaviors, including dress, language, religion, celebrations, eating, studying, and even medical practices. For example, think of how music contributes to a wedding, graduation ceremony, or sporting event. Music has been shown to affect the amount of food we eat, contribute to steady exercise, contribute to feelings of hate and joy, and influence our reading comprehension (Radocy & Boyle, 2003). Because of music's power over human behavior, it needs to be better understood and not accepted as a status quo phenomenon. Thus, music education is needed to present music as important phenomena itself, and a social entity that can affect human actions and thought.

Why Do We Need Music?

Can you imagine a world without music? The sociologist Max Kaplan (1990) stated that, while music may not be as essential as food and water, "One can live without music; one hardly does" (p. 19). The debate over why humans need music extends to why music exists. As musicians, music is so apparent in our lives that we may believe that our world would be an empty void if music were not present. However, music in the United States may be so pervasive that even musicians, including music educators, are not always aware of music's presence. Indeed, there are few activities or places in society where we can go and not hear music. Music may be so common, so expected, we may not appreciate its value and thus its role in our lives. We may fail to be aware of its connection to humans, that humans alone determine what is considered music. In doing so, as teachers we may fail to recognize music's importance in the lives of our students. This failure can lead to a narrow musical scope in terms of musicianship and acceptance of musical diversity. A narrow perception can have a limiting effect on the experiences we provide our students.

People presumably create music, for some reason, to serve some function or purpose. Many scholars suggest music exists due to its enculturation powers (Johnson, 1985; Nettl, 1956; Wallin, Merker, & Brown, 2000). The enculturation process informs us of how music functions in a particular culture. Music's functions are often purposeful and reflect the unique value and relationship individuals have to participating in music, whether this participation is active or passive, including performing, listening, composing, and teaching. We find music in ceremonies and the media, at work and in restaurants, in hospitals and schools, and even in the military. Consequently, we use music in a multitude of ways, to both stimulate and sedate our activities and thoughts, to entertain, educate, provoke, eat, wage war, motivate, persuade, heal, and reward.

The anthropologist Alan Merriam (1964) identified ten broad ways in which music functions in every society throughout the world. In essence, Merriam's functions of music demonstrate why all humans need music. Merriam, like other anthropologists (Johnson, 1985; Nettl, 1956; Wallin, Merker, & Brown, 2000), stated that music is everywhere humans exist, and has been everywhere humans have existed. However, while music is a global entity, it is used differently throughout the world.

Merriam stated that the term *function* denotes *reasons* for engaging in music activity. The functions reflect how humans use music in their lives throughout the world. While reflecting an anthropological perspective, each function illustrates the broad array of uses in which music serves humans in various cultures. Furthermore, Merriam suggested that music has served to function in these capacities since its beginnings and is still applicable to contemporary cultures. According to Merriam, the ten functions of music in society are as follows.

Alan Merriam's Functions of Music

Function	Description
Emotional Expression	Music serves as a vehicle to express ideas and emotions that people might not be able to do in ordinary interactions.
Aesthetic Enjoyment	Contemplating music in terms of its beauty, or meaning and/or to provoke a feeling.
Entertainment	Music serves to engage our attention or divert attention to some other aspect.
Communication	While music is not a language, it is used to convey reference and meaning.
Symbolic Representation	Music functions to represent some nonmusical thing, idea, or behavior.
Physical Response	Music elicits, excites, and stimulates behavior.
Enforcing Conformity to Social Norms	Music functions to help individuals to learn and accept cultural expectations and proper behavior.
Validate Social Institutions and Religious Rituals	Music helps to emphasize proper behaviors and attitudes associated with cultural organizations and ceremonies.
Contributing to the Continuity and Stability of Culture	Music serves to assure individuals of a continuation of norms and security in society.
Contribution to the Integration of Society	Music draws people together by inviting, encouraging, even requiring individuals to work together.

While Merriam's functions represent an anthropological perspective, Max Kaplan (1990) presented music as a global phenomenon from a sociological perspective. Accordingly, because music is so influenced by humans and influences humans so greatly, music serves social functions within every society. Kaplan's social functions of art, including how music functions in society, are:

1. A form of knowledge
2. Collective possession
3. Personal experience

4. Therapy
5. A moral and symbolic force
6. An incidental commodity
7. A symbolic indicator of change
8. A link between the past, present, and future.

Kaplan agreed that music, like all of the arts, has a global function. Similar to Merriam, Kaplan stated that the functions of art change as the various needs of society change. However, the social needs of culture may alter the function of music at any time. Accordingly, the intentions of the art's creator (e.g., music composer) are frequently overridden by the public's intentions, which may find their own meaning in what is seen, heard, or read (Kaplan, 1990, p. 28). Consequently, as culture changes, so does the function of art within society, including music. Thus, a true reciprocal relationship exists between art (music) and society where each affects, and reflects, the other. Both music and society depend on each other to some extent. The same relationship exists between music education and society. The functions of music education must change with the needs of society if our profession is to be relevant.

Music Education's Role in Society

Music may be so pervasive that humans take it for granted. We become unconcerned with where or how the music started, as long as it is there. This attitude exemplifies a degree of apathy regarding music's role in various cultures, further demonstrating a lack of relevancy between music and members of society. Apathy affects music education, where a lack in relevancy of school music experiences to everyday music experiences may also be occurring. People are participating in musical behaviors; they are just not necessarily participating in music behaviors that relate to school music experiences (Gallup, 2003a). This reaction was presented in the Vision 2020 conference, where discussion focused on how people value music deeply as an aesthetic and entertainment force in their lives, they just don't value school music because it offers few musical options and choices, and is different from the music personally consumed by society (Jellison, 2000; Madsen, 2000). If such attitudes indeed exist, our profession must question the value and role of music in the schools and the product resulting from these experiences.

Apathy among society, including among music teachers, may be one of music education's greatest challenges. Apathy was addressed in the Vision 2020 conference with the perception that the more pervasive music has become in our culture, the more irrelevant the study of music has become in our schools (Madsen, 2000). If society and schools reflect each other, it is reasonable to assume that music and music education reflect each other. If society takes music for granted, it may also take the process of learning music for granted. The lack of awareness or concern can lead individuals being unaware of music's contribution to their lives.

Furthermore, if Haack (1997) is correct, many in society are unaware of music's power and influence on their behavior and attitudes. We frequently allow various societal components such as businesses, politicians, the military, the media, and even schools to use music to convey and manipulate certain meanings or actions. Consider the messages music helps present in various advertising or political campaigns. Because many individuals are unaware of music's power and have a lack of knowledge regarding the diversity of music available, components of society can exert tremendous control over their musical choices and music's affect. This control is the essence of the conflict theory of the "haves" controlling the "have-nots." If power is knowledge, then having more knowledge of music's influence and diversity enables individuals to choose what is best for them. Power through musical knowledge enables individuals to maintain self-control over a potentially controlling substance.

Thus, music education becomes a compelling tool in contemporary society. Knowledge and skills learned through music education are useful throughout life, and though they function in varying manners among our cultural groups, music skills do not discriminate based on cultural characteristics such as race, gender, ethnicity, religion, or socioeconomic status (Radocy & Boyle, 2003). From a sociological view, music education provides an opportunity for lifelong learning and participation in ways unique to each individual; both should be among the primary goals of music education.

Throughout life, participation in music should be based on individual desire. Desire should not be impeded by a restriction on what is defined as a quality music experience. Restricting music to only experiences judged to be "good" experiences limits the diversity of musical experiences that can be meaningful to everyone. Confining music to "good" experiences further conveys the message that music participation is only for those who cannot only excel, but must be able to excel at a high degree. Christopher Small (1997) uses the term "musicking" to describe any musical behavior as a valid form for musical participation. Small uses musicking as a verb denoting music as an act, any act of participation in music behavior. Accordingly, musicking defines a "good" music experience as any music experience that is meaningful to an individual. Musicking would include performing, listening, and composing, and reading or talking about music. Musicking provides for a "quality" music encounter to be experienced either passively or actively. The means of musicking would be served through either formal venues such as a performance hall or rehearsal room, or informally through driving in your car, eating, studying, or simply having a conversation with friends about music.

Musicking enables individuals to participate in "good" meaningful music experiences for their entire life. By simply enabling individuals to participate in music by whatever means or abilities they desire, it de-mystifies music as something only for individuals with "talent." Anyone can participate in music. The key is that the individual determines the level of music participation, as any degree of participation is a valid choice! Consequently, music education becomes more relevant to members of society. Enabling lifelong participation in music connects music education to music in people's lives, throughout their lives. The reciprocal relationship between society and schools, and between music and music education, becomes evident. Relevancy occurs because everyone can use and participate in music whenever and however they want to, to whatever degree they desire.

Nevertheless, neither the average United States' citizen, nor perhaps even many of our music teachers, view or understand music in a musicking manner. Music education often fails to allow for diverse individualism or the concept of musicking. Music is not often included in studies or valued as important core courses by many components of society. Typically, knowledge and skills considered as core educational goals include mathematics, English, science, and social studies. While these studies are necessary to the success of individuals in society, they are not by themselves sufficient. The ability of music to control or be part of so many aspects of our lives goes unnoticed and thus is frequently omitted from core educational curricula. Any other aspect of society that exerts such power is included in the core of school curricula. However, due to the power and influence music has in society, it would appear to be a necessary component in curricula for all students to learn and experience.

Re-Defining a Music Education Experience

Placing music at the center of education requires a re-evaluation of what is defined as "music education." The traditional role of public school music education is based on a large ensemble performance and dates back to Lowell Mason. This model has worked well and provided music experiences to unknown numbers of American students. Still, in this model, the end product of a performed concert becomes more important than the process leading to the performance. This view is still maintained in contemporary music education by many educators, school administrators, parents, students, and members of the general public.

However, society has changed since 1838, yet the role and practice of music education in our schools has altered very little. Music education has at times lost its reciprocal relationship to society. Unlike other curricular areas, which often change to reflect society, music education has failed to reflect changes in music within our society. Hence, public school music education has been criticized as being out of touch with the music behaviors of its students (Madsen, 2000). The foundation of the American music education curriculum remains focused on large performing ensembles. Opportunities for individuals to discover their unique relationship with music are often limited at best. Individualism suffers due to the traditional group ensemble experience. An unbalanced emphasis on the product becomes the focus.

To reverse this trend, music education must be willing to change its role to better reflect contemporary societal values, including the changing role music plays in our society. Music education must reflect the needs and desires of the school and community by reaching out to all students by incorporating individual opportunities into traditional group ensemble experiences, thus making participation in music more accessible to a greater number of students. Accomplishing this goal will require a change in what music educators, administrators, and the public define as a music education experience. While the traditional value of the large performing ensemble may still serve as the core foundation of any music education curriculum, diversification of the curriculum must occur.

Diversifying the music curriculum should begin with understanding the variety of roles that music plays in our society, including the music experiences and behaviors being practiced and sought after by members of our society. One study by the American Music Conference (1997) of 6,000 high school students found the following data on students' music attitudes:

1.   96% wanted to be able to read music
2.   93% wanted to be able to play the music they read
3.   91% wanted to compose their own music
4.   90% wanted to be able to record the music they composed.

These data illustrate the need for music educators to rethink the definition of a music education and its role in the lives of their students. Music education, as it has historically and traditionally been taught, does not reflect the needs and desires of contemporary society. While performance may remain the essence of music education, other modes of musical behavior and participation are wanted and need exploration. Much of music teaching involves telling students information while not allowing students to discover for themselves. Alternate, perhaps more efficient, ways of teaching need investigation. New experiences that challenge existing experiences/knowledge for learning must occur (Woodford, 1997). Music educators need to empower students to think for themselves, to make their own musical decisions, and encourage lifelong learning of and participation in music. Music educators might consider that learning occurs best when:

1.   It is personal
2.   It involves authentic participation
3.   It involves both individual & group processes
4.   The focus is on *both* process and product.

Any likely change in music education could start with providing additional experiences through an expansion of the music curriculum. Traditional music education curricula frequently offer varying opportunities in large ensembles, including band, choral, and strings. Additional offerings commonly include music theory and small ensembles. Certainly traditional music education experiences are still relevant to many students, thus forming the foundation of any school music program. However, an expansion of the curriculum could increase the relevancy of school music to a broader cultural scope. A more diversified contemporary music curriculum may include non-traditional opportunities such as music composition, electronic music (including MIDI), popular music performance ensembles (yes, even rock 'n' roll ensembles or country and western bands!), music appreciation classes, and world music ensembles. Students could receive individual instruction in guitar, piano, or any traditional wind, percussion or string instrument. Justification for these types of curricular experiences can be found in one study that asked high school students to select what music experience they would most like to participate in (Lentsch, 2000). The results found most students would like to learn to play the piano. One implication of this study is that by diversifying the curriculum, music can become more relevant to contemporary music roles that may provide more direct transfer of school experiences to out-of-school usages for both large ensemble groups and individuals.

Redefining music education will meet many challenges in order for ideas to become reality. Ideas to expand music's role in school and society are not new. In the 1960s, Comprehensive Musicianship sought to broaden music offerings in the schools (Mark, 1996). Many educators were excited about possibilities, yet Comprehensive Musicianship faltered. Music education failed to justify its new role as more meaningful than traditional instructional concepts. Failure was frequently associated with performance expectations of school administrators, the public, and music educators themselves, a lack of funding, and an inability to provide opportunities for all students (Mark, 1996). Marching bands were still expected to perform at football games, choruses were still required to perform for various schools functions or singing the *National Anthem* for pep rallies, and ensembles to perform at festivals or contests. Many problems faced by Comprehensive Musicianship are also challenges to redefining music's role and offerings today.

Proposed changes in schools are frequently first met with challenges associated with a lack of funding. Certainly sufficient funding is needed to purchase supplies and equipment, but funding may also be needed for additional staff and possible teaching space. Physical space and class scheduling are common challenges, as is meeting existing expectations of the community and school. The traditional focus on large performing groups is enculturated into the perceptions and expectations of school administrators, faculty, staff, and students. The same expectations extend to the general public, as school ensembles are frequently asked to perform for various functions in the community. Activities that do not perform a service or perform in public venues may not be perceived as valid school music experiences. Altering perceptions that music curricula can include nontraditional music experiences will require demonstrating the value of these experiences from both an academic and musical perspective.

Perhaps the greatest challenge to re-defining music education will come from music teachers themselves. Like other school personnel and community members, teachers have been enculturated to what traditionally constitutes music education. This socialization process began when they first started music instruction and continued throughout their teacher-training experiences (Woodford, 1997). Consequently, teachers must consider music education in ways that are very unfamiliar. While maintaining a focus on traditional forms of music-making, teachers will need to overcome enculturated attitudes about what is "good" or appropriate music, and be willing to become familiar with music their students enjoy. Subsequently, music teachers will need to defend new approaches and experiences to administrators, parents, the community, and even students so that funding, space, and scheduling issues will not be obstacles to implementing new curricula. New experiences help the general school and community members to see what can be accomplished in music education, thus contributing to a new perception of what constitutes a music education experience.

Summary

Music education succeeds best when it functions within the reciprocal relationship with our American society. The historical development of music education in the United States reflects a sociological perspective that music has always been valued by our society, and we have always interacted with music. When considering a broader perspective of the role that music serves in a contemporary global society, the music anthropologist Bruno Nettl stated:

> There is probably no other human cultural activity which is so all-pervasive and which reaches into, shapes, and often controls so much human behavior. (1956, p. 6)

Music may be so important that throughout human evolution we have continuously created music to reflect our needs, emotions, and behaviors (Blacking, 1973). Music has bonded us together, helped us to relax, contributed to our rituals, and made us think about our existence. We have participated in music individually, but we usually share (or at the very least intend to share) the experience with others. Thus, music may arguably be one of the most basic human behaviors, indeed a fundamental social behavior with global uses (Merriam, 1964). Also, because the relationship of music to humans is an indication that the act of music has been passed down from generation to generation, music education, in some form, may arguably be one of the oldest forms of education associated with humans.

Because music is such a social experience, music education is also a social phenomenon. If indeed music exists in many cultures, then a case may be made for education being the best role for music. It is important for educators to remember that most students receive formal music instruction through the schools. The purpose of school music is to provide instruction and experiences, enabling students to transfer learned skills to other musical interests. Perhaps music education's best role is to connect music experienced in the schools to music experienced outside of schools. In this manner, the role music plays in our society, and the awareness that music education contributes to this role, can become more vibrant and purposeful.

Key Items

Merriam's Functions of Music
Singing Schools
Singing School Masters
Comprehensive Musicianship
Horace Mann
Sputnik
Wiley Housewright
Visions 2020: The Housewright Symposium on the Future of Music Education

Kaplan's Functions of Music
Bay Psalm Book
Musicking
Common Schools
Lowell Mason
Tanglewood Symposium
Goals and Objectives Project
Progressive Era

Questions for Consideration

1. How can music teachers convince school boards that music education is equally important as other academic classes, such as math and science?
2. What is the relationship of music in society to school music? Do music educators have a professional obligation to connect societal music to school music?
3. What are current issues in music education that may be viewed as parallel issues to historic events that have affected music education?
4. What can contemporary music educators learn from Lowell Mason?

5. Why haven't the Tanglewood and Vision 2020 conferences been more successful in securing music's place and role in school curricula?
6. How might Merriam's and Kaplan's functions of music be used to develop and justify school music curricula?
7. What may be various uses of music in organizations such as the media, businesses, sports, and the military?
8. How might musicking be used to broaden school music curricula?
9. How might school music experiences change or be re-defined to better reflect changes in societal music?
10. In what ways does music serve as a symbol in our culture? In what ways does it influence our emotions?

Web Resources

Early Music Education

Journal of Historical Research in Music Education: http://www.ithaca.edu/music/education/jhrme/
Smithsonian Institute: http://smithsonianeducation.org/educators/lesson_plans/shapenote/index.html

Lowell Mason

Lowell Mason Fellows: http://musiced.nafme.org/about/lowell-mason-fellows
Lowell Mason House: http://www.lowellmasonhouse.com/
The Boston Handel and Haydn Society: http://imslp.org/wiki/The_Boston_Handel_and_Haydn_Society_Collection_of_Church_Music_%28Mason,_Lowell%29

Role of Music

National Association of Music Merchants: http://www.nammfoundation.org/
National Endowment for the Arts: http://arts.gov
Society for American Music: http://www.american-music.org/conferences/

Chapter 5

Equality of Education

Our profession rests on the assumption that music study is not only valuable but necessary.
—J. Terry Gates

Most Americans are taught, and therefore perceive, that society is open, fair, and full of opportunities for all citizens. Anyone with sufficient drive can achieve anything. Data from one survey showed that the majority of individuals believe that hard work and a good education are keys to getting ahead in life (Pew Research, 2014). The belief in opportunities for individuals to improve their social and educational status and mobility remains strong despite their chances being highly related to socioeconomics, ethnicity, and gender (Banks, 2001). Chapter 5 discusses equality of opportunity in education and music education. The chapter's main idea is that a diverse society is not necessarily an equal society, as different groups have different opportunities. Is music and music education truly for everyone? What factors within society promote and also limit school music experiences? Can limitations be overcome to explore music in ways unique to each individual?

An Overview of Educational Models of Equality

The United States is a nation of ideals that frequently contrast with actual practices. Our country has historically been based on the premise of equal opportunity for all citizens. However, access and treatment are keys to equality. Equality of opportunity requires everyone having access to the same choices. Equality of opportunity has meant all members of society have an equal chance and equal access to enter an occupation or social class (Spring, 2006). Equality of educational opportunity refers to all students having equal access to the same education (Spring, 2014). However, equal access is influenced by equal treatment. For equality to occur, everyone should receive equal treatment without special privileges due to race, gender, religion, ethnicity, or wealth. This democratic premise (embedded in the Fourteenth Amendment to the U.S. Constitution) has been applied to the our school system, where all children are believed to have an equal opportunity to learn and fulfill individual potential through the equivalent access to instruction, resources, and activities (Levine & Levine, 1996). The premise of equal opportunity applies to music educators and is the fundamental philosophy of the National Association for Music Education (2014), which stated that music instruction should be for everyone and benefits all students.

Conceptually, American schools have been designed to help students overcome inequalities in order to achieve occupational and social goals (Oakes & Lipton, 1999). Horace Mann considered education as the great equalizer that enabled individuals to overcome variables such as race and socioeconomics (Keene, 1987). However, much of the current American educational system is based on a factory model developed in early 1900s that frequently fails to differentiate between student abilities, backgrounds, expectations, and resources (Darling-Hammond, 2010). As changing skills and demands evolved, questions exist as to whether schools can actually provide equality for all students. Furthermore, do circumstances outside of schools, such as economics, influence equality more than educational opportunity? It is possible that schools reduce social differences for some while increasing differences for others.

It is doubtful any child may have a reasonable chance to succeed if they are denied an opportunity for education. Ironically, beginning with Horace Mann in the 1830s, American public schools have been viewed as the gateway to equality by providing opportunities to reduce cultural differences (Feinber & Soltis, 1998; Swift 1976; Thayer & Levit, 1966). John Dewey (1900) envisioned education as the opportunity for all individuals to develop their capacities to the fullest extent; no one had a monopoly on truth or value. Yet evidence suggests our society, including our schools and music programs, is riddled with inequalities (Darling-Hammond, 2010; Ravitch, 2010; Robinson, 2000; Serow, Castelli, & Castelli, 2000; Woodford, 2005). Conflicts arise over different choices, treatment, and unequal outcomes of the educational processes regarding wealth, occupational status, and opportunities. Differences exist between gender, socioeconomic levels, race, ethnicities, and individuals with disabilities, among many other groups.

Public schools in the United States are mandated to teach all students, regardless of ability or disability. In 1974, Congress passed the Equal Education Opportunities Act, which called for all students to have equal educational opportunities regardless of race, color, gender, or national origin (Law & Higher Education, 2010). Later, the No Child Left Behind Act (2001) required that all students achieve the same minimum standard. Most recently, the Common Core Initiative (2014) purported that students across the country should receive the same training and skills, no matter where they live. However, is it possible for schools to teach all students equally well? Considering the pluralistic nature of our population, there are many variables influencing a child's learning, including influences both controlled by school, and out of school's control.

Ideally, schools evaluate student skills and behaviors based on achievement alone, with no influence from social background. In principle, teachers encourage the "best and brightest" students to pursue the most challenging courses, while guiding students with more ordinary abilities toward programs most suited to their specific talents (Ballantine, 2001; Thayer & Levit, 1966). There is no single selection criterion, as many factors affect the determination of individual skills, including past achievement, creativity, motivation, aspirations, and self-concept. However, evidence suggests other factors, including gender, race, ethnicity, social class, parental influence, and even physical attractiveness also affect perceptions of ability (Kozol, 2005b; Pole, 1993; Ravitch, 2010).

To provide equal opportunity requires that all participants begin at the same starting place. But is this possible? Achieving an equal starting point for all students can be difficult, if not impossible. Family variables such as socioeconomic status, cultural expectations, and access to resources frequently create inequalities before some individuals even begin school (Kozol, 1991; Pole, 1993). Early childhood programs such as Head Start attempt to overcome early inequalities by providing special instruction for underprivileged students in reading, writing, and other skills in order to develop a level of preparedness to enter school (Kozol, 2005a; Meier, Stewart, & England, 1989). Yet differences concerning opportunity continue to affect students differently.

Common School and Sorting Machine Models

When a child enters school, it is often assumed all students will have the same access to experiences and knowledge. However, two different models of equality, offering very different experiences and opportunities, frequently affect schools: the common school model and the sorting machine model. The common school model is based on the democratic ideal that everyone should have access to the same educational opportunities (Spring, 2006; Swift, 1976). The basic philosophy is that education is intended to improve the quality of life for all individuals. Theoretically, each individual begins at the same starting place. Social class, race, gender, disabilities, or other factors do not determine or affect educational opportunities, as success for all students is the primary goal. All students are given the same choices and taught to think individually. The goal is to prepare all students to function equally in society and have an equal opportunity to obtain a vocation after graduating. It is assumed the universal application of experiences will eliminate social class differences due to everyone having equal access to skills, instruction, and resources.

Another model of educational opportunity is the sorting machine model. This model has been increasingly used in American schools due to the need to educate a large number of students whose backgrounds and abilities differ widely (Spring, 2006; Swift, 1976). In the sorting machine model, schools classify, divide, and group students according to individual talents and abilities based on teacher assessments, counselor recommendations, and test scores, including standardized test scores, which are presumed to be impartial. Thus, students are given fewer opportunities to make choices and are directed into specific curricula. Justification of the assigned group is based on the school's prediction of the student's ability to succeed in a particular group (Spring, 2006; Swift, 1976). This classification placement or ability grouping is known as tracking (Burnett, 1995). Students are placed into a specific curriculum or program that best "fits" their abilities and then guided or tracked throughout their school careers in these curricula. The classification and tracking creates homogeneous groupings used to separate students for different levels of instruction (Ballantine, 2001; Burnett, 1995). For example, some students may be placed into college preparatory classes while others receive vocational training classes. Students may be further separated into "gifted" classes or "learning disabled" classes.

Sorting and tracking is a common practice in American schools. Many teachers believe it is easier to teach groups of homogeneous students with similar backgrounds and abilities (Ballantine, 2001). However, problems arise when efforts to deal with diverse abilities frequently result in low-income and minority students ending up at the bottom of the ability group system (Burnett, 1995; Darling-Hammond, 2010). Furthermore, once placed into a specific curriculum it is difficult for individuals to change into another curriculum (Spring, 2006). Some studies have suggested that students not classified into gifted or college preparatory classes do not receive as much exposure to more rigorous classes, more individual instruction, or access to advanced technology resources (Burnett, 1995; Coleman, 1990; Hallinan, 1990). As a result, the sorting machine model produces an unequal and different education for students.

There are defenders of both education models. Defenders of the sorting machine model assert that student-grouping assignments are based on objective criteria and that classes and curricula that are disproportionately one-sided due to race, gender, or other cultural variables are due to individual student backgrounds and abilities (Ballantine, 2001). Individuals promoting the common school model state that unlike homogeneous groupings, schooling based on heterogeneous groupings promotes a more multidimensional educational experience, leading to better social understanding and awareness of population diversity (Ballantine, 2001).

Groups Affected by Inequalities

Many educational inequalities are connected with attitudes, mostly negative, associated with discrimination and its components of prejudice and stereotypes (Oakes & Lipton, 1999; Renzetti & Curran, 2000). Each attitude revolves around groups or categories of people and is usually based on cultural variables such as race, ethnicity, religion, gender, socioeconomic status, political views, geographic location, special needs, and sexual orientation (Meier, Stewart, & England, 1989; Oakes & Lipton, 1999). Additionally, groups may also include cultural differences in intelligence or academic accomplishments, and music ability. Discrimination is a behavior broadly defined as the act of treating particular groups of people unequally (Gollnick & Chinn, 1994; Oakes & Lipton, 1999). Prejudice represents an attitude resulting in a generalization or irrational judgment regarding a category of people (Oakes & Lipton, 1999). Prejudicial judgments can be both positive and negative. Even a positive prejudice can lead to an exaggerated view of an individual or events. For example, believing that a certain race or ethnicity has more musical ability than another race or ethnicity is positive prejudice. The results of negative prejudices may range from mild aversion to hostility. Stereotypes evolve from prejudice. A stereotype is an idea or perception of a particular group or category of people (Gollnick & Chinn, 1994; Oakes, & Lipton, 1999). Because prejudice and stereotypes usually reflect learned cultural values, they become part of our thinking process and are difficult to overcome (Renzetti & Curran, 2000).

Common Types of Discriminating Attitudes

Discrimination: a behavior that may be broadly defined as the act of treating particular groups of people unequally

Prejudice: an attitude resulting in a generalization or an irrational judgment regarding an entire category of people

Stereotype: an idea or perception of a particular group or category of people

---

There are many variables, including low expectations and self-esteem, learned helplessness, and cultural expectations resulting from resistant cultures that affect inequality among cultural groups (Robinson, 2000). Social, educational, and psychological research regarding variables affecting educational opportunity among different cultural groups is extensive and beyond the scope of this introductory material. The following is a brief overview for select groups. Individuals seeking more in-depth information are encouraged to consult the resources at the end of the chapter.

Family Influences

The influence of family is the greatest influence on learning outside the classroom and contributes as much to student opportunity and success as individual ability and ambition. Most Americans end up in social and occupational positions similar to their parents (Alwin & Thornton, 1984). Families who have existed in a lifelong and intergenerational web of poor education, substandard housing, low income, bad nutrition, and overall repression have long become disillusioned at prospects to escape their conditions and frequently acculturate their children into a similar sense of hopelessness. A home environment that does not provide children basic skills needed to start school is a frequent explanation for academic problems and a lack of opportunity to escape family conditions (Ballantine, 2001).

Early parental involvement in children's educational decisions and experiences is important to educational opportunity and success (Alwin & Thornton, 1984). Active parental interaction with children assists in the development of verbal skills, the ability to focus attention, fundamental problem-solving abilities, and elementary social skills that contribute to a sense of "school readiness" and a positive attitude toward learning (Alwin & Thornton, 1984). Furthermore, study results have shown that parental influence can have tremendous effect on student and teacher expectations (Alwin & Thornton, 1984; Cooper & Conswella, 1995; Phillips & Zimmerman, 1990). Students whose parents are highly educated frequently perceive education as more valuable, achieve higher educational levels, and seek more rigorous classes (Ballantine, 2001; Cooper & Conswella, 1995). Schools with higher parental involvement have higher academic achievement rates and lower absenteeism, truancy, and dropout rates (Alwin & Thornton, 1984; Ballantine, 2001).

Variables related to family socioeconomic status can be powerful dimensions in cultural differences related to education equality (Harrington, 1962). Census data show the sharpest divisions in socioeconomic levels are between suburban and inner city schools (National Center for Education Statistics, 2003a). The highest family income has been found in school districts outside of inner cities, whereas high poverty levels are found in inner city communities (Kozol, 2005a). Frequently, parents at higher socioeconomic levels tend to be more involved with their children's education than parents at lower economic levels (Ballantine, 2001). The lack of participation is often due to the need for lower socioeconomic parents (usually both) to work, and thus they do not have as much time to become involved. Some research has demonstrated that family socioeconomic variables can overcome other differences, such as race and gender (Pole, 1993; Meier, Stewart, & England, 1989; Renzetti & Curran, 2000). For example, upper-class African- and Hispanic-Americans typically attain higher academic achievement and are less likely to drop out of school than individuals from their same cultural group in lower socioeconomic classes (Meier, Stewart, & England, 1989). When socioeconomic levels are considered along with family variables such as a positive parental attitude toward education, academic achievement is even higher (Meir, Stewart, & England, 1989).

Gender

Differences in academic roles among gender are an international phenomenon (Jones & Dindia, 2004). Many of the world's societies consider schooling more important for males than females (Woolfolk, 1998). However, in recent years, females in the United States have replaced males in many roles (Fulcher & Scott, 2011). In the United States, achieving gender equity in classrooms has received much political attention through federal legislation such as the Civil Rights Act in 1964 and Title IX of the Education Amendment in 1972 (Jones & Dindia, 2004; Spring, 2006). Title IX has perhaps been the most powerful, as this policy seeks to provide males and females equal opportunities to pursue training and career paths, including those traditionally thought to be female occupations (elementary general music teacher) or male occupations (construction worker or manager). However, while opportunities have increased, and the academic achievement gap between males and females has narrowed, differences still exist in social expectations between genders (Fulcher & Scott, 2011).

Boys and girls have different socialization experiences from birth, and by the time they enter school they already have concepts of gender identity (Macionis, 1997). Learning gender roles initially takes place in the home through observing and imitating parental figures and siblings, playing with certain toys, reading books and seeing pictures in the books, and being exposed to various media forms (Macionis, 1997). Later, when students attend school, gender roles are further learned and reinforced by observing teacher interactions and reactions to students, interacting with peers, reading textbooks, and experiences through curriculum tracking (Levine & Levine, 1996).

Research has shown that classroom equality is affected by the social context of the class environment. Males and females are treated differently in the classroom, but not always due to their gender (Sadker & Sadker, 1995). Frequently the teacher's gender and sex biases influence classroom opportunity. While research is mixed, much data suggest teacher-initiated interactions with students, particularly those by male teachers, are more frequent with male students than female students (Jones & Dindia, 2004; McCormick, 1994; Sadker & Sadker, 1995). This appears to hold true across students' educational lifespans. Furthermore, biased behavior often affects teacher expectations, which can influence students' self-images and expectations (Jones & Dindia, 2004).

Studies have demonstrated males and females attending the same school can come out of that situation with very different experiences, interests, achievement levels, and expectations (Jones & Dindia, 2004; Sadker & Sadker, 1995). Much of this research has focused on the socialization processes occurring in schools that "teach" gender-role identity within social norms and expectations (McCormick, 1994; Spring, 2006). Gender-role identity is the image each individual has of him or herself, and has been shown to affect students academically (Renzetti & Curran, 2000). Some research findings suggest girls perform equal to or better than boys in most academic areas until the high school years. By the end of high school girls have fallen behind boys in several areas, including scores on college entrance exams, science, and mathematics (Marsh, 1990; Muller, 1998). One explanation for this decline are data suggesting females receive less encouragement from teachers, parents, and peers to succeed academically than males, resulting in low self-esteem (Muller, 1998). A positive feeling about one's self appears to correlate with greater academic success (Woolfolk, 1998). During elementary school, girls and boys appear to feel equally positive regarding self-perceptions. Perceptions begin to change for girls in middle school and steadily decline through high school (Woolfolk, 1998).

Research inquiries have shown girls perceive they do not have freedom and respect to perform the same activities as boys (Estrich, 1994; Jones & Dindia, 2004). This perception reflects stereotype generalizations of the "correct" roles boys and girls should perform, which often begin in the home where girls are expected to meet certain cultural expectations considered female (and vice versa for boys) (Alwin & Thornton, 1984; Macionis, 1997). Perceptions are frequently reinforced by exposure to the media and peers. The stereotypical perception of cultural expectations extends to classrooms, where girls are often expected to perform certain roles, including not achieving as high in certain academic areas considered male domains (Estrich, 1994; Spring, 2006). Some research demonstrates boys may actually receive better instruction because teachers believe boys can achieve more than girls (Jones & Dindia, 2004; McCormick, 1994). Consequently, girls often report a poor self-image, constraints on views regarding their future, and less confidence in their abilities (Estrich, 1994; Sadker & Sadker, 1995).

Race and Ethnicity

Racial and ethnic changes occurring in the American population are reflected in the changing population of its schools (Lee, 2014; Oakes & Lipton, 1999; U.S. Census, 2013). The U.S. Department of Education estimated that in the fall of 2014, minority students will outnumber white students in public schools for the first time in history. The Department of Education further reports that while whites will still outnumber any single racial group, their overall enrollment numbers were expected to drop to under 50% for the first time.

An individual's race and ethnicity are two different cultural categories. Race is a category of people sharing biologically transmitted traits such as skin color, facial features, and body shape (Macionis, 1997). In the United States the concept of race is becoming increasingly blurred as more interracial marriages occur, resulting in an increased number of interracial individuals (Oakes & Lipton, 1999). Ethnicity is a shared cultural heritage commonly linked to geographic orientation (Macionis, 1997). A single ethnic group can be comprised of many different races.

A racial or ethnic minority is a category of people, distinguished by a physical or cultural trait, who are socially disadvantaged (Oakes & Lipton, 1999). Individuals in this group are typically highly distinctive in their cultural traditions and physical appearance and are subordinate to a more dominant cultural group. In the United States, racial and ethnic minorities are typically in lower socioeconomic classes and have received more limited educational opportunities (Levine & Levine, 1996).

Racial and ethnic groups are frequently subjected to various forms of discrimination, prejudice, racism, and stereotypes. A common form of discrimination is racism, which is defined as an act of oppression from one racial group toward another (Oakes & Lipton, 1999). Racism affects all races, including Latinos and Asian-Americans, but in the United States, racism is perhaps most frequently thought to be discrimination between Caucasians and African-Americans (Ballantine, 2001). Much of this oppression involves perceived stereotypes. In education, oppression based on stereotypes was exemplified in the book *The Bell Curve* (Herrnstein & Murray, 1994), which created great controversy when it argued a direct link exists between race, intelligence, and resulting social problems. The authors implied that race, primarily African-American, and income are principle factors linking low intelligence and social ills to poverty.

Because many minority groups are also economically disadvantaged, many of the same social class variables also affect race and ethnicity. A brief review of the data reveals race and/or ethnicity can have an effect on an individual's educational opportunities (Darling-Hammond, 2010; National Center for Education Statistics, 2001). Indeed, Darling-Hammond (2010) creates a strong case for the existence of a race- and class-based achievement gap in the United States. A general pervasive finding is that African-American, Latino, and low-income students are consistently overrepresented in low ability, remedial, and special education classes (Carey, 2004; Coleman, 1990). Additional data frequently name cultural variables such as home background, socioeconomic factors, and school environments as leading contributors to educational opportunity among different races and ethnicities (Gollnick & Chinn, 1994). Furthermore, data suggest schools serving predominately minority populations receive less funding than schools serving mainly white students (Carey, 2004; Darling-Hammond, 2010). The report, *The Funding Gap 2004: Many States Still Shortchange Low-income and Minority Students* (Carey, 2004), indicates that racially isolated schools serving low-income and minority students typically have smaller curricular offerings and larger vocational programs, in part due to lower funding from local and state school administrations.

Additional findings related to educational opportunity toward race and ethnicity reveal the following:

1. Typically, schools primarily attended by African-Americans and Hispanics offer limited college preparatory courses, such as advanced mathematics or science classes, and fewer musical options (Kozol, 1991; Walker & Hamann. 1995).
2. Some research has suggested schools attended primarily by minority populations place less emphasis on developing critical thinking and problem-solving skills (Coleman, 1990; Marzano, 2003).
3. Students tend to have teachers who reflect the racial makeup of the school population (Marzano, 2003).
4. Schools with large minority populations have greater turnover in teaching staff and have less experienced teachers (Marzano, 2003).
5. Lower ability groupings tend to include a disproportionate number of lower-class and minority students (Meir, Stewart, & England, 1989).
6. The socioeconomic makeup of the school's student population and the students' home backgrounds has tremendous influence on the school's achievement levels. Curriculum and the school facilities make little difference in student achievement (Marzano, 2003).

7. Language barriers greatly affect certain minority groups, the exception being Asian-American students (Morrow, 1991).
8. At almost every educational level white/non-Hispanics earn higher incomes than other racial categories, even when all races achieve the same education level (Kozol, 1991, 2005a, 2005b).
9. Despite attempts to desegregate schools to achieve more racially balanced populations, schools that were deeply segregated 30 years ago are still deeply segregated today. In California and New York, only one black student in seven goes to a predominately white school (Kozol, 2005b).

Students With Disabilities and Diverse Learners

That all music teachers will work with a student with a disability is not simply possible, but likely. Data from the National Center for Education Statistics (2013a) show that the number of students with a disability in public schools has more than doubled from 1976–2011. Annually, the number of students with disabilities educated in regular education classrooms, including the music classroom, increases at a steady rate. According to the U.S. Department of Education, in 2002 almost half of all students with disabilities in this country were educated in ordinary classrooms for at least 80 percent of the day. These students represent a diversity of learning challenges, ranging from more obvious characteristics such as physical disabilities or mental retardation to more mild disabilities, such as limited English proficiency. More mild disabilities present unique challenges, because teachers may not be aware that the student has a disability (Adamek & Darrow, 2005). However, the most common disabilities encountered in regular classrooms are specific learning disabilities, speech or language impairments, including students whose primary language is not English, mental retardation, and emotional disturbance (Adamek & Darrow, 2005).

The labels of "learning disabilities" or "special needs students" have at times been confusing and controversial terms that have been interpreted and used as catchall education phrases (Woolfolk, 1998). There is growing thought regarding the term "special," as it could place an unintended label on individuals. Darrow (2014) states that the label of "ordinary" is more accepted by students with disabilities, as they rarely view themselves as different from other students. Darrow states that the use of disability-related labels unnecessarily describes students in ways that may contribute to isolation or segregation, which diminishes the overall attributes of students. Darrow further states that "Reframing disability as a natural form of human variation—one characteristic among many possible human characteristics—can recast the image of students with disabilities and consequently promote their assimilation into school culture" (p. 37).

There are many definitions and qualifications for individuals to be labeled as having a learning disability. The American Psychological Association (2010) defines students with disabilities as students having a physical, emotional, intellectual, or social challenge. The criteria to have a child classified as disabled requires that an existing health condition or impairment (1) limits the ability of the child to perform a major life activity, and (2) affects the individual for an extended period of time (Ballantine, 2001). Such conditions or impairments include learning disabilities, speech, hearing, orthopedic and visual disabilities, mental retardation, and serious emotional disturbances (Ballantine, 2001; Hardman, Drew, & Egan, 2002).

A learning disability is a cognitive disorder resulting from the brain's inability to process information at a higher efficiency (Hardman, Drew, & Egan, 2002). Students classified as learning disabled (LD) have difficulty accomplishing certain standard tasks considered routine for other students. Students with learning disabilities are limited regarding social adjustment, vision, hearing, physical-motor coordination, speech and language, and learning efficiency and are thus categorized as students with disabilities (Hardman, Drew, & Egan, 2002). There are different categories or groups within the umbrella of special needs, including individuals with disabilities and gifted students.

Few may think of gifted students as disadvantaged, but if their skills are not challenged or developed, these students do not achieve their potential, thus placing them in the disadvantaged category (Hardman, Drew, & Egan, 2002; Raywid, 1989). PL 95–561 defines "gifted" as a specific academic aptitude, creative or productive thinking, leadership, and visual and performing arts talents (U.S. Department of Education, 2002b). However, the general nature of this definition frequently leaves the labeling of gifted students up to the individual school or academic program. Many states provide special funding for gifted and talented educational programs, and nearly all schools have some type of program where the highest achieving students are grouped together for enrichment or accelerated instruction (Ballantine, 2001). One problem in working with gifted students is singling out this special student at the possible alienation of other students. This special treatment can cause an elitist view, or academic jealousy, to develop among the students and peers (Hardman, Drew, & Egan, 2002; Raywid, 1989).

Two federal laws have helped bring attention to the importance of considering children's needs and designing programs suited for providing educational opportunity. The role of children with disabilities within school organizations began in 1975 with the passage of PL 94–142, the Education for All Handicapped Children Act (1975). This law stated all children with disabilities must be educated in the "least restrictive environment" possible. The provision forces schools to place students with disabilities into classrooms with peers who have no disabilities as much as possible. More recently, the Individuals with Disabilities Education Act, or IDEA, (U.S. Department of Education, 1997) extended the rights for equal education opportunities for students with disabilities by requiring school districts to educate all disabled children between the ages of three and 21. Some reports have indicated that laws pertaining to students with disabilities have resulted in 95 percent of those students now receiving instruction in regular school buildings and classrooms (Ballantine, 2001). Approximately 30 percent of these students are in regular classrooms all day, while another 38 percent spend a portion of the day in resource rooms that provide special assistance.

Most research on the integration of students with disabilities indicates positive results, especially regarding social skills and learning expectations (Johnson, & Darrow, 1997; U.S. Department of Education, 2002b). However, one concern is self-esteem as related to academic achievement (Hardman, Drew, & Egan, 2002; Woolfolk, 1998). The effects of labeling students as having special needs may be detrimental to achievement, thus meeting the self-fulfilling prophecy (Hardman, Drew, & Egan, 2002; Woolfolk, 1998). Research on strategies to best provide the most effective educational challenge for gifted students appears to be mixed. Some studies have shown gifted students benefit from being integrated into homogeneous ability classrooms (Ballantine, 2001; Hardman, Drew, & Egan, 2002). Other researchers purport that individualized instruction combined with some joint classroom activities best serves this population (Ballantine, 2001; Hardman, Drew, & Egan, 2002). Still, most findings suggest a program providing a variety of learning styles is most effective in working with gifted student populations (Ballantine, 2001; Hardman, Drew, & Egan, 2002).

Teacher Influence on the Equality of Opportunity

Teachers are the single greatest influence on learning inside the classroom. Teachers are socialization agents, influencing attitudes and behaviors as strongly as academic and musical knowledge. Individuals who are our earliest and most fundamental influences are known as primary socialization agents. These individuals provide a framework of reality for later development, including personal values, dress, language, even musical preference (Macionis, 1997). Initial primary socialization agents include close family members—parents or parental figures, and siblings. As we age, the number of primary socialization agents increases as we spend more time with others outside of immediate family, including peers, the media, and teachers.

As contact with others begins to diversify, we develop secondary socialization agents. These individuals influence how we apply the behaviors and attitudes learned from primary socialization agents to various aspects of our new expanded world (Macionis, 1997). Consequently, these influences begin as we go to school or spend significant time away from family. Secondary socialization agents frequently change roles as we grow and mature. Because schooling frequently begins in preschool or daycare settings, the influences of secondary socialization agents can begin much earlier. Thus, many of these agents, including teachers, become primary socialization agents due to the amount of time spent together (Ballantine, 2001; Macionis, 1997). Other secondary socialization agents remain strong influences because we develop a strong admiration for them and desire to emulate their lives. This group can include teachers, musicians, business, civic and religious leaders, and pop culture figures.

Understanding the roles and influence that teachers occupy requires an awareness of the environment in which teaching occurs. Educational opportunity begins with the curriculum. Since individuals most responsible for presenting the curriculum are teachers, they become a major influence on the quality of education in classrooms (Coleman, 1990; Kozol, 1991). Due to the amount of time spent in schools, teachers play a major role in the socialization of students (Ballantine, 2001; Levine & Levine, 1996). Because of the rise in single-parent and two-career families, teachers frequently function as parental figures (Ballantine, 2001; Alwin & Thornton, 1984). When considering issues such as parental divorce, child abuse, and teenage pregnancy, it is easy to understand that teachers often deal with issues that once stayed outside the walls of schools.

Due to the teacher's input through the sorting machine model, the influence of teacher-student dynamics on educational opportunity is apparent (Kozol, 1991). This educational approach draws attention to an inherent problem: teachers are human and thus affected by human biases. Biases may be most frequently observed in how teachers interact with and label students, resulting in defined student expectations and roles (Ballantine, 2001). Teacher expectations are influenced by various factors, including a student's name, past work and test scores, dress, physical appearance, attractiveness, race, sex, spoken language and accent, parent's occupation, parental, marital, and motherhood status, and manner in responding to the teacher. Expectations are manifested in the teacher's behavior toward and treatment of students in class (Jones & Dindia, 2004). Students quickly realize cues, causing them to believe they possess or do not possess certain abilities that can result in future behaviors, attitudes, and achievement. The combination of teacher expectations, labels, and students learning their roles can lead to the development of a self-fulfilling prophecy where the teacher expects certain behaviors from a child and the child responds to the expectations (Ballantine, 2001). This action results in the child achieving and behaving as he or she perceives is expected. Research has shown that this behavioral pattern is difficult to alter once established.

Inequality Among Schools

There are many differences among schools, even schools within the same school district. Many variables impact difference in school quality. Perhaps one of the greatest influences is funding. Economic factors appear to affect the quality of education at the school level. Demographics show most students from low-income families attend schools that spend less in per-pupil expenses than those attended mostly by higher-income families (Ballantine, 2001; Carey, 2004; Darling-Hammond, 2010). This lack of funding has resulted in computers with no keyboards, science classes without laboratories or microscopes, and music classes without music stands or playable instruments (Carey, 2004). Low-income schools tend to have more difficulty attracting and retaining better qualified teachers, are less likely to provide educational opportunities such as preschool programs and more challenging curriculums, have lower expectations and standards, and lack current technology and modern facilities (Carey, 2004; Coleman, 1990; Darling-Hammond, 2010; Harrington, 1962; Kozol, 2005a, 2005b).

Furthermore, equality of opportunity may be affected by the approach of schools themselves. Schools have been accused of reinforcing social expectations and norms through social reproduction (Kozol, 1991; Spring, 2006). This approach is a method of providing skills and experiences intended to maintain current conditions while not providing experiences to advance or improve the quality of life. Whether intentional or not, this process can affect education opportunities for students and contribute to maintaining differences between social classes (Levine & Levine, 1996).

Another factor in school quality is school choice. Traditionally, citizens in the United States have been educated by a public school system based on the concept of neighborhood schools where students attend schools located in the communities where they live (Levine & Levine, 1996). The concept of selecting a different school for their children to attend has long been an option for parents. Since the 1960s, the concept of school choice has granted parents the right to select the school they believe is best suited for their children's needs and interests (Spring, 2006). School choice allows students to attend any public school within or outside of their school district, a magnet or charter school, a private school, or home school. Additionally, virtual education has expanded with 22 states offering virtual schooling as a form of school choice in 2005 (National Forum on Educational Statistics, 2006). Thus, school choice has given parents a range of options as to where their children may receive the best opportunity for a quality education. Consequently, Americans have embraced this alternative to public schools (Spring, 2006; U.S. Department of Education 2000).

Interest in school choice has been fueled by the growth of high-stakes testing mandated by No Child Left Behind (NCLB; 2001) and Race to the Top (U.S. Department of Education, 2009). Parents, political leaders, and business leaders have advocated school choice as a way for students to escape "failing" schools and as an impetus for public schools to improve instruction and teacher quality (Spring, 2006). Critics of high-stakes testing suggest the testing is part of failed school reform policies that create innate unequal education opportunities (Ravitch, 2010). School reform policies place additional responsibility on schools for ensuring every student is given an equal chance to succeed. Under NCLB, public schools are required to provide accountability information regarding student achievement and conditions for each school, so that parents may make a decision as to whether to keep their child at that school or move the child to another school. Yet students receive different experiences due to different access to instructional levels, resources, activities, and even family expectations (Marzano, 2003; Ravitch, 2010). Standardized methods do not allow for differences, resulting in some students having more advantages for success than others.

The premise of many school reformers is to improve school quality through comparison and competition, much like American business models. Business models in the United States frequently assume equal access and treatment. Everyone has the potential to succeed, and those who fail simply shut down. Education is different. Unlike a business, a student who is having trouble cannot be cast aside to fail. Schools must cope with individual differences, often affected by non-school experiences. The business model approach holds schools accountable for differences not always directly associated with school experiences. Consequently, competition does not ensure that every school will have the same rate of success.

The majority of students attending private schools attend parochial schools or church-related schools (U.S. Department of Education, 2000). According to the National Center for Education

Statistics (2013b), private schools represent about 24% of all schools in the country and about 9% of the total student populations. There were an estimated 33,366 private elementary and secondary schools in this country in 2011, which represents an increase from 20, 764 private schools in 1976. Private schools were primarily affiliated with religious or nonsectarian groups, and most were located in the southern United States. However, enrollment in private schools decreased from 12% of all school-aged students in this country in 1995–96 to 10% in 2011–12 (National Center for Education Statistics, 2013c). Seventy-six percent of the enrolled students were labeled as white. Parents favor private schools because they want their children's academic experience to include a religious focus and believe they can have more input into their child's education (U.S. Department of Education, 2000). However, many parents also believe education at a private school is higher quality than at public schools.

Are private schools better than public schools? The answer is both yes and no. Educational statistics illustrate that when comparing school to school, student scores at many private schools are higher than similar scores at public schools (National Center for Education Statistics, 2001). A study conducted for the National Center for Education Statistics (2006) found students from private schools routinely scored higher in math and reading than those at public schools. However, many students at private schools come from cultural and family backgrounds that encourage, support, and provide resources for their children's education.

However, when comparing student to student differences, scores become more equal. The 2006 study for the National Center for Education Statistics found that when adjusting for differences in student characteristics, students from private schools did not perform significantly better than students from public schools in math and reading. Another study found that mathematics scores of students attending private schools were higher than similar students attending public schools (Lubienski & Lubienski, 2005). However, when adjusting for family variables such as socioeconomic status, the same study demonstrated that students from public schools actually scored higher than their counterparts attending private schools. In short, many students attending private schools would succeed at a higher level even if they were attending public school. Furthermore, many advocates of public schools cite a type of "brain drain" of higher achieving students choosing to leave public schools to attend private schools, thus causing public school scores to fall (Muller, 1998; Renzetti & Curran, 2000).

Another option of school choice is for parents to home school their children. An estimated 1.5 million children were home schooled in this country in 2007 (National Center for Education Statistics, 2008). This amount grows approximately 7–15 percent annually, making home schooling the fastest growing type of education in the United States. In the home schooling approach, parents have the responsibility to take charge of their children's education. Home schooling rejects the traditional approach of public schooling. Whereas historically the common school approach has been the center of schooling in the United States (Serow, Castelli, & Castelli, 2000), home school advocates reject the belief that children should receive a common education and culture. They believe the traditional public school approach to education is too factory-like and not flexible enough to meet specific instructional or individual learning needs. Values are often at the center of the home school movement. The three most common reasons parents cite for choosing to home school their children are (1) parental concerns about the school environment such as safety issues, drugs, or negative peer pressures, (2) a desire to provide religious or moral instruction, and (3) dissatisfaction with academic instruction (National Center for Education Statistics, 2008).

While school choice has been an option for many years, it has recently encountered critics due to the increased involvement of the federal government in education issues. A controversial component of the No Child Left Behind Act (2001) is the use of tax-based vouchers that families may use in faith-based and for-profit schools to help cover the costs of tuition, transportation, and other education-related expenses. Critics of vouchers say that taking money away from public schools in the form of vouchers is an abandonment of the nation's commitment to public education (Campbell, 2006; Feller, 2005). Many critics also question the constitutionality of this aspect of the Act due to the issue of separation of church and state. Their concern is that taxpayer monies will promote specific religious beliefs (Campbell, 2006; Feller, 2005). Proponents say that while they do pay taxes to support schools, they should have more input into how this money is spent (Hamilton & Stecher, 2004; Spring, 2006).

Other critics say that private schools are held to different standards and expectations than their public school counterparts. Critics state that private schools are not held as accountable for student performance and the fiscal use of tax-based vouchers. Many states do not require private schools to administer state-sponsored high-stake tests to demonstrate student learning and teacher effectiveness. Indeed, many private schools are not required to employ certified teachers. Many states do not require private schools to make the same disclosures as public schools regarding their use of funding received through the vouchers or other state and federal funding sources. Still other critics say that school choice is more for wealthy families because many poor students do not have the transportation or financial means to attend other schools. This has led some to suggest that school choice is segregating our society between the haves and have-nots. One effect of school choice has been on enrollment in public schools, where a four percent drop occurred between 1993 and 1999 (National Center for Education Statistics, 2003b). This trend was most evident among low-income families. Some reports stated that when poor and minority students do use vouchers to attend different schools, many frequently encounter social resistance from other students and subsequently transfer back to their original school (National Center for Education Statistics, 2003b).

Equality of Opportunity in Music Education

Music education is not exempt from issues of equal opportunity, as equity gaps persist throughout groups within music education. Concerns regarding both access and treatment plague many music programs. Music educators are frequently criticized for focusing on students perceived to have talent while ignoring those with less ability. This affects the access students may have to quality music instruction, resources, and experiences. The question of who we will teach requires our profession to broaden its scope if we are to live up to the philosophy that music is important for everyone. Therefore, issues relating to the common school or sorting machine models do affect music classes. Additionally, equality of opportunity in the music class is affected by attitudes associated with discrimination, prejudice, and stereotypes. Furthermore, variables such as race, gender, family background, and special needs can influence opportunities that students have in the music class.

In theory and practice, both the common school and sorting machine models exist in music education curricula. The opportunity to succeed to some degree is a necessary component of both models. However, the amount and quality of opportunities each student receives in order to achieve success differs depending on which model is used. A music curriculum based on the common school model provides all students with the same opportunities to participate in music, regardless of ability. This model provides every student with opportunities to try music at their own level by exploring their unique relationship to the experience. Without an opportunity to experience as many musical relationships as possible, a student may never find the hint of success or interest that can develop into the desire to investigate further, thus extinguishing their intrinsic motivation to learn (Jellison, 2000).

However, the common school model is difficult to implement due to the time necessary to allow students to experiment. The efficient and effective use of time is a major concern for.

educators (National Education Commission on Time and Learning, 1994). Preparing for performances requires large amounts of classroom rehearsal time (Goolsby, 1999). While performance may be a focus of most music classes, music education based on the common school model does not necessarily place emphasis on formal performance before an audience in order to demonstrate success. Performance may come within the class, or on an individual basis. Thus, time is needed to explore individual relationships and interests with music. One study found that an approach to music rehearsals incorporating composition and listening positively affected both individual and ensemble achievement in musical performance (Riley, 2006). The method in this study reflects a common school model approach to teaching music.

Desire, either as a single variable or in combination with other variables, is frequently cited in research as the greatest determining success factor in music experiences (Hedden, 1982). Desire is a unique variable that the common machine model can allow to influence music opportunity because it provides for music experiences most relevant to individuals. If students have a strong desire to participate in music, they will more often than not overcome obstacles that may prevent them from participating to the extent they desire (Brand, 1986; Hedden 1982). This includes physical obstacles, such as injury or disability, and intellectual obstacles. However, the variable of desire must still overcome the obstacle of either parents or teachers who may think the student cannot succeed in music (Brand, 1986; Guerrimi, 2005; Zdzinski, 1996).

The sorting machine model is perhaps the most widely used approach in music education. Music teachers are frequently forced into this model due to limited rehearsal time and heavy performance demands. Consequently, the sorting machine model approach can create an unbalanced focus on performing at the expense of education and individual interest. With a large number of performances constantly being prepared, students may be forced into experiences that do not connect personal interests with musical desires. Thus, students may fail to understand the

Photo Figure 8 A strong sense of desire is one of many variables influencing musical success.

relationship of the music they are experiencing in school to the music they participate in outside of school.

The influence of the sorting machine model frequently begins with early music instruction (e.g., beginning band or orchestra, even elementary general music). Teachers may start to track students as musical abilities begin to develop. As in other educational areas, teachers begin to form perceptions of different individuals based on emerging musical abilities. Students may then be sorted into different ability groups, which can affect access to and type of musical opportunities for individuals. One example is that some students may receive opportunities for more advanced experiences that may enhance creative development, such as performing solos, playing certain instruments, or opportunities for individual lessons. Other students may participate in music, but in situations more conducive to support roles, such as an ensemble.

Similar to other education areas, the sorting machine model in music education may use some form of testing to help determine the specific musical experiences or the extent to which students may participate in music. Music students may experience testing as a way to determine if they have the ability or aptitude to succeed in music (Gordon, 1967, 1968, 1979). While such testing may not involve formal written tests or grades, this type of informal testing can be used to determine the type of instrument a student might play or the type of musical experience received, thus minimizing the variable of student desire or motivation. (Abeles & Porter, 1978; Delzell & Leppla, 1992). Testing students' ability to succeed does not allow for the development of desire or for individual potential ability to arise. Forcing students to play instruments or participate in activities they do not desire to be involved in can have a negative initial experience that can affect future participation (Abeles & Porter, 1978; Delzell & Leppla, 1992). Testing students for placement in music experiences can create unintended consequences of failure, possibly resulting in students not participating in or withdrawing from music class.

Once again, much research exists on the many social, educational, and psychological variables affecting equality of opportunity in the music class. Frequently these variables include race and ethnicity (Lind, 1999; Walker & Hamann, 1995), gender (Abeles & Porter, 1978; Delzell & Leppla, 1992), family background and involvement (Brand, 1986; Custodero & Johnson-Green, 2003; Fitzpatrick, 2006; Guerrini, 2005), which includes socioeconomic level and expectations, and groups associated with special needs such as individuals with disabilities and those labeled as gifted (Adamek & Darrow, 2005; Ebie, 1998; Johnson & Darrow, 1997). There are many shared characteristics among such groups that affect opportunities, including low expectations and self-esteem, learned helplessness, and cultural expectations resulting from resistant cultures. Research regarding the variable and characteristics of musical opportunity is extensive and beyond the scope of this introductory material. The following is a brief overview of findings for each cultural variable relating to opportunity in music education. Individuals seeking more in-depth information are again encouraged to consult the resources at the end of the chapter.

Family Influences

A musical home nurtures musical behavior. The foundation for musical opportunities and life-long association with music begins with family involvement, especially with parental figures (Brand, 1986; Custodero & Johnson-Green, 2003; Guerrini, 2005; Kinney, 2008; LeBlanc, 1982; Mehr, 2014; Zdzinski, 1992, 1996). Parents influence children's decisions regarding education, including music participation, throughout their lives. The family context provides a nurturing environment that stimulates musical interest in children (Custodero & Johnson-Green, 2003; Guerrini, 2005; LeBlanc, 1982; Mehr, 2014). According to anthropologist John Blacking (1973), musical culture is transmitted through interaction with other human beings. This transmission begins with each child's parents or parental figures. Because parents in the United States are usually the primary caregivers of young children, they become our first music teachers and thus affect initial opportunity for music experiences. Musical communication between parents and children defines our earliest cultural concept of what constitutes musical sounds and distinguishes these sounds from other environmental noises (Custodero & Johnson-Green, 2003; Guerrini, 2005; Mehr, 2014). Parental attitudes toward music instruction and activities affect our perceptions of our musical self-concept and our confidence to initiate musical behaviors (Custodero & Johnson-Green, 2003; Guerrini, 2005; Mehr, 2014; Wilson & Wales, 1995).

Studies have suggested that the most productive period for musical development is between the ages of birth and age five, stabilizing around age nine (Gordon, 1968; Sloboda, 2003). Thus, the preschool years are most important for musical growth. Young children need exposure to music activities, with opportunities to explore and experiment (Wilson & Wales, 1995). Frequently, exposure to and experience in musical activities begins with imitating parents (Custodero & Johnson-Green, 2003; Guerrini, 2005). Positive musical behaviors and interactions such as parents singing to and with their children, providing elementary musical instruments, helping children to learn songs, and taking children to musical activities and events give children motivation to explore music. Parents frequently initiate music activities by talking about music, playing music themselves, or providing music-listening opportunities in the home (Brand, 1986; Custodero & Johnson-Green, 2003; Guerrini, 2005; LeBlanc, 1981, 1982).

Research has shown that early influences are not confined to parents with musical backgrounds and appear across socioeconomic levels (Brand, 1986; Kinney, 2008, 2010; Zdzinski, 1996). Parents who perform music themselves do not influence their children's musical activities more than parents who provide a musical environment through encouragement and support (Brand, 1986). Data show family influences are frequently related to the desire to provide a nurturing, positive musical environment where parents are supportive and encouraging of their children's musical involvement (Custodero & Johnson-Green, 2003). Additionally, it is not uncommon for parents to feel deprived, confused, or inadequate about their own musical ability (Custodero & Johnson-Green, 2003; Guerrini, 2005). Subsequently, these parents tend not to make music or provide a musical home environment, thus affecting the development of musical skills and interests. In these situations the music educator must provide opportunities and information regarding the importance of musical experiences, which will motivate parents to encourage their children's participation in music experiences.

Despite the apparent strong influences of parents on the children's musical development, their degree of influence may be limited. Age appears to be a factor, as younger students seem to benefit more from parental involvement than older students (Custodero & Johnson-Green, 2003). For example, elementary students whose parents are more involved in their children's musical behaviors tend to be more influential on their children's participation in music activities (Bowles, 1991). Studies have suggested that these students have a tendency to achieve music outcomes at a greater pace than students with less parental involvement (Bowles, 1991; Duke, Flowers & Wolfe, 1997). However, this influence is stronger with elementary students than high school students.

To what extent does heredity play in the acquisition of musical skills? If an individual is thought to have musical ability due to genetic heredity, then parents may be more encouraging of musical participation. However, if parents can be convinced that environmental factors may also lead to the development of musical interests, and therefore music participation, then this may encourage parental enthusiasm. The nature versus nurture issue is frequently debated even among music educators. Little physical evidence exists supporting the acquisition of musical skills through the inheritance of DNA genes (Radocy & Boyle, 2003; Sloboda, 2003). Yet many music researchers conclude they cannot discount this possibility. They explain the existence of musical skills as a combination of nature (innate ability) and nurture (environmental interactions), including family influences (Radocy & Boyle, 2003).

Gender

Gender associations regarding equal opportunity in music tend to revolve around the issue of occupational choice or instrument selection. Gender association with musical instruments is a common sociological phenomenon. Typically, research has shown that instruments associated with females are the flute, violin, clarinet, piano, and cello. Instruments associated with males are drums, brass instruments, and saxophones (Abeles & Porter 1978; Delzell & Leppla, 1992). Students learn associations through various socialization interactions, including parental influence, the media, and teachers, including music teachers (McCormick, 1994). The reasons for gender associations vary and include the size of the instrument, the instrument's timbre, a person's physical characteristics, and simple biases such as "that's an instrument for girls" (Abeles & Porter 1978; Delzell & Leppla, 1992; Kelly, 1997a)

Gender associations with instrument selection hinder an individual's desire to learn a specific instrument, which may affect the choice to participate in music. The reasons for directing an individual toward a specific instrument may include the availability of a certain instrument, the need for balanced ensemble instrumentation, or the teacher's belief that a student may achieve better success on a certain instrument (Abeles & Porter 1978; Delzell & Leppla, 1992). However, recalling that desire is the primary reason for musical success, biases related to gender associations and musical instruments may not provide students with an equal opportunity to experience music in a meaningful manner.

Biases and gender association are also apparent when individuals seek to become music teachers. Stereotypically, females teach elementary and choral music classes. Males teach high school and instrumental classes, especially band. While there are far more high school male marching band directors than female directors, few elementary music teachers are male. Vocational statistics throughout education reflect these trends. Many of the same biases affecting instrument choice affect occupational choice in music. Equality of opportunity is affected by discrimination when an individual desires to teach in an area outside of the stereotypical gender norms and subsequently encounters resistance (Oakes & Lipton, 1999).

Race and Ethnicity

Unfortunately, the continued growth of diversity in the United States and its public schools is not always reflected in school music programs. There is often a disparity between the racial makeup of a schools' population and the students enrolled in its music classes, particularly its performing ensembles (Chipman, 2004; Robinson, 2000). By not appealing to a broader student base, many school music programs reinforce the view that school music is only for specific populations, not necessarily for all students (Ebie, 1998; Walker & Hamann, 1995).

While many characteristics that influence music participation are shared across racial and ethnical lines, cultural differences do appear to affect the degree of participation among various races and ethnicities. Studies have shown that equality of opportunity in the music class is affected by the classroom environment (Chipman, 2004; Robinson, 2000; Walker & Hamann, 1995). These factors include the teacher's attitude toward various styles of music and student interactions, as well as the social aspects of the classroom, such as peer relations and the sense of affiliation with music. Additionally, the teaching approach used appears to have some influence on the level of participation by minority students (Walker & Hamann, 1995). Some research data suggest an environment that is less competitive but that takes into account the cultural heritage of the students provides minority students with more opportunities and encouragement (Robinson, 2000; Walker & Hamann, 1995).

With the American population becoming increasingly pluralistic, the need to diversify music education programs will be essential if all students are to receive equal opportunity in music. The Vision 2020 conference called for music programs to recognize cultural diversity by advancing education programs that recognize the equality of cultural traditions (Madsen, 2000). Music education was challenged to provide transitional opportunities for students to experience music that is relevant to their lives, yet still based on traditional and historical foundations (Jellison, 2000). In many ways, this approach calls for music educators to recognize that classes can be both multicultural and multi-musical. Since a goal of education is to teach the transfer of learned knowledge to new situations (Music Educators National Conference, 1994), teaching musical skills for transfer to a variety of cultural situations would be an important element if students from all racial and ethnical backgrounds are to receive an equal opportunity in music education.

Music Students With Disabilities and Diverse Learners

Music educators at every level are required by law to provide an effective quality music education for all students, including those with disabilities (Adamek & Darrow, 2005). Consequently, music educators are responsible for providing music experiences for students, regardless of ability or disability, in their general music classes, performance ensembles, and sometimes even general education classes. Often, this responsibility requires the music teacher to develop new or adapt existing materials, pedagogical approaches, and attitudes for working with this diverse student culture. The adaptation of curricular and instructional aspects frequently requires specialized training, usually either at the undergraduate level or through inservice training. It is advisable to consult a registered board certified music therapist for advice on adapting activities and teaching strategies to meet the needs of the broad spectrum of disabled students that music educators may encounter.

Since the implementation of both the Education for All Handicapped Children Act (PL 94–142) and the Individuals with Disabilities Act (PL 99–457), music educators have faced the challenge of integrating all students into the least restrictive environment possible (Adamek & Darrow, 2005). Still, these policies continue to provide music opportunities for a growing number of students (Darrow, 2014). Music educators have learned that factors such as teacher preparation, creating a positive environment, repetition, and appropriate attitudes toward working with students with disabilities are necessary, as well as adequate resources to achieve the goals of these laws (Adamek & Darrow, 2005; Gerrity, Hourigan, & Horton, 2013; Gfeller, Darrow, & Hedden 1990; Salvador, 2013).

Music teacher preparation should include participation in developing the Individual Education Plan (IEP) with other teachers involved in the outcomes of each student's education (Adamek & Darrow, 2005; Gfeller, Darrow, & Hedden, 1990). Research has shown that with exposure and meaningful inclusion, both students and teachers benefit from students with disabilities in the music classroom (Darrow, 1993; 2014; Darrow & Johnson, 1994; Ebie, 1998; Gfeller, Darrow, &,Hedden, 1990; Johnson & Darrow, 1997; VanWeelden & Whipple, 2014). These benefits extend to all areas of music instruction, from instrumental to choral to general music education.

Another area of classification is "at-risk" students. While the number of students referred to as at-risk has dramatically increased in recent decades, there is no commonly supported definition of this label (McWhirter, McWhirter, McWhirter, & McWhirter, 1998). Generally, all children may be considered "at-risk" due to societal issues such as divorce, violent behavior, physical and emotional abuse, low socioeconomic status, minority race and ethnicity, gender stereotypes, drug use, early pregnancy, and even degree of academic success, as with "gifted" students (McWhirter, McWhirter, McWhirter, & McWhirter, 1998). At-risk labels apply to student dropout. Music participation has been cited as a factor in helping all students remain in school and improve their self-esteem (Chipman, 2004; Ebie, 1998; Robinson, 2000). Music can provide social experiences and challenges that are important to personal development. These opportunities can be encountered through all types of musical participation. For example, research has shown that participation in large performing music ensembles provides opportunities for at-risk students to experience leadership roles and group responsibility (Chipman, 2004; Robinson, 2000). Participation can have a positive effect on at-risk students' social acceptance and their attitudes toward school, as well as improve their attendance and reduce disruptive behaviors (Ebie, 1998; Robinson, 2000). Experiences in music composition have also been shown to be effective in developing self-esteem through creativity and decision-making skills. According to students, the arts, including music, provide a supportive environment where it is safe to take risks and still attain acceptance (Chipman, 2004; Ebie, 1998).

Teacher Influence

The potential influence of a single music teacher is enormous. It is not unusual for students to have only one music teacher throughout a specific period of time (e.g., one band director during all of middle school). This extended time with a single teacher increases the teacher's influence over students and provides the teacher with many opportunities to serve all students. Music students frequently spend more time with their music teacher than any other teacher (Adderley, Kennedy, & Berz, 2003; Morrison, 2001). The power of this individual to develop broader musical perceptions and preferences affects the amount of opportunity for all students. Studies demonstrate that students become intrinsically motivated and eager to learn from someone they respect and trust as both a musician and a teacher (Asmus, 1986; Deisler, 2011; Kantorski, 2004; Legette, 1998).

Social reasons, frequently controlled or affected by the teacher, have also been shown to influence students' participation, motivation, and success in music. No single factor appears to influence a student's participation and success in music (Hedden, 1982; Walker & Hamann, 1995). A combination of any number of factors appears to be most influential, including a positive individual attitude, self-concept, and desire toward music; family members, peers, media, and classroom influences. Among these factors are a student's cumulative grade point average and instrument choice, and a teacher's personality and instructional style (Hedden, 1982). Ironically, some researchers have suggested that a primary reason students become both involved in music and stop participating in music is their relationship with the music teacher (Kantorski, 2004; Lind, 1999; Walker & Hamann, 1995). Additional factors affecting participation and success include the student's socioeconomic status and expected outcomes because of the music experiences (Deisler, 2011; Fitzpatrick, 2006; Kinney, 2008; Walker & Hamann, 1995).

Music Teacher Influences on Equal Opportunity	
Positive Personality	Teaching Style
Open Attitude	Avoiding Biases & Labels
High Expectations	Learning Student Names
Willingness to Work With All Students	

Music Education Among Different Types of Schools

Overall, music education appears to be maintaining its presence in American public schools. A study by the U.S. Department of Education found that 94% of elementary schools and 91% of secondary schools offered specific instruction in music between 2008 and2010 (National Center for Education Statistics, 2012). However, music education has not been exempt from school reform issues, including high-stakes testing and resulting consequences. For example, a study by Abril and Gault (2008) found that standardized tests and No Child Left Behind were two of the most negative variables affecting secondary music programs across the United States. Another study by Elpus (2014) found that while overall music enrollments in public schools remained relatively stable after the implementation of No Child Left Behind policies, its influence was negatively highlighting non-speakers of English and special needs students.

The issue of school choice has helped create differences in the music education experiences available to all students. While musical opportunities can be found in most school situations, the extent of those experiences varies depending on the type of school a student attends (U.S. Department of Education, 2000), and location. For example, Miksza and Gault (2014) found that urban and rural schools provided fewer music opportunities for elementary students than their suburban counterparts. Musical opportunities also vary widely among schools considered among the best in the country (Kelly & Heath, in press). Music education has frequently followed other curricular areas in public schools by expanding and specializing to attract and retain students who otherwise may choose to attend a different school. However, drops in overall school enrollments have frequently affected the number of students interested in participating in music classes (National Center for Education Statistics, 2003a; Woodford, 2005). Decreases in enrollment have led to a reduction of opportunities in many public schools that do not specialize in music or arts instruction. Music offerings in private schools are often limited due to small enrollments or program costs. However, many private schools have found that offering music to some degree appeals to parents and attracts students.

The variety of music experiences in all school settings is subject to teacher attitudes and qualifications, overall school costs or tuition and related expenses, parental attitudes, classroom space, and the school's perception of need or interest (Austin, 1997b). The music curricula in traditional public schools is perhaps the most varied and typically consists of broad areas of instruction in band, choral, and orchestral music. Within these broad areas experiences in jazz, small chamber ensembles, and solo opportunities are often offered. Increasingly, traditional public school music curricula are providing more diverse experiences, including music theory, electronic music, and guitar. Subsequently, students in these schools have a wide variety of musical experiences from which to select. Additionally, while some ensembles may require students to pass auditions to participate, most traditional public schools have ensembles or music classes that are open to all students.

As the popularity of school choice has grown, traditional public schools have lost students to other school settings (National Center for Education Statistics, 2003b). Since the tax-based funding for public schools is based on the number of full-time enrolled students, lower enrollment affects funding for public schools (Carey, 2004). Among the characteristics traditional public schools have been forced to change to attract and retain students is their curricula (Spring, 2006). Whereas some schools have broadened their curricular offerings, others have altered their approach to a more specialized curriculum. Two alternative formats to public schools have evolved: the magnet school and the charter school (Spring, 2006). Both schools seek to provide students with more specialized instruction and parents with more input than traditional public schools. Magnet schools have very specialized curricular tracks within a traditional curricula. Students zoned for that school may still attend and partake in the traditional curriculum. However, students from outside the zone may attend the magnet school due to its specialized curriculum. Magnet schools specialize in a variety of curricula, including music, science, mathematics, and technology. Students attending music magnet schools are frequently required to audition for acceptance. The curriculum is more specialized and often includes large, small, and individual experiences, music theory and history, composition, technology, and private lessons.

Students attending charter schools have an even more specialized curriculum, which is often intentionally limited (U.S. Department of Education, 2000). Traditional and magnet public schools are under the governance of the local school boards, and much of the power and funding related to those schools is based on decisions made by the boards. However, charter schools are governed by their charter while still funded by local school districts (Spring, 2006). A charter is an organizational constitution or mission that outlines learning philosophies, goals, approaches, and assessments used at that school. The school's administration, teachers, parents, and community leaders form the charter. In essence, participation in forming the charter gives parents more input into their child's education. Thus, charter schools have more autonomy over their curricular offerings than more traditional public schools. Furthermore, due to the nature of a school's charter, curricular offerings frequently reflect community values.

For music education, charter schools can be precarious in part because they have been endorsed by the No Child Left Behind Act (2001) and Race to the Top (U.S. Department of Education, 2009) and are rapidly growing in number. In the year 2000, the U.S. Department of Education reported over one million students were enrolled in more than 3,500 charter schools in 40 states. This number continues to increase annually. While a charter school must still abide by state standards, music frequently falls into the category of fine arts. Many other courses within the fine arts can satisfy this requirement. Thus, musical opportunities are subject to the desires of those individuals forming the charter and may not exist (Austin, 1997b). If the governing body values music instruction, then musical opportunities exist; otherwise, the fine arts requirement can be satisfied by other classes with no music opportunity for students.

The extent of the musical opportunities in private schools is frequently subject to the same values as those in charter schools. Because most private schools have smaller enrollments than public schools, their curricula are also smaller and more specialized. Costs also become more of a factor, as most private schools are tuition-driven and operational expenses frequently affect curricular offerings. Thus, similar to charter schools, many private schools offer only limited, if any, music experiences. However, private schools are increasingly offering limited music instruction to attract students.

Home schooling is a school choice option growing in popularity. Many parents view this option as the ultimate opportunity to ensure their children will obtain the level and quality of education they desire. The curricular offerings by home schools are limited to the skills, knowledge, and attitudes of the parents. The extent of music instruction is thus affected by these same characteristics. If parents feel comfortable with their musical skills, then music instruction is valued and offered; otherwise, students do not gain these opportunities. However, as the popularity of home schools has grown, many parents have sought to expand offerings to their children by forming home school associations. For example, students may go to one house for English, and then move to another house for math, then another for music.

A growing organization pertaining to music education is the privately funded El Sistema USA (2014) program. El Sistema originated in Venezuela and was brought to the United States in 2008. Its purpose is to bring classical music to school-aged children in low socioeconomic areas through the use of classically trained musicians. The goal is to involve children in music and bring about social change because of this involvement. The program has grown in major cities across the United States, but has received criticism for its teachers lacking educational training.

Recent Issues Concerning Educational Equality

The "achievement gap" in education refers to the disparity in academic performance between groups of students, primarily based on race and socioeconomic variables. However, a more recent broad focus of the achievement gap now pertains to differences in gender, English-language proficiency, and groups with disabilities (Education Week, 2011). Gaps in educational achievement have always existed in our country. Efforts to close achievements have been made with some degree of success. For example, the Elementary and Secondary Education Act of 1965 (re-authorized in 2001) provided resources to schools in low socioeconomic communities (Darling-Hammond, 2010). Later, the 1975 Education for All Handicapped Children Act created educational access for students with disabilities. However, with budget cuts to school and social programs in the 1980s, America's investment in education declined, resulting in a growing lack of access for many underprivileged students, minorities, and students in urban and rural communities (Darling-Hammond, 2010). Additionally, as funding was reduced, teacher salaries begin to drop, resulting in fewer teachers and fewer qualified teachers. Students attending less affluent schools began to fall behind in many core academic subjects. Funding declines also resulted in the reduction of more broad curricular offerings such as music and other arts, resulting in more narrow educational opportunities (Elpus, 2014).

No Child Left Behind was intended to address the growing achievement gap, and indeed some progress was made. Yet equity gaps in reading and mathematical achievement scores continue between African-American and Hispanic student and their white peers, and dropout rates between the groups remain large even as Race to the Top school reform policies have continued to focus on achievement for all (Education Week, 2011; National Assessment of Education Progress, 2011).

Evidence suggests the achievement gap exists among many groups pertaining to music education. For example, Miksza & Gault (2014) found wide variances in the amount of musical offerings among elementary schools based on location, race, and socioeconomics. Furthermore, according to data from the 2008 National Assessment of Educational Progress (NAEP), average scores in music were 22 to 32 points higher for white and Asian students than for black and Hispanic students. Female students scored ten points higher than male students. Interestingly, this same report found significant differences in the musical curricula of schools, with white and Asian students attending schools that offer a wide variety of musical opportunities. The NAEP states that curricular opportunities could also be a reflection of a school's location and socioeconomic variables. The achievement gap appears to have negatively affected enrollment in music education classes. Due to the need to take more academic subjects, many Hispanic students, students from low socioeconomic families, low English-language proficiency students, and low-achieving students have been prevented from participating in school music experiences (Elpus & Abril, 2011; Gerrity, 2009; Lorah, Sanders, & Morrison, 2014; West, 2012).

The concept of social justice formulated in the 2000s. Social justice promotes common humanity and equitable treatment among all people regardless of gender, sexuality, religion, political affiliations, age, race, belief, disability, location, social class, or any other background or group membership (Robinson, 2014). In essence, social justice views everyone as having equal economic, political, and social rights and opportunities (National Association of Social Workers, 2015). Social justice promotes tolerance, freedom, and equity. Issues related to social justice often include bullying, prejudice, and unequal access. Bullying presents one of the greatest health risks to all American citizens. The American Educational Research Association (AERA) (2013) reported that schools of all levels are at the epicenter for bullying due to the amount of time individuals spend at school each day. Still, the AERA states that many teachers and other education personnel lack training in addressing bullying.

In addressing social justice issues, Allsup and Shieh (2012) called for teaching of dispositions against acts related to inequality. Music is viewed as being an effective venue for promoting social justice due to data that showing people under 18 years old spend more than six hours per day interacting with or listening to media (Cahill, 2008). As such, Allsup and Shieh cited schools' music experiences as being ideal for teaching democratic ideals that promote acceptance and equality.

Summary

All students deserve the same opportunity to learn. Equality of education requires equal access, treatment, and opportunity to achieve success in our society regardless of race, gender, socio-economic status, or other cultural or philosophical view, or biological factors. In schools, equal opportunity also includes equal facilities, financing, curriculum, and availability of resources.

Equity is a democratic ideal not confined to education, but a common value throughout our society. From a social perspective, schools and society again mirror each other in both positive and negative ways. Opportunities have become more open for different cultural groups, including individuals with special needs, different races and ethnicities, and genders. Yet discrimination and biases pervade both society and education settings. Consequently, some people may never overcome the disadvantages with which they began (Hallinan, 1990). Many social policies that keep the social playing field uneven also exist in our schools and music classes (Coleman, 1990; Kozol, 1991).

Human biases exist in every aspect of American culture and affect opportunity. However, after an individual's home environment, biases may exist in schools more than any other institution in society, a realization that often surprises many new teachers. Practices of sorting and tracking students, providing different access to resources and knowledge, and high-stakes testing are often discriminatory based on race, gender, home environment, socioeconomic level, language, and even physical and intellectual abilities. Such practices are too common, contribute to biases and injustices, and deny students opportunities to make decisions on their own. Biases extend to the attitudes and behaviors of teachers, administrators, parents, business leaders, and politicians.

However, despite partialities in the education system, schools may be a student's best hope for learning to overcome biases. Through schools, children may learn to appreciate diversity, think for themselves, and create new dimensions to society that are equal for all. Schools can provide opportunities for students to improve their self-image, break away from stereotypes, and develop confidence to overcome societal challenges such as self-fulfilling prophecies.

As socialization agents, teachers may have the best opportunity to initiate student equality. Due to the amount of time spent together, music teachers have a tremendous chance to provide experiences for all students. Equality of opportunity begins with teachers giving opportunity for students to explore music at their own level. In this manner, students learn from their own mistakes, take ownership of their progress, and become self-motivated to explore music further (Jellison, 2000). Music becomes accessible not only for those with "talent," but for everyone.

Key Items

Equality of Education
Sorting Machine Model
High-Stakes Testing
Primary/Secondary
   Socialization Agents
Discrimination
Stereotypes
School Choice

Achievement Gap
Magnet Schools
Traditional Schools
Common Core Initiative
Common School Model
Tracking
El Sistema
Social Justice

Prejudice
Gender-role Identity
Racism
Attribution Theory
Charter Schools
Home Schools
Vouchers

Questions for Consideration

1. What are ways that schools limit educational opportunity for certain students while providing opportunity for others?
2. Is it possible for all students to receive the same music education? Why or why not?
3. How might school music experiences differ for males and females?
4. How does music education reflect both the sorting machine and common schools models of education?
5. How might a student's home environment affect his/her music educational opportunity?
6. What are ways that music teachers might work with special needs students in order to provide an opportunity for a quality music experience?
7. How might school choice pose a threat to music education?

Web Resources

Common Core Curriculum

Common Core Initiative: http://www.corestandards.org/

Education Equality

Education Trust: http://www.edtrust.org/
Leadership for Educational Equity: https://educationalequity.org/
National Association of Education Progress: http://nces.ed.gov/nationsreportcard/
People for the American Way: http://www.pfaw.org/issues/equality-for-all

Individuals with Disabilities

American Association of People with Disabilities: http://www.aapd.com/
American Music Therapy Association: http://www.musictherapy.org/
National Organization on Disability: http://nod.org/

School Choice

Friedman Foundation for Educational Choice: http://www.edchoice.org/School-Choice/What-is-School-Choice.aspx
Alliance for School Choice http://allianceforschoolchoice.org/
International Association for K-12 Online Learning: http://www.inacol.org/

School Reform

Annenberg Institute for School Reform: http://annenberginstitute.org/
Bill & Melinda Gates Foundation: http://www.gatesfoundation.org/

Chapter 6

Social Components of Music Learning

Education is the most powerful weapon you can choose to change the world.

—Nelson Mandela

As teachers, how do we know students have learned material or acquired skills? How are students different after they have been exposed to new information or possibilities? In music, we frequently assume if students can demonstrate skills through performance then knowledge is learned. Yet we know that not all demonstrated skills are retained and transferred to different situations. If they are not retained, have they been learned? Transfer of knowledge to different situations or new music does not always occur. Simply performing in ensemble does not ensure that learning is occurring. Instruction is frequently repeated, as new music containing previously presented concepts is distributed. Consequently, teachers may incorrectly assume that because students can demonstrate skills, they have actually learned those skills. Chapter 6 presents information on theories and variables influencing how humans learn, and what influences learning music. The chapter's premise is that our students learn in diverse ways. Subsequently, effective music teachers must be aware of the many methods through which learning occurs.

Teachers should be knowledgeable of as many ways as possible that students learn. No single approach to learning contains all the answers, as students learn in multiple manners, formally and informally. While schools may be considered more formal structured learning, it may be that less structured more informal approaches could be more effective (Green, 2008). Effective teaching begins with an understanding of how children think and react to new information. What works for first graders does not work for sixth graders. To understand the difference requires knowledge of theories regarding how humans acquire skills and knowledge.

Principle Learning Theories

Learning is an intentional act, an embodied constructive process based on experiences (Wiggins, 2015). Humans construct mental concepts or schemas, which enable us to understand new information and experiences (Boardman, 2002). According to Wiggins (2015), schemas are interactive networks of ideas that help organize information and experiences into understandable concepts. Because humans perceive information differently, schemas for each individual are different. Consequently, the unique nature of schemas helps explain how humans learn in different manners.

Learning results in change in an individual's knowledge or behavior. Change that results in new knowledge or abilities is in relation to previous information or past experiences (Wiggins, 2015). Connections create a frame of reference, leading to new understanding. More specifically, learning is an observable change in behavior, due to experience, which is not attributed to anything else (Radocy & Boyle, 2003). Humans construct new ways or changes to use and exhibit as new skills and information is learned. Without changes between two points of time, no learning can be said to have occurred. Consequently, when a student has learned new knowledge or skills, an observable change in behavior, thought, or emotion can be seen or experienced.

Humans learn every day of their lives, but what are the best ways to learn? Where is learning best facilitated? Learning often occurs relative to contextual parameters that are frequently affected by cultural settings and resources (Boardman, 2002). Thanks to the efforts of educational psychologists and sociologists, teachers have access to a wealth of information regarding how to best teach music. Educators can more clearly understand the processes involved in human musicality, including psychoacoustical, physiological, and affective processes. Understanding how individuals learn has clarified how humans give meaning to music, what and how we feel during musical experiences, and why we like the music we do. We now better understand what can be expected of students at different ages and how to better stimulate musical participation. This information enables teachers to design better classroom and rehearsal strategies, leading to more meaningful experiences.

From a developmental perspective, music involvement can occur at any stage and age of human growth. Many factors influence musical learning, including auditory acuity, genetics, home environment, individual physical features (e.g., teeth alignment, finger size), creativity, maturation, fatigue, intelligence, gender, race, and ethnicity (Bower & Hilgard, 1981; Radocy & Boyle, 2003). Learning occurs informally and formally, deliberately and unintentionally, for better or for worse, and at varying times and stages of life, often including the interaction of many diverse variables.

Hunt and Sullivan (1974) suggest a taxonomy of factors influencing learning in a classroom that illustrates the interrelationships of variables involved in learning processes. By understanding classroom interrelationships, teachers may better develop a culture of learning by establishing an environment where teaching can occur and learning can be experienced.

Hunt and Sullivan Taxonomy for Learning

1. Cultural Setting	Includes societal and cultural norms and values
2. Current School Setting	Includes culture if the school, class, and community location (e.g., rural, urban, etc...), size of school
3. Characteristics of Classroom	Includes size of class, age and sex of students, age and sex of teachers, physical setup of room (e.g., chairs and music stands)
4. School and Classroom Organization	Includes decision-making processes, communication patterns, relationship among staff and students, peer influences
5. Personal Characteristics of Teachers	Includes personality, attitudes, philosophy of life
6. Student-orientated Teacher Attitude	Includes education goals, concept of teacher and student roles, acceptance of student diversity
7. Teacher Behavior	Includes teaching approaches, techniques, and responses to student behavior and changes in teaching strategies

There are many theories regarding how humans learn. As with all theories, no single perspective has all the answers. While each theory may be predominantly based in psychological perspectives, each contains a strong social component. Although there are similarities among all theories, the differences create great debate in how humans learn and the most effective methods to teach. Each theory has the following similarities.

1. People develop at different rates.
2. Development is relatively orderly.
3. Development takes place gradually.
4. Some element of social/cultural experience.

The following are perhaps the most well-known and fundamental theories on how humans learn. Each theory is complex and extensive. The explanations presented are intended to be more of a brief introduction. For more information, please refer to the cited works at the end of the chapter.

Basic Learning Theory Groups

There are two basic groups of learning theorists: behavioral learning theorists and social learning theorists. Behavioral learning theorists believe that external events cause changes in observable behaviors (Woolfolk, 1998). The outcome of learning is a change in behavior. If a student could not play the tuba until after receiving lessons, then performs a scale, this action would constitute a learned behavior. One area of behavioral theory is classical conditioning, where a stimulus activates an observable response that can be either voluntary or involuntary. This method is most frequently associated with Ivan Pavlov's experiments with dogs in the 1920s.

Another form of behavioral learning is operant conditioning, where humans learn to behave in certain ways based on environmental situations (Woolfolk, 1998). Edward Thorndike and B. F. Skinner are the principle pioneers of this theory. Thorndike (1903/2007) suggested the law of effect, where any act that produces a satisfying effect will tend to be repeated. Skinner (1974) extended operant conditioning to include operants, which are voluntary behaviors affected by antecedents and consequences. Antecedents are events preceding an action, such as asking questions that enable students to explore a creative process. Consequences are actions brought about by antecedent actions, such as composing a piece of music based on the earlier questions. Reinforcement is used to strengthen or weaken desired or undesired consequences. Providing rewards or praise for a well-performed musical concert of the composition is a form of positive reinforcement.

Social learning theory emphasizes learning through observing others. Interactions with people and environments are important. To learn, students must have opportunities to interact (Wiggins, 2015). Unlike behavioral learning theory, social learning theory requires more than an observable change in order to understand that learning has occurred (Woolfolk, 1998). Albert Bandura (1976) developed the concept of social learning theory, where there is a distinction between the acquisition of knowledge and observable actions based on that knowledge. According to Bandura, behaviors are only a single component of learning; expectations, beliefs, and thoughts also reflect learning. Environmental events, personal factors, and behaviors interact in the learning process. Learning can be a result of interacting with and imitating others. Individuals create or construct an understanding of new information that is unique to each person. Teacher modeling of a performance technique and students imitating the concept is an example of this approach. Constant interactions facilitate new experiences that stimulate learning.

Jean Piaget: Theory of Cognitive Development

A Swiss psychologist, Jean Piaget, devised a learning model describing how human beings go about making sense of their world by gathering and organizing information (Piaget, 1950). Piaget was perhaps the first to conclude that humans construct understanding. According to Piaget, children think differently from adults. It is important that children are developmentally ready for the information being presented, or no understanding will occur. Piaget's Theory of Cognitive Development describes how human thinking processes change radically, though slowly, from birth to maturity because we are constantly trying to make sense of our world. In its basic form, Piaget's theory is that individuals construct their own understanding, as learning is a constructive process.

Accomplishing cognitive change is based on four factors: biological maturation, activity, social experiences, and equilibration, or the interaction between cognitive perception and environmental interactions that influences changes in thinking (Piaget, 1950). Piaget stated that all humans have the ability to organize information and experiences, and adapt by adjusting to their environment. We organize information and experiences into schemas that are mental representations of our world. As a person becomes more organized, he/she develops new schemas. This new development helps us to adapt to the new information about and perception of the world. This is known as assimilation, or the understanding of how we fit into the new information, and helps us to make sense of the situation. We then begin to accommodate or make necessary changes in existing schemas to respond to the new situation. Both assimilation and accommodation are processes that construct new ways to understand the situation or world around us.

Piaget's approach to learning is known as stage theory. There are four stages of cognitive development in Piaget's theory. Piaget (1950) believed all people pass through the same four stages in exactly the same order, which is associated with specific ages. Piaget was careful to note that the cognitive stages are general guidelines and that individuals could go through long periods of transition between stages. Knowing a child's age is no guarantee a teacher will know how a child will think.

Piaget's Stages of Cognitive Development

Stage	Approximate Age	Characteristic
Sensorimotor	0–2 years	Begins to make use of imitation, memory, and thought. Recognizes objects do not cease to exist when they are hidden. Moves from reflex actions to goal-directed activity.
Preoperational	2–7 years	Gradually develops the use of language and ability to think in symbolic form. Able to think operations through logically in one direction. Has difficulty seeing another person's point of view.
Concrete Operational	7–11 years	Able to solve concrete (hands-on) problems in logical fashion. Understands laws of conservation and is able to classify and seriate. Understands reversibility.
Formal Operational	11 —Adult	Able to solve abstract problems in logical fashion. Becomes more scientific in thinking. Develops concerns about social issues and identity.

For educators, the implication of Piaget's theory is that if we understand how children think, we will be better able to match teaching methods and activities to children's abilities at an age-appropriate time. Additionally, Piaget's theory informs educators that development occurs in a series of stages, which are universal to humans in all cultural contexts. All students have some capacity to learn if material is presented in a manner that can be understood during the appropriate time in development. It is important that information or skills required of students are neither too easy nor too difficult. Students need challenges to constantly reconstruct their schemas and make necessary accommodations to their world based on the new knowledge. However, if the requirements are too easy students will become bored, if too difficult frustrated (Woolfolk, 1998).

A component of Piaget's theory, conservation, has received attention from music researchers. Conservation occurs in the concrete operational stage (ages 7–11) when most children in society begin formal music training in schools. Conservation is necessary to form perception and musical analysis (Pflederer, 1967). It is the time when children begin to understand that an object can convert to a different property but remain the same. The musical form of theme and variation is an example, as you can play "Mary Had a Little Lamb" in different keys and different ranges, but through conservation children will still recognize the melody as "Mary Had a Little Lamb."

Piaget's work reminds educators that children are not miniature adults. Music teachers must present information and materials in appropriate ways and at the proper time, when children are ready to learn. Thus, Piaget's work affects the time when musical concepts should be presented, how difficult music should be taught at a certain age, and how students may react to music form.

Lev Vygotsky: Sociocultural Theory of Learning

The work of Russian researcher Lev Vygotsky is becoming increasingly influential, as his theory highlights the important role teachers and parents play in the cognitive development of children. Vygotsky (1978) believed higher cognitive processes differ from fundamental sensory processes. He believed social interactions are critical for intellectual development, and thus all knowledge is socially constructed. Vygotsky (1978) argued that a child's development could not be understood by solely studying the individual. We must also examine the external social world that the child is experiencing. Vygotsky stated that learning is embedded within social events and occurs as children interact with people, objects, and events in the environment. Vygotsky's concepts are the basis for the sociocultural theory of learning (Vygotsky, 1978).

Vygotsky shares Piaget's constructivist perspective. However, Vygotsky's approach to learning differs from Piaget's; where Piaget believed cognitive development occurred over four main stages with a definite endpoint, Vygotsky believed learning processes are too complex to be defined within only four stages. According to Vygotsky, development is dependent on social interactions, which are internalized, leading to cognitive development. Basically, children are a product of their environments and the interactions occurring within them.

The basis for Vygotsky's theory is the concept of the zone of proximal development (ZPD). ZPD is the gap between a learner's current or actual level of development, determined by independent problem solving, and the learner's potential level of development (Vygotsky, 1978). The "Zone" is the gap between what a person knows, and what they are capable of learning. Stated otherwise, the ZPD is a set of knowledge and abilities the learner has, but is unaware of. Social interactions with more capable humans (e.g., parents or teachers) produce shared experiences during which humans use tools, such as speech and writing, to learn their environments. By learning their environments, humans internalize the knowledge necessary to exist successfully within the setting. ZPD theory implies that a person's capacity to learn has no upper boundary and while individuals can learn on their own, humans learn better with the aid of others. Furthermore, what is learned with assistance from others today can be demonstrated independently tomorrow. The more an individual experiences, the more they can learn.

Vygotsky's theory requires teachers and students to plan and collaborate to create meaning in ways unique to the student. Instruction should be designed to be just above the student's current developmental ability. The social context should be open to interactions. Collaborative learning, where a group of peers strive to understand each other, is part of the learning process. Teachers mediate these interactions with the focus less on direct instruction and more on discovery. Through discovery, students should be put in situations where they will be challenged to understand, but where support from more experienced students and teachers is available. Motivation occurs when individuals support others to attain understanding and achieve the goal. (Woolfolk, 1998).

Zone of Proximal Development

1. The gap between current level of development and the learner's potential level of development.
2. Learning occurs through human interactions and discovery.
3. There is no limit on how much a person can learn.
4. Music should be presented in a manner that promotes individual experience and relevancy.

Vygotsky's work encourages music educators to reconsider how they present music and the environment in which the music is being experienced. Discovery learning places less focus on group ensemble instruction and more responsibility on teachers to provide students opportunities to create meaningful ways to experience music. This does not mean that large ensemble instruction cannot occur. However, the music class will include more opportunities for individual music experimentation and focus on more musical relevancy for individuals.

Jerome Bruner: Spiral Curriculum

Jerome Bruner's work emphasized the importance of understanding the holistic structure of a subject. A subject's structure refers to fundamental ideas, relationships, or patterns that would be considered essential information regarding the topic. According to Bruner (1977), by understanding a subject's structure a student can see the relationship between the different components. Understanding relationships helps make learning more meaningful, useful, and memorable. A student who sees the relevance of a particular skill to his or her own purpose will more readily engage in the type of behavior needed to improve that skill (Caine & Caine, 1997).

Bruner's theory reflects many of Piaget's ideas. Understanding when a student is ready to learn is important and requires presenting information in an age-appropriate manner based upon how the child views his/her world. Bruner (1977) proposed that the essential information of a subject can be taught at the earliest of abilities and ages, then revisited at a more complex level as the student grows and develops. Like Piaget with his theory of cognitive development,

Bruner stated that as a child's cognitive abilities develop, new material can be presented in a more complex manner and in different situations. Because students are ready to learn, they experience less frustration and failure, and are more willing, which increases stimulation to learn more.

Bruner's approach is known as the spiral curriculum (Bruner, 1977). The spiral curriculum is a degree of understanding that applies what is learned in a progressively more complex manner. Transfer of information and skills from one situation to another is essential as the student becomes ready for more advanced instruction. Teachers are the principle agents of instruction and transfer. The spiral approach begins by breaking down advance skills or complex knowledge to their most fundamental concept or skill. The initial learning of basic knowledge or skills is the foundation for subsequent learning. Information should be presented in ways that demonstrate relationships of similarities and differences. By showing relationships, Bruner believed new information is structured in a manner that enables students to easily remember the information. Stimulating further exploration in a subject is the goal of the initial presentation, as material is shown as increasingly important. Constant review is essential and should be done in different contexts so transfer of information and skills to new situations can be accomplished. Demonstrating the connection of information and skills to "real" world experiences further enhances transfer. Consequently, new information and skills become relevant and meaningful outside the formal school setting.

Spiral Curriculum

1. Understanding relationships is important for relevancy and later transfer.
2. Knowing when a child is ready to learn is essential; presenting information in age-appropriate manners is necessary to motivation and continued learning.
3. Information is initially presented in its simplest form, increasingly more complex as the student develops; transfer is essential.
4. Music instruction may begin with rote-to-note learning that sets the foundation for more advanced concepts to be presented later.

Bruner's theory encourages music educators to carefully consider standards and expectations for all students. Bruner is similar to Vygotsky in that teachers and students must work together. How concepts are presented can enable students from elementary school through high school to achieve higher goals. For example, beginning band students can be expected to perform advanced rhythms if not constrained by having to read notation. This rote-to-note approach helps to break down an advanced concept into its simplest form. Notation can be added to complete the instruction as students progress. The spiral approach to learning suggests that while music teachers should have larger objectives for students to learn, they should also carefully plan how they will present the material in an elementary manner so that simple foundations can be laid for later advanced learning.

Benjamin Bloom: Taxonomy of Learning

Benjamin Bloom created a classification of intellectual behavior to help individuals learn. In his research, Bloom (1956) found that over 95 percent of test questions required students to only think at the lowest, most basic level: the recall of information. He believed learning should focus on the mastery of subjects and promote higher levels of thinking. In order to master a subject or concept, a more in-depth knowledge and application of material was needed.

Bloom developed a taxonomy that explains higher order thinking processes. A taxonomy is a framework of categories along a continuum that helps organize a process. According to Bloom (1956), there are three different domains of learning:

1. Cognitive: mental skills; how to think; intellectual ability
2. Affective: growth in feelings or emotions; attitude
3. Psychomotor: manual or physical skills.

Within each domain are categories or levels of acquiring and demonstrating learned knowledge or skills. The categories are in sequential order, from most basic or lowest complexity to most complex. Each category must be mastered before progressing to the next level (category). Below are the three domains of learning and categories within each.

Cognitive Domain

Category (lowest to highest)	Description
Knowledge (lowest complexity)	Simple recall of data or information
Comprehension	Understanding the meaning, translation, and connection of information; be able to state a problem in one's own words
Application	Uses a concept or knowledge in a new situation
Analysis	Separates material or concepts into parts so its organizational structure can be understood
Synthesis	Builds a structure or pattern from diverse elements to create a new meaning
Evaluation (highest complexity)	Makes judgments about value of ideas or materials

---

Affective Domain

Category (lowest to highest)	Description
Receiving Phenomena (lowest complexity)	Awareness, willingness to hear, selected attention
Responding to Phenomena	Active participation; attends and reacts to particular phenomena
Valuing	Establishes or demonstrates a worth to a particular object or phenomena
Organization	Organizes values into priorities by contrasting different values; emphasis on comparing, and formulating, values
Internalizing Values (highest complexity)	Has a value system that controls behavior; behavior is pervasive and consistent

Psychomotor Domain

Category (lowest to highest)	Description
Perception (lowest complexity)	The ability to use sensory cues to guide motor activity
Set	Readiness to act mentally, physically, and emotionally (mindsets)
Guided Response	Early stages of learning a complex skill that includes imitation, and trial and error
Mechanism	Intermediate stage in learning when responses become habitual with some degree of proficiency
Complex Overt Response	Skillful performance of motor acts that require complex movement; performing without hesitation and automatic response
Adaptation	Skills are well developed and can be modified to fit special requirements
Origination (highest complexity)	Creating new movements to fit a particular situation or problem.

Using Bloom's taxonomy to teach requires the instructor to know what objectives students should learn (Bloom, 1956). Learning objectives are what students should know and be able to do as a result of instruction. Put another way, learning objectives help describe what students will be able to do or know because of the class experience. Thus, within the taxonomy, teaching is an intentional and purposeful act that facilitates learning specific knowledge or behaviors. Students are assumed to be active learners with the goal of constructing new knowledge based on prior knowledge.

Having an understanding of Bloom's taxonomy can help music educators to better plan for how students will learn. The taxonomy assists in organizing rehearsals and instruction so learning occurs in all areas and domains. By challenging students to think on a higher level, more abstract and meaningful musical skills can be achieved and demonstrated. Music educators may find it easier and clearer to explain to nonmusicians what is being experienced and learned in class.

Erik Erikson: Psychosocial Theory of Development

Erik Erikson (1963, 1980) believed all humans have the same basic needs and that society must provide for those needs. The psychosocial theory of development's premise is that every individual, regardless of culture, evolves through a series of choices made in developmental personality stages occurring throughout life. Within each stage, individuals encounter unique developmental conflicts that must be resolved through choices. Resolutions may be successful or unsuccessful, but how they are accomplished influences an individual's sense of self. Through the theory, Erikson explains how all individuals have basic needs throughout their lives. Through social interactions, needs are met in some manner of selection by the individual, resulting in the emergence of a self-identity that is in relation to other human beings (Erikson, 1963, 1980). Erikson believed that emotional changes and their relation to social environments follow similar patterns in every society. He believed that within every society each person must accomplish specific tasks at different stages of life. Resolving these tasks determines an individual's emotional relationship with his or her environment.

Similar to Piaget's, Erikson's theory is based on a series of stages, each with a specific goal, concern, accomplishment, and danger. He also expanded most stage theorists' concepts of development by suggesting that humans have room for growth over an entire lifespan. Erikson's stages are interdependent: accomplishments at later stages depend on how conflicts are resolved in earlier stages (Erikson, 1963). Erikson suggested that each individual faces a developmental crisis at each stage. A developmental crisis is a specific conflict whose resolution prepares the way for the next stage. Each crisis involves a conflict between a positive choice and a potentially unhealthy alternative. How an individual resolves each crisis will have a lasting effect on that person's self-image and view of society. There are eight stages to Erikson's psychosocial theory of development.

Erik Erikson's Eight Stages of Psychosocial Development (Woolfolk, 1998)

	Stage	Approx. Age	Important Event	Description
1)	Basic trust vs. mistrust	Birth to 12–18 months	Feeding	Infant must form a loving, trusting relationship or develop a sense of mistrust
2)	Autonomy vs. shame/doubt	18 months to 3 years	Toilet training	Child's energies are directed toward development of physical skills. Failure to learn control may result in shame and doubt if not handled well.
3)	Initiative vs. guilt	3–6 years	Independence	Child continues to become more assertive and take initiative, if too forceful guilt can develop.
4)	Industry vs. inferiority	6–12 years	School	Child must deal with demands to learn new skills or risk developing a sense of inferiority/failure.
5)	Identity vs. role confusion	Adolescence 12–20 years	Peer relationships	Must achieve identity in occupation, gender roles, religion, etc.
6)	Intimacy vs. isolation	Young Adulthood 20–35 years	Love relationships	Must develop intimate relationships or suffer feelings of isolation.
7)	Generativity vs. stagnation	Middle Adulthood 35 years to retirement	Parenting/Mentoring	Must find some way to satisfy and support the next generation.
8)	Ego integrity vs. despair; oneself as one is	Late Adulthood Retirement years	Reflection on and acceptance of one's life	Culmination is a sense of fulfillment and acceptance of oneself as one is.

Erikson's emphasis on the development of one's self is important to educators. It appears that students with higher self-esteem are more likely to succeed in school (Marsh, 1990). Other studies suggest that students with higher self-esteem have better attitudes toward school and better classroom behavior (Cauley & Tyler, 1989).

The psychosocial theory of development has direct implications for individuals seeking to become music teachers. The transformation from an adolescent high school student to mature music educator begins to occur during Stage Five, when individuals begin to develop a sense of identity. Research by Mead (1934) and Cooley (1902), presented in Chapter 2, describes how identity and personality develop within a social context. Interactions with people in settings where they are expected to function effectively help to develop how individuals will perceive themselves. Thus, Stage Five, which covers the time of high school and college years, is the time when teachers need to provide experiences that help individuals form their classroom personality and self-image of how they will perceive themselves as a teacher. Erickson's theory was tested on the development of music educators (Bergee & Grashel, 1995). The study found that using Erikson's theory could assist in profiling future music educators' personality and potential success. The research suggested undergraduate students need opportunities in their teacher-training experiences that provide interactions in order to build a strong sense of identity as a teacher. These opportunities might include direct experiences in music classroom settings where the student would be challenged to assume adult roles and responsibilities.

Howard Gardner: Theory of Multiple Intelligences

Howard Gardner (1985) developed and later refined a learning theory based on human intelligence. According to Gardner, intelligence is not a single variable, but is multiple variables in many forms. Gardner was influenced by Piaget, and suggested that intelligence develops along a developmental sequence similar to Piaget's. Gardner's theory has become known as the Theory of Multiple Intelligences. Intelligence is defined as innate potential activated by cultural values, opportunities, experiences, and personal decisions (Gardner, 1985). Thus, intellectual potential is a genetic endowment developed through environmental and social experiences. Originally, Gardner (1993) suggested each individual has a set of seven intelligences: linguistic, logical-mathematical, musical, spatial, bodily-kinesthetic, interpersonal, and intrapersonal. Gardner later (1999) revised his definition of intelligences to include more biological and neurological potentials.

The debate over how human intelligence and ability are acquired is the essence of the nature versus nurture concepts. Is intellectual ability an innate genetic capability or solely developed through environmental and human interaction? The Theory of Multiple Intelligences contains both concepts. According to Gardner (1985), every human being, in every known culture, has the same capabilities through genetic endowment. However, development of intellectual potential is based on environmental experiences. Simply stated, the Theory of Multiple Intelligences asserts that all humans have potential in all of the abilities (genetic), but some are developed (or not) based on environmental factors/experiences. Thus, individuals have strengths and weaknesses in one or several areas. This explains why though we all have potential for musical ability, the potential develops more in some individuals than others.

Original Seven Intelligences in the Theory of Multiple Intelligences		
Linguistic	Logical-Mathematical	Musical
Spatial	Bodily-Kinesthetic	Interpersonal
Intrapersonal		

An important implication of Gardner's theory for music educators is that music is an intelligence possessed by every person, in every society and culture. Accordingly, every individual has some degree of potential for music ability (Gardner, 1985). The development of this innate potential is influenced by environmental factors, including family members, peers, teachers, the media, and simple experimentation with or exposure to music. Musical experience and exposure, especially at younger ages, is important to developing potential. The importance of a strong elementary music experience is crucial. However, research is showing that even earlier experience and exposure is good (Custodero & Johnson-Green, 2003). Experiencing music from birth to school age (0–5 years) could have an impact on developing music abilities.

Gardner's theory may be most important to music educators because it challenges American society's notion that music is a divine gift and thus only for a few select individuals (Austin, 1997a). Gardner suggests that every student has the potential to develop music skills to some degree. Thus, when recruiting students into music programs, music teachers can explain to other teachers, parents, administrators, and students that all students have potential to develop and experience music skills. This is especially important to parents who may believe their child has no family background or aptitude in music and therefore cannot succeed in music class. Knowledgeable music teachers can explain the Theory of Multiple Intelligences by focusing on the importance of exposure and experience to developing music ability.

Intelligence and Musical Ability, Preference, and Taste

Intelligence and ability are frequently linked together. However, they can be very different and distinct. Every child is unique in his or her abilities, talents, and limitations. This realization is not new; the idea that people vary in intellectual abilities has been in existence for a long time. Intelligence can be defined as capacity to acquire and use knowledge for solving problems and adapting to the world (Woolfolk, 1998). Some theorists believe intelligence is related to the ability to perform a single cognitive task, such as a paper and pencil test or computing mathematical problems. This ability is referred to as general intelligence or the capacity to perform specific mental tasks (Woolfolk, 1998). Other theorists suggest intelligence is the capacity to perform a combination of tasks at a single time, or multitask (Gardner, 1985; 1999). A combination may include cognitive, as well as psychomotor and affective, tasks. Whichever theory is accepted, humans vary in demonstrating their intelligence and how it is acquired.

The term "ability" suggests being able to do something. An individual with music ability is able to perform, create, and analyze if given the opportunity. However, society often uses ability interchangeably with the terms "aptitude" and "talent." Ability refers the facility to do something regardless of how an individual acquired the skill, knowledge, or experience. However, developing musical ability involves some degree of training or instruction. Musical ability varies widely in humans and is very imprecise, making it difficult to objectively assess or predict (Radocy & Boyle, 2003).

Music aptitude is more of the capacity or potential of an individual to develop musical ability. Demonstrating aptitude does not require any instruction or training. If students are being measured for their musical aptitude, the teacher is trying to predict the extent that ability will develop. Music talent is a more imprecise term used to describe a demonstration of ability. It is a cumulative term demonstrating what has been accomplished, often due to instruction (Radocy & Boyle, 2003).

How an individual acquires intelligence and ability appears to be a great debate. There has never been a concrete answer to why some people appear to have learned more musical skills than others. The center of this debate focuses on genetic endowment or environmental influences: nature versus nurture. Is an individual born with ability or, as sociologists assume, is music

Photo Figure 9 An individual with music ability is able to perform, create, and analyze if given the opportunity.

ability something we learn from our environment and interactions with other humans? A purely sociological view suggests that music ability is developed from environmental influences, with no genetic contribution, learned from members of various cultures. However, music researchers have not been able to totally discount the possibility of any genetic influence (Radocy & Boyle, 2003). Most psychologists believe both hereditary and environmental influences combine to affect the development of intellectual ability, including music ability (Radocy & Boyle, 2003; Sloboda, 1985).

Variables possibly influencing the development of music ability are diverse and numerous. The perception of musical ability is frequently affected by social beliefs, stereotypes, and cultural expectations. While factors such as gender, race, ethnicity, or age have been shown to have no influence on the development of musical ability (Radocy & Boyle, 2003), stereotypes and social beliefs regarding these issues frequently influence the public's perception of ability (Koza, 1994; Radocy & Boyle 2003). Many individuals believe music ability is a divine gift that only a few people possess (Austin, 1997a). Some research suggests the American sociocultural belief is that music talent is only demonstrated by extraordinary exhibitions (Austin, 1997a). Thus, the principle violinist of the Chicago Symphony is an individual with "true" music ability while the first chair trumpet player in the Jones High School Band is just "having fun."

The best way to develop musical skills is also debatable. To begin with, intellectual abilities are affected by experiences and open to future changes (Woolfolk, 1998). Humans have the capacity to learn at different times and in different styles. The learning theories of Piaget (1950) and Gardner (1985) suggest musical ability is best learned sequentially, beginning at a young age. In addition to possible genetic contributions, cultural influences on the development of musical ability appear to include parents and home environments, siblings, peers, teachers, the media, and experience through exposure and practice (Radocy & Boyle, 2003; Sloboda, 1985). It is important that parents and teachers provide an open, positive environment that encourages exploration. Criticism and judgmental approaches can create frustration and embarrassment, thus turning young students away from music. Interestingly, research has shown that having musical parents has little influence on children's musical development. However, having parents who promote musical activities is very influential on encouraging children to try music and develop a positive self-perception that they can succeed in music (Brand, 1986; Custodero & Johnson-Green, 2003; Zdzinski, 1992).

It is important that music educators have an understanding of music ability and remember that ability, however defined or acquired, can always improve (Sloboda, 1985). Music educators constantly encounter issues related to music ability when they perform responsibilities related to assigning grades, selecting soloists, choosing music, and deciding on section leaders. If there are questions regarding these decisions, then the music educators will need to explain and often justify their decision to administrators, parents, and students. This explanation will be based on the educator's definition of what constitutes music ability. The problem is that defining music ability is subjective. Is the demonstration of ability only playing correct notes and rhythms? Should intonation, phrasing, diction, and tone quality be factors in judging music ability? Does ability also include knowledge of composers, history, and musical styles? Everyone seems to have an opinion of what constitutes musical ability, who has musical ability, and to what extent people have musical ability. While there may be many perceptions, the teacher must have a clear concept of what skills or behaviors constitute music ability in the classroom. Equally important, the teacher must clearly articulate these skills and behaviors in a manner that individuals with little or no musical experience can understand (e.g., parents, administrators, and students).

A relationship exists between music ability and the development of music preference. In general, the better students are able to perform a piece of music (ability), the more they enjoy the music (preference). Over time and continued performance, the development of taste occurs. Furthermore, when students perform music they enjoy they are more motivated to practice and be attentive in class and thus improve their ability. Consequently, the concepts of aptitude, ability, preference, and tastes are reciprocally connected.

Humans vary in their musical preferences due to cultural standards, training, and expectations. Preference is an immediate, short-term choice of specific objects or events that can change at any time (Abeles, 1980; Radocy & Boyle, 2003). Musical preference is a value judgment influenced by factors such as time of day, peers, the media, gender, teacher approval, exposure and experience, race, ethnicity, age, auditory sensitivity, and musical complexity (LeBlanc, 1981, 1982). Developing musical taste may be the ultimate goal of music education. Taste is a more long-term or permanent commitment to a broader group of objects or events (Radocy & Boyle, 2003). Consequently, an individual can have a taste for classical music, but have a preference for Mozart in the morning and Stravinsky during dinner.

Musical taste and preference can be altered, but not always in predictable patterns, and any change appears to require some degree of experience (LeBlanc, & McCrary, 1983; LeBlanc, Sherrill, 1986). Repetition and familiarity are two influential techniques used to broaden student preferences. Students frequently express dislike for music they are unfamiliar with upon first performing. However, as they become more accustomed to the sounds, rhythms, and general music design, they often become more agreeable to the music and enjoy rehearsing. Familiarity through repetition does not guarantee increased preference. Exposure can also be effective. Studies have shown that elementary students exposed to sounds, musical concepts, and general performance information prior to attending classically orientated music concerts were consistently more positive about the new musical experiences than students not receiving this information (Hornyak, 1966; Sims, 1992).

Pedagogically, music educators should provide students with a wide variety of direct music experiences in listening, performing, and creating various musical styles. Research has shown that musical elements such as style, genre, tempo, range, and authenticity, language, and performance medium (e.g., voice, instrumental) can influence student musical preference (Brittin, 2000; Demorest & Schultz, 2004; LeBlanc, 1981; LeBlanc & McCrary, 1983; LeBlanc & Sherrill, 1986). Student characteristics that may affect musical preference include the student's gender, race, ethnicity training, and exposure (Fung, 1994; Morrison, 1998; Siebenaler, 1999; Radocy & Boyle, 2003). Teaching techniques that appear to be influential include the mode in which music is presented (live music as opposed to recorded music) and the authenticity of the performance (Fung, 1994; Killian, 1990; Siebenaler, 1999; Sims, 1992).

Summary

In the United States, teachers are viewed as the individuals most responsible for organizing and presenting materials in ways that students can acquire knowledge and skills. Good teaching involves knowing how students acquire musical information, organize and process information, and use information. Effective instruction is dependent upon the teacher possessing knowledge of children's intellectual development, as much as their development of physical skills and imagination. This knowledge enables age-appropriate planning, sequencing, and presentation to influence learning. Knowledge includes an understanding of age-appropriate responses.

Nearly all music experiences reflect the theories of teaching and learning to some degree. It seems obvious that learning occurs best when teachers provide multiple opportunities for interactions and hands-on experiences. We tend to learn best by actively doing rather than passively listening. Teachers need to understand multiple theories of learning as they guide instruction and link the teacher to the student-learner. There are disagreements regarding the manner in which humans learn. How much intellectual capacity can be attributed to genetic endowment and what is the role of environmental influences on abilities? While these questions may never be definitively answered, most learning theorists propose that learning is accomplished most effectively within a cultural setting and is dependent upon cultural resources, most important of which is interactions through experience.

Music is more than recreation; it is a creative and intellectual process involving most likely a combination of innate abilities and environmental interactions. Consequently, musical intelligence does not develop independently of other intellectual processes and is acquired in multiple ways and through different venues. Musically, students not only learn through performance, but also learn through listening, creating, describing, and reading music. Experimenting with playing kitchen pots, imitating music on the radio, making up silly songs with parents are examples of learning theories within music experiences. Thus, music learning can occur anytime and anywhere, at home and in schools.

Key Items

Learning
B. F. Skinner
Behavioral Learning Theory
Jean Piaget
ZPD
Schemas

Albert Bandura
Edward Thorndike
Social Learning Theory
Lev Vygotsky
Sociocultural Theory of Learning
Jerome Bruner

Spiral Curriculum
Psychosocial Theory of Development
Assimilation/Accommodation
Music Ability, Aptitude, & Talent
Benjamin Bloom
Music Preference & Taste

Erik Erikson
Theory of Cognitive Development
Intelligence
Taxonomy of Learning
Nature vs. Nurture

Questions for Consideration

1. How might you use antecedents, consequences, and reinforcement to manage rehearsal behavior in your music class?
2. What are indicators of music ability?
3. What musical behavior might be appropriate for children during Piaget's concrete operational stage?
4. How might rote-to-note instruction be used to teach complex musical concepts in a K-6 music curriculum based on the spiral curricular approach?
5. Using Bloom's taxonomy, what might be music-related questions that represent each category with the three different learning domains?

Web Resources

Learning Behaviors

Association for Talent Development: https://www.td.org/
Behaviorism: http://www.learning-theories.com/behaviorism.html
Bloom's Taxonomy: http://www.celt.iastate.edu/teaching-resources/effective-practice/revised-blooms-taxonomy/
Social Learning Theory: http://www.simplypsychology.org/bandura.html

Chapter 7

Social Characteristics of Effective Teachers

Whenever and wherever humans have existed music has existed also.

—Bennett Reimer

What is effective teaching? How does an individual become an expert music teacher? Are teachers "born" or "made?" Is effective teaching simply applying common sense to a given situation? There are as many different answers to these questions as there are teachers. Chapter 7 presents the knowledge and characteristics of effective music teachers. This information includes awareness of student and classroom characteristics, motivation theories, and attributes of effective music teachers. The chapter's premise is that not everyone can be an effective teacher. While individuals can learn effective teacher behaviors, effective teaching requires much more than pedagogical skills.

"Can I be a good teacher?" is a question every individual should ask themselves before entering the teaching profession. Teaching is a challenging professional vocation requiring broad knowledge, with very few absolute answers. Being an effective teacher requires a commitment to broadening individual knowledge and skills related to the many ways in which humans learn in order to reach every student, in every situation. While some may say this goal is impossible, others might use this high measure as motivation to reach students on every level. Whichever perspective is accepted, it is clear that effective teaching is a multidimensional, complex commitment requiring many different skills and behaviors.

One view of effective teaching involves technical competence. Technically good teachers are concerned about planning, creating lessons, solving problems, and making decisions. Selecting appropriate music and carefully deciding how to teach the concepts presented in the music is a method reflective of a technically competent view. Effective teaching is also viewed as a reflection of personal competence. Personal competence includes knowing when to change facial expression and voice fluctuations, moving around the room to create a sense of proximity to control students' attentions, or knowing when to use humor and smile or make a joke in order to affect a classroom or rehearsal environment.

Most people would probably agree that effective teachers are both technically and personally competent. Effective music teachers not only know subject matter, but are also able to relate content to the world around them while keeping their students engaged in learning. They are aware of a variety of classroom variables, including student characteristics, motivational techniques, classroom management styles, and effective teaching techniques that include both personal and technical behaviors.

Good teachers tend to be good teachers no matter what subject they teach. All effective teachers combine good planning, organization, and decision-making and are able to use a variety of existing teaching strategies and develop new strategies when necessary. A music teacher's ability to initiate and maintain an effective classroom or rehearsal environment is dependent upon the interaction of many factors, including musical, emotional, intellectual, physical, and social components. Effective music teachers must be able to manage classrooms, be able to establish rehearsal routines and schedules, and be willing to break away from established routines when situations require change.

Student Characteristics

Many preservice students state they want to become teachers because they enjoy working with students (Madsen & Kelly, 2002). Yet, while working with students is immensely rewarding, understanding students can be one of the most challenging aspects of becoming an effective teacher. Students represent a variety of cultures, as they come in all shapes and sizes, and reflect a wide diversity of characteristics, making it impossible to approach any music class with a single instructional perspective. Each student brings different values, attitudes, beliefs, abilities, and behaviors into classrooms. Students have different interests, abilities, intellectual capacities, and musical skills. Due to so many differences, it is every music teacher's challenge to attract students into their classes. For example, a 1991 study by Stewart found that 30.9% of high school seniors in the United States were enrolled in a music performance class. This is in contrast to a 2011 study by Elpus and Abril, which cited data from 2004 showing that high school music enrollment had fallen to 21%. Another study showed that 67.9% of all students at the age of 13 have never participated in band, and 91.3% have never participated in orchestra (Nierman & Veak, 1997).

The reasons for joining music vary widely. Some students are more interested in learning, while others are more passive. For instance, Adderly, Kennedy, and Berz (2003) found students participated in school music ensembles for a wide variety of reasons including family influence, enjoyment of music, performing, and social benefits. Other students join music classes because they want to be with their friends, their parents made them join, administrators and counselors placed them in the class, they wanted to go on trips, or they perceived music as an "easy A." Additional research indicated students join music because it makes them feel good about themselves (Austin, 1997), it provides meaningful connections (Abril, 2011), or they have a familiarity with a music professional (Abeles, 2004). Furthermore, students enjoyed tasks that were creative, involving performance-related activities (Boswell, 1991). Based on research findings, it is clear students participate in music for numerous reasons, including many nonmusical factors often associated with social influences.

Frequently, a student's decision to join music is based on music's perceived value. It is important to realize that music is highly valued among American students, particularly for its identification elements, emotional and life benefits, and social benefits (Campbell, Connell, & Beegle, 2007). Music education's value also appears to be influenced by a variety of variables including a student's gender, musical self-concept, class or rehearsal activities, and home environment. For example, research findings (Elpus & Abril, 2011; Stewart, 1991) have shown that females participated in music more than males. Not surprisingly, Boswell (1991) found that middle school females have better attitudes toward music than males. However, the value of school music education is not always realized. Wayman (2005) found that public school students felt music class was fun and provided a sense of stress relief, but did not view music as a serious academic subject. Wayman's research found that students believed music class was more important for individuals perceived as more talented and that music's main purpose was to entertain.

Two other characteristics affecting students' music participation are race and ethnicity (also see Chapter 5). Data (Elpus & Abril, 2011; Stewart, 1991) indicate white students participate far more in school music than any other race. With steady increases in school enrollments, non-white minority participation in music classes does not reflect this growth. Racial and ethnic minority music enrollment in primarily Caucasian schools is frequently lower, as students are often not encouraged to participate due to differences in cultural expectation, including musical values (Minear, 1999; Spearman, 2000). Many barriers such as socioeconomic factors, cultural perceptions of different music styles, teaching approaches, and cultural expectations are among the variables inhibiting many minorities from participating in school opportunities, including music (Albert, 2006; Cartledge, 1996; Spearman, 2000). Socioeconomic variables are frequent major factors that influenced all students' decisions to participation in music (Albert, 2006; Elpus & Abril, 2011; Fitzpatrick, 2006; Kinney,2008, 2010; Miksza & Gault, 2014; Nierman & Veak, 1997; Stewart, 1991).

Students learn many roles in school that can be influential throughout their lives, such as class leader, athlete, musician, traffic guard, bully, homecoming queen, and valedictorian. While in school, individuals learn routines, follow orders while learning obedience, learn how to deal with disagreements, interact with the opposite sex, and generally identify with being a good student. Students who refuse to submit to school routines are labeled as rebels (Gracey, 2011). Frequently, roles are learned through cultural expectations based on variables such as gender, race, parental influences, and teacher expectations (Ballantine, 2001). Students have opportunities to learn many roles in music classes. Morrison (2001), as well as Adderly, Kennedy, & Berz (2003), points out that music classes often resemble families where students develop abilities and self-images of roles within the family structure.

Music teachers play a major role in attracting and shaping student experiences and role development in school. Music often presents ways for students to experience leadership responsibilities through ensemble officers, section leaders, and soloists. Like other classes, interactions with other students, teachers, and activities through the curriculum provide students with perceptions of abilities and relationships. Perceptions of musical abilities can enable some students to be

Photo Figure 10 Schools provide opportunities for students to learn many roles.

viewed with higher regard than others. Hallinan (2012) states that when students perceive that teachers care about them, respect them, and praise them, they achieve higher academic goals. Boswell (1991) noted that teachers were more influential than either a student's gender or grade level in developing a positive perception of music. A more positive perception increases the likelihood an individual will participate in music.

Learning roles can have negative influences as well. Students are frequently aware of where they stand academically, and musically. Teachers place labels on students that can have a detrimental effect on students' self-perceptions. Furthermore, self-fulfilling prophecy can become a reality as students meet what they perceive as expected behavior and academic achievement. Thus, by learning or meeting specific roles, students may not be able to expand their interests or abilities.

Unfortunately, not all students succeed in school. Data from the National Center for Education Statistics (2014b) show that the overall dropout rate for high school students declined from 12 percent in 1990 to seven % in 2012. The dropout rate was lower for whites than blacks and Hispanics, and lower for females than males. According to the National Dropout Prevention Center/Network (2014), most students who drop out of school do so because they (1) are pressured by individuals or situations to either pull or be pushed out of school, or (2) become apathetic or disillusioned regarding their academic situation. Most concerns involve school-related, family-related, or employment-related reasons. Generally, students frequently cited a dislike for school and an inability to get along with teachers as reasons for dropping out of school (National Center for Education Statistics, 1999). Specifically, Ballantine (2001) cited isolation, a feeling that no one cares, and low expectations as primary reasons for dropping out. A 2006 nationwide survey found that almost two-thirds of high school dropouts stated schools did not expect enough of them and that they would have worked harder if standards had been higher. The survey found 69% of dropouts did not feel motivated in classes, 47% found their classes uninteresting, 43% missed too many days to catch up on schoolwork, and 42% spent time with people who were not interested in school (USA Today, 2006).

While some schools are attempting to bribe students with new cars, movie tickets, and gas vouchers (Tallahassee Democrat, 2006), individual teachers can have tremendous influence in retaining students. Setting high expectations, connecting with students inside and outside of class, and learning then recognizing early warning signs of potential dropout (e.g., repeatedly skipping class) can help keep students in school. Music has frequently been cited as a subject that can be effective in keeping students in school. In a nationwide survey, 96 percent of school principals reported participation in music education encourages and motivates students to stay in school. Another 89 percent of principals believe a high quality music education program contributes to higher graduation rates. This finding correlates with additional data showing schools with music programs have significantly higher attendance and graduation rates (Music Educators National Conference, 2006b).

Motivating Students to Learn

Research has shown that students who like school tend to achieve higher academic goals and have a lower incidence of discipline problems (Hallinan, 2012). Thus, finding what interests and motivates students is a major goal for every educator, as most would agree that the desire to learn is a critical component in academic and musical achievement. Researchers and educators frequently disagree on the source of motivation. Motivation is usually defined as an internal state that arouses, directs, and maintains behavior (Woolfolk, 1998). What variables energize and direct behavior? Possible influences on motivation include personal needs, incentives, fears, specific goals, social pressure, self-confidence, interests, curiosity, beliefs, values, and expectations

(Hruska, 2011; Woolfolk, 1998). Certain people have fears of tests, performance anxiety, or a strong need to be accepted or to succeed; each trait affects an individual accordingly. Individuals work hard to achieve, avoid tests, or spend hours practicing to not fail.

It is possible that some explanation of motivation relies on internal or personal factors such as needs, interests, curiosity, or enjoyment. These factors are based on a natural tendency to achieve or please, otherwise known as intrinsic motivation. The goal of intrinsic motivation is to derive desire from within the learner. Intrinsic motivation assumes the learner is making decisions concerning the amount of effort to learn or act in a certain situation (Ciskszentmihalyi & Nakamura, 1989). When an individual is intrinsically motivated, no reward or punishment to perform or reach a goal is needed.

Other motivational factors may be more environmental, such as rewards, social pressures, and punishment. These factors cause individuals to do something to avoid a consequence, earn a reward, or please someone. This type of influence is known as extrinsic motivation and is associated with factors outside the learner. When individuals seek to avoid punishment, earn a goal, or please a teacher, they are behaving due to external factors that are part of the environment or situation. When extrinsically motivated, individuals are not interested in the activity for its own sake, but rather about what it will gain them. (Woolfolk, 1998).

Both intrinsic and extrinsic motivations are important in education. Students do not always come to the classroom with a natural desire to learn or to participate. Why would a student be motivated to study for a test or practice for a music performance? Poor student performance, either musically or academically, is often a source of frustration for teachers attempting to stimulate students to achieve higher goals. In addressing student performance, Albert Bandura (1993) stated teachers have three goals in developing motivation in their students:

1. To create a state of motivation to learn
2. To develop the trait of being motivated to learn throughout their lives
3. To encourage students to be thoughtful about what they are studying or participating.

Teachers are concerned about developing the motivation to learn in all students; consequently, a balance of both extrinsic and intrinsic motivational approaches is necessary. This aim requires students to perceive activities and knowledge as meaningful and worthwhile. Different types of activities are interesting to different students. Teaching can create intrinsic motivation by stimulating student curiosity and making individuals feel competent due to their own work. However, there are situations where external rewards can support and contribute to students' learning. For example, working to achieve a superior ranking for a school or group can create a tremendous sense of accomplishment.

What might be methods for motivating students? Sloboda (2003) suggested an individual is motivated to achieve musically by first experiencing pleasure with the experience. Enjoyment leads to a level of commitment that leads to achievement. Adding to this knowledge, Coffman and Adamek (2001) suggested musicians are motivated in three different varieties: (1) Personal Motivation—includes self-expression, leisure, and recreation; (2) Music Motivation—includes a professed love of music, learning about music, and performing music; (3) Social Motivation—includes meeting new people, being with friends, and having a sense of belonging. Research also gives an indication as to when students are being motivated. Maeher, Pintrich, and Linnenbrink (2002) stated four specific actions indicate motivation is at work: (a) Choice and Preference—a deliberate response by students in selecting one activity over another; (b) Intensity—the degree that a student becomes involved in an activity; (c) Persistence—the extent an individual continues in a choice and desires additional learning opportunities; and (d) Quality—the degree the new actions affect achievement.

One important factor in developing motivation is teacher praise. The authoritarian role teachers have makes their words and actions highly influential in motivating students to strive for higher learning. Most students attempt to please teachers. Research has shown that specific positive praise is influential in providing specific feedback to students as to what they have done correctly. By having a clear understanding of what is acceptable, students become more motivated to keep doing positive tasks in order to continue to please the teacher (Madsen & Madsen, 1981). Many novice teachers provide students with praise that is more generalized, does not provide specifics, and therefore provides less motivation (Goolsby, 1997). Furthermore, research has shown that many teachers provide more specific negative criticism than specific positive praise (Goolsby, 1996; 1997). It seems teachers find it easier to point out wrong notes and rhythms than to praise good tone production or phrasing. While recognizing that error-free learning is virtually impossible, teacher recognition of positive aspects may help sustain a student's desire to correct errors and improve.

In addition to praise, goals are important to both motivational concepts. A goal is what an individual strives to accomplish (Woolfolk, 1998). When a student strives to perform a music solo or make a 4.0 grade point average, this is goal-directed behavior. Goals that are specific, moderately difficult to achieve, and are likely to be attained in a relatively short time span tend to enhance motivation and persistence (Pintrich & Schunk, 1996). Specific goals provide clear standards for judging performance. Moderate difficulty provides a challenge. Goals that can be reached quickly are less likely to be pushed aside for more immediate concerns.

Beliefs about our ability and effort affect the kind of goals we set. Our beliefs about what is happening, and understanding the reasons or attributes as to why we succeed or fail, affect our motivation. In schools, most students try to explain their successes and failures to themselves. When successful students fail, they frequently attempt to explain the results by controllable factors within them (Woolfolk, 1998). These internal attributes include that they did not study or practice hard enough or they misunderstood directions. If students see themselves as capable once they eliminate these deficiencies, they become motivated to focus on methods to succeed next time. Conversely, if students believe they have no control over the factors affecting their success or failure, they are less likely to be motivated to work and achieve. Receiving praise from a teacher for a good performance when no individual practice occurred could lead the student to think the performance was lucky. No sense of personal achievement was gained due to individual effort. This leads to the greatest motivation problem, as the student attributes failure to uncontrollable causes (Woolfolk, 1998).

Understanding the attributes of success or failure is the basis for the attribution theory (Weiner, 1974; 1979; 1992). The attribution theory describes how an individual explains and justifies success or failure, resulting in an influence on motivation. According to Weiner (1974), students attribute most causes of success or failure to three dimensions: locus (location of the cause internal or external to the person), stability (whether the cause stays the same or changes), and responsibility (whether the person can control the cause). In the locus dimension, if success or failure is attributed to internal factors, success will lead to pride and increased motivation. However, failure may lead to a decrease in self-esteem. The stability dimension is related to expectations about the outcome. If students believe they can control the factors, they will be more motivated to work to achieve. However, if the outcome is perceived as unstable, then success or failure will be attributed to luck. The responsibility dimension is related to emotions such as anger, happiness, or shame. If students fail at something they believe was controllable they will feel guilt; however, success would have resulted in pride. Failure at a task perceived as uncontrollable could lead to shame, while success would lead to a feeling of luck (Weiner, 1992).

Attribution theory research has been used to help explain student beliefs about their success and ability in musical activities. A summary of this research indicates that music teachers need to place emphasis on developing a student's sense of effort more than ability to explain success or failure. For example, Asmus (1985) found that sixth-graders attributed success and failure in music to internal reasons associated with effort. Effort was seen as a factor in overcoming perceptions of musical ability, the difficulty of the task, and luck. Legette (1998) investigated K-12 public school music students' beliefs about their success and failure in music classes. In each grade level, students placed more importance on ability and effort as reasons for their success or failure in music. Interestingly, Legette found females placed more emphasis on ability and effort than males, and students in city schools placed more importance on ability and effort than students in county schools, who perceived environment as more important. Research has notably demonstrated that a person's ego and competition do not correlate with long-term attributes toward success or failure in music (Schmidt, 2005).

Abraham Maslow (1970) suggested that when attempting to reach goals, humans have a hierarchy of needs ranging from lower-level needs for survival and safety to higher-level needs for intellectual achievement and self-actualization. Human needs are internal to the individual and motivate behavior when the needs are not satisfied. The hierarchy provides a basis for considering the physical, emotional, and intellectual needs as interrelated when attempting to motivate a student to reach goals. Self-actualization is Maslow's term for self-fulfillment, or the realization of personal potential. Maslow's hierarchy of needs is a model of seven levels of human needs, from basic physiological requirements to the need for self-actualization. Maslow (1968) called the four lower-level needs—survival, safety, belonging, and self-esteem—deficiency needs. These needs must be satisfied before further motivation can occur. When the lower-level needs have been met motivation does not cease; instead an individual becomes motivated to seek more fulfillment in the high-level needs or growth needs—intellectual achievement, aesthetic appreciation, and self-actualization.

Maslow's Hierarchy of Needs

Growth Needs	Self-Actualization Needs
	Aesthetic Needs
	Intellectual Achievement: Need to Know and Understand
Deficiency Needs	Esteem Needs
	Belonging and Love Needs
	Safety Needs
	Physiological Needs

The implications of Maslow's hierarchy are important in understanding students and creating an effective motivational strategy. Students who come to school without eating breakfast, or who have been hurt, are more unlikely to be motivated to learn or achieve goals because they have needs that are more basic to survival. If a child feels unsafe or unwanted due to parental divorce, this event may hinder motivation to learn academic knowledge or musical practice. If a classroom is fearful or unpredictable, students may be more likely to be concerned about safety than learning.

Characteristics of Effective Music Teachers

What makes an individual an effective music teacher? There is no single factor or trait that creates effective teaching. It is difficult to state precisely what traits constitute effective teaching, yet it appears easy to recognize effective teaching when it is experienced (Madsen, Standley, Byo, and Cassidy, 1989). Effective teaching is a multidimensional art, requiring individuals to know a broad array of knowledge in many different forms. Good teachers know their subject matter, understand human growth and motivation, and are aware of the social influences affecting their profession. Truly effective music teachers also know how to apply their knowledge in many different ways, at different times. They have built a "big bag of tricks" to teach a whole note in many different ways. Shulman (1987) addressed the multidimensionality of teaching by identifying seven areas of professional knowledge that all successful teachers have and know:

1. The academic subject they teach.
2. General classroom strategies that apply in all subject areas (classroom management, effective teaching, and evaluation).
3. The curriculum materials appropriate for their subject and grade level.
4. Subject-specific knowledge.
5. The characteristics and cultural backgrounds of their learners.
6. The settings in which students learn (pairs, small groups, teams, classes, schools, and community).
7. The goals and purposes of teaching.

Philosophically, effectively teaching music involves social components through student-teacher interactions with curricular activities. The *National Standards for Arts Education* (1994) state it is "essential" that music educators address various social and cultural issues such as ethnicity, national customs, religion, and gender (p. 14). Vision 2020 (Madsen, 2000) presented the need for teachers to implement curricular changes reflecting a more diverse society that would connect "school" music with "real" music. The new music standards within the *National Coalition for Core Arts Standards* (National Association for Music Education, 2014) call for educators to create opportunities for students to make musical connections between different cultures and music in daily life. Both the national standard documents and Vision 2020 reflect the earlier writings of John Dewey (1915), who stated that effective education should be based on students learning a process or method that can adapt to changing knowledge and situations in society.

Generally, all effective teachers have developed solutions for common classroom problems such as motivating students, disciplining students so the desire to learn is not affected, creating class environments that contribute to learning and not inhibiting success, and assessing student learning and teacher effectiveness (Woolfolk, 1998). Good teachers work hard to develop time-efficient classroom environments containing a quick instructional pace with a focus on fast teacher delivery of information (MacLeod & Napoles, 2012; Napoles & MacLeod, 2013; Silveira, 2014) and specific praise to motivate students (Droe, 2012).

Effective teachers understand the importance of the teacher-student relationship. They focus on student success, not teacher success, and are able to change behaviors and strategies to adjust to the classroom conditions. They provide specific, clear feedback and praise, help develop students' abilities to discriminate between good and bad, better and excellent, all while maintaining high expectations and standards. Effective teachers seek to help students discover the answer to problems rather than telling the solutions. Enabling students to think for themselves and make knowledgeable decisions while transferring information to different situations is a goal all effective teachers have for their students (Madsen & Kuhn, 1994).

Effective teacher characteristics are successful with any subject matter, including music. Many of the same personal traits, as well as subject matter skills and behaviors, in general education can be applied directly to developing effective teachers of music. The most successful music teachers are student-centered, maintain well-organized and creative classrooms, encourage student creativity and music independence, encourage intrinsic motivation, and carefully plan and organize each rehearsal based on constant evaluation of students' abilities and progress (Madsen, & Madsen, 1981).

Many of the traits associated with effective teaching reflect a strong social component, yet this component is often overlooked (Kelly, 2002). A developing view of effective teaching is one that affects the social skills of teachers as they interact with students (Johnson, 2014). Based in neuroscience, researchers have suggested that human brains are designed to be sociable when interacting with other humans. During social interactions (such as teaching), our brains act as modulators to gage our emotions and how humans react behaviorally to these feelings in different situations. This form of neural behavior has been termed social intelligence (Goleman, 2006). The researchers suggest that the more socially we are of situations we encounter, the more effective we can be in handling the experiences in a positive manner. Studies that have applied social intelligence to music teaching found that effective music teachers demonstrated more social characteristics, especially instructional communication skills, when interacting with students in their classrooms (Juchniewicz, 2008, 2014).

Social components of teaching involve multiple forms of human behavior, attitudes, and interactions, including characteristics such as eye contact, gender, race, dress, facial expressions, and personality (Macionis, 1997). Additional social variables involve more classroom-related activities such as teacher/student interactions, a teacher's proximity to students, verbal fluctuations, instructional pace, and involving students in the learning process. These traits may reflect an individual's personal characteristics, including personality, interactions with students, approach to classroom or rehearsal environment, or subject delivery or presentation style. Because so much of teaching reflects a social perspective, it is no surprise that teaching is often considered a social phenomenon.

Much of the contemporary research related to social aspects of teaching demonstrates the importance of personal characteristics to effectively teach music, often indicating that social characteristics are more desirable teacher qualities than musical, academic, or instructional knowledge (Gordon & Hamann, 2001; Rohwer & Henry, 2004; Teachout, 1997). A teacher's personality often appears to affect their effectiveness. The development of a teacher personality is considered one of the most important skills influencing the success of a music teacher (Froehlich, 2007; Haston & Russell, 2012; Kelly, 2010; Raiber, & Teachout, 2014; Roberts, 1991, 2000; Russell, 2012). A teacher personality may be defined as how individuals perceive themselves as educators (Froehlich, 2007).

A personality may include an individual's belief and values, and can be evident through dress, nonverbal and verbal communication, classroom preparation, and class management style (Macionis, 1997). Teachout (2001) found that effective music teachers are artistic, social, and inquisitive. Other studies on teacher personality highlight the importance of an extroverted personality, especially overt energy and enthusiasm, in effective teaching (Gordon & Hamann, 2001; Isbell, 2008; Killian, Dye, & Wayman, 2011; Madsen, et. al, 1989; Mark & Madura, 2010; Rohwer & Henry, 2004; Teachout, 1997; Yarbrough, 1975). The importance of personal maturity, a drive to achieve, a positive attitude, and a strong desire to help others (Gordon & Hamann, 2001; Rohwer & Henry, 2004) has also been shown to affect music teacher effectiveness. Teachout (1997) found that social and personal skills were among the highest rated characteristics of forty teacher skills and behaviors, with "Enthusiastic & energetic" rated as the most desired skill. Other highly rated social skills included "Involving students," "Sense of humor," and "Frequent eye contact." Ironically, many music skills involving direct pedagogical applications (e.g., ear training skills, use of secondary instruments) were rated as mid- to lower-level skills.

Research has shown a relationship between a teacher's appearance and perceptions of effective teaching. Education sociologists have found that teachers perceived as physically attractive are considered more effective (Clifford & Walster, 1973; Rueda & Stillman, 2012). Interestingly, VanWeelden (2002) found a music conductor's body shape and size, and gender, had no significant effect on perceived effectiveness. However, teacher dress, posture, and facial expression are

Photo Figure 11 Personal characteristics can influence a teacher's effectiveness.

appearance variables that have been shown to influence the perceptions of effective teachers (Clifford & Walster, 1973; Rueda & Stillman, 2012; VanWeelden, 2002).

An awareness of classroom environment and interactions has been shown as influential toward effective teaching. This knowledge leads to the conclusion that socially, it is often not what an individual knows, but how well knowledge is presented that makes an effective teacher (Madsen, 2003). Yarbrough (1975) and Madsen et. al (1989) showed that effective teachers demonstrate the ability to dramatically change their social behavior at precisely the right time to affect student behavior, motivation, and performance. These changes include teacher body movement, voice fluctuation and speed, movement around the class, eye contact, and facial expressions. These variables create an active, dramatic human presence termed teacher magnitude.

Teacher intensity and time on-task are part of effective ensemble conductors as well. Studies indicate that effective ensemble teachers talk less in class (Goolsby, 1996; 1997; Hendel, 1995; Juchniewicz, Kelly, & Acklin, 2014; Price 1983; Skadsem, 1997) because students, when given the opportunity, are capable of understanding and responding to many basic nonverbal gestures without the need for verbal explanations (Cofer, 1998; Kelly, 1997b). This could explain why clear nonverbal communication, on and off the podium, appears to affect students' perceptions of ensemble conductors' effectiveness (Byo, 1990; Johnson, et. al, 2000; Juchniewicz, Kelly, & Acklin, 2014; Skadsem, 1997; Yarbrough, 1975).

Despite strong research on an individual's effect on teaching, music teachers cannot ignore their community's influences on their teaching (Mark & Madura, 2010). The effectiveness of any teacher may begin with an awareness of societal standards. What and how information is taught, and what is defined as success, is often determined and affected by community expectations and requirements (Spring, 2006). Accordingly, what defines effective teaching is frequently determined by community standards, state testing programs, and college teacher preparation programs (Spring, 2006).

Common Social Classroom/Rehearsal Skills of Effective Music Teachers

Able to Connect with Students	Inquisitive
Enthusiastic/Energetic	Outgoing Personality
Mature	Positive Perspective
Desire to Help Others	Sense of Humor
Frequent Eye Contact	Involves Students in Learning
Clean Professional Appearance	Good Posture
Variety of Facial Expressions	Awareness of Classroom Interactions
Movement around Room	Voice Fluctuations & Speed
Keeps Students on Task	Aware of Community Standards

Developing Effective Teacher Characteristics

Can anyone learn to teach effectively? Madsen and Duke (1993) suggest that teacher behaviors are learnable. Still, becoming an effective teacher takes commitment and an understanding of a multitude of variables. Making the transition from student to teacher can be a difficult process for some, while others may find teaching a natural extension of their everyday lives. Many preservice teachers have difficulty understanding the role of teacher; therefore, while they may want to teach, they do not necessarily understand what a teacher really does (Paul et al., 2002; Raiber & Teachout, 2014). Perhaps the best way to understand the role of a teacher is to teach. Teaching is an active art. While many individuals may study the act of teaching through reading books, observing other teachers, and talking about education, perhaps the only way to understand being labeled a "teacher" is to engage in behaviors and experiences that are expected of teachers (Haston & Russell, 2012; Isbell, 2008; Mark & Madura, 2010; Paul, et al., 2002). For instance, in addition to curricular teaching experiences, working with young people in churches or summer camps, teaching private lessons, and being around schools are experiences that help develop characteristics of future effective teachers.

What distinguishes a novice teacher from an expert, experienced teacher? All beginning music teachers have concerns and frequently encounter "reality shock" when encountering the harsh conditions sometimes experienced in the everyday classroom (Bell-Robertson, 2014; Conway, 2015; DeLorenzo, 1992; Madsen & Kaiser, 1999). Research findings have consistently shown that beginning teachers in all subject areas are most concerned about classroom management and discipline, motivating students, accommodating differences among students, evaluating and assessing student achievement, and dealing with parents (Woolfolk, 1998). Some research (Conway, 2015; DeLorenzo, 1992; Draves, 2013; Kelly, 2000b; Krueger, 2000; Madsen & Kaiser, 1999) has indicated similar concerns among new music teachers, who reported concerns handling classroom discipline, working with administrators or principals, and dealing with non-teaching responsibilities.

Teachers often express concerns such as overcrowding and scheduling regarding adapting to their classroom responsibilities and environments (Bell-Robertson, 2014; Conway, 2012, 2015; DeLorenzo, 1992; Krueger, 2000; Veenman, 1984). DeLorenzo (1992) reported many first year music teachers are overwhelmed with the barrage of responsibilities, especially non-teaching duties such as preparing budgets, maintaining instrument and music inventories, and documenting student and parent conferences. The only "on the job training" comes during the student teaching experience, which can be short and casual compared to many other professional fields. Seldom do individuals student teach in the school where they will begin as a music teacher. Furthermore, the student teaching experience is frequently very different from the initial full-time inservice position (Kelly, 2000b). Adjusting to a new situation requires a learning-while-doing philosophy.

Complicating the entrance into teaching is the immediacy of the experience. Unlike many professions, teachers do not have the luxury of easing into teaching positions through apprenticeships. It is typical that an individual is a student in June and a full teacher in August (Lortie, 2002). Teachers are immediately responsible for their classrooms and the students within these rooms. Thus, during the first day on the job, new teachers encounter the same challenges as expert, experienced teachers. New teachers frequently learn that the first ten minutes of a class can determine their success for an entire year! Thus, new teachers encounter "sink-or-swim" situations where they are the Chief Executive Officers of their classrooms, responsible for the musical, academic, and personal well-being of their students.

Adjusting to the life and role of a music teacher can challenging. Frequently, beginning teachers experience problems adjusting to the new demands and responsibilities associated with the teaching profession. Among the problems encountered include many non-instructional responsibilities such as preparing a budget, relating to school personnel and administrators, and becoming aware of general operating procedures. Other problems include a feeling of isolation, and few opportunities to continue their musical growth (DeLorenzo, 1992; Krueger, 2000; Conway, 2003, 2015).

Despite challenges, most new teachers meet the demands of their classroom. Experience provides them with confidence to experiment with new methods and establish relationships with expert teachers from whom they can seek advice. Many new teachers become associated with more experienced mentor teachers. Research has shown that guidance from mentors helps new teachers cope with classroom realities, including class management, administrators, and other non-teaching duties (Conway, 2003, 2015; Smith & Ingersoll, 2004). However, as Conway (2015) stated, new teachers must be proactive in finding help and creating solutions. One way to be proactive is to connect with other teachers. For example, researchers have shown that music teachers who are active in professional organizations adapt more easily and remain stimulated in their careers longer (Madsen & Hancock, 2002).

Classroom Characteristics

Have you thought about what you will do when you meet your first music class? What will the first ten minutes of that class be like? Will you introduce yourself and tell the students your interests? Will you be firm and hand out the class rules? Perhaps you will have some music for the class or ensemble to perform? Will that music be easy to give the students a sense of ease, or more difficult to cautiously assess how much the students know and are able to do? Will your classroom be colorful, with lots of posters? How will the physical configuration of the class be set; will chairs and stands be already in place, or will you require the students to set these up?

There are many decisions to be made before the first music notes are performed. Each decision will affect a student's perception of a teacher's effectiveness and the overall classroom environment. Such perceptions have been shown as important for all teachers, as a student's first impressions of a teacher appears to be long-term and difficult for individuals to overcome (Robinson, 2000).

Classroom Environments

There are many different music class environments. Consider the different settings associated with large performing ensembles, lecture-style classes such as music theory or music history, small chamber ensembles, and choral, strings, jazz, guitar, and band classes. Consider how classrooms for beginners differ from those designed for advanced students. How do different technologies and use of social media influence an environment? How might the cultural backgrounds of students influence classroom interactions? Each music class is a different experience, requiring a different teaching approach and instructional skills, and different ways to communicate information. Additionally, because of different subject matter, classes may have different physical set-ups, instructional goals, student-teacher interactions, and learning processes. Research findings have shown that effective music teachers place a good deal of importance on creating the proper environment for each class (Juchniewicz, Kelly, & Acklin, 2014). Consequently, music teachers need to be flexible when creating the most effective classroom environment (Raiber & Teachout, 2014).

Music classrooms are vibrant, diverse cultures representing the overall school society (Kelly & Heath, in press). Music classes are multidimensional, simultaneous, involve immediacy, are public, and have histories. All classrooms are crowded with people and materials, involve multiple tasks, and contain time pressures. It seems that everything happens at once! While teachers are explaining a concept, students react to the instruction while the teacher assesses the extent they are understanding information and decides how far to go into the next topic. All of this action frequently occurs while music is being presented, students are fingering or silently voicing their parts, and audible sounds are being presented. Due to the fast pace of most music classes, immediacy is a characteristic often encountered. There are literally hundreds of interactions between teachers and students, and students and other students, in a single day. For example, some research estimates teaching requires individuals to participate in more than 1000 interactions with other people each school day (Ballantine, 2001). Because of the fast pace, even with the most careful planning many exchanges are unpredictable. A music stand may fall over, music may be dropped, and a student may be called to the office. Immediacy requires teachers to be prepared to make decisions quickly that may affect a single student, or an entire class.

Music classes are public environments. Because of the public nature of music performances, and the use of music ensembles to promote school and community activities, music teachers constantly have their lesson plans on public display and open to public scrutiny. The quality of the music program can be judged based on the public's perception of "good" music. Such "critics" often affect students as much as the teachers.

Like all cultures, music programs are filled with their own commonalities and shared values. These commonalities constantly shift as older students graduate and new students take their places. Yet traditions remain in some form, as school music programs have their own customs, lore, conventions, and language (Morrison, 2001). Similar characteristics often serve as an instant bond between current and former students, or music students from different parts of the country who quickly connect due to familiar experiences. These experiences include several common cultural themes within most music programs (Morrison, 2001), including:

1. Identity—music students tend to take ownership of their program, as the program becomes a reflection of their self-identity.
2. Transmission—the expectations and standards of a program's performance skill level and activities, as well as dress, language, structure, and values, are passed down from exiting students to incoming members.
3. Social Dimension—every ensemble is a social unit, as members get to know each other in great part due to the large amount of time spent together during and after school or in rehearsals.
4. Organizational Hierarchy—most programs possess a formal power structure where students are elected to positions and roles including president, treasurer, section leader, drum major, and soloist.

5. Traditional Songs—all ensembles are known for a specific style of performance and music reflecting this expectation, including fight songs, contest or festival lists, and music that has been commissioned by that organization.

Recognizing the cultural dimension of a music class helps the teacher become more effective by realizing the broader influence music has on students. A broader perspective assists in choosing more meaningful teaching approaches and activities.

Finally, all music classes have some degree of history. Tradition is a frequent standard for students, as well as parents (especially former music students) and administrators. Much of what a teacher or student does depends on what has previously occurred. Understanding the history of a classroom or program can affect the entire school year. No matter how experienced the teacher, any changes to tradition must be slow and students must be shown that changes can improve on previous traditions.

Classroom Organization and Management

Generally, music teachers may have as many as 15 to 100 students in a room at a single time, depending on the age and the type of class. What concerns might you have with this number of students? How will you prepare your instruction, the type of experiences you will present, and what you will say? Many novice teachers underestimate the importance of good organization, and the amount of time that thorough class preparation requires.

Classroom management begins with deciding the class culture through organization and management style (Madsen & Madsen, 1981). Classroom management techniques are approaches used to maintain a healthy learning environment, relatively free of behavior problems (Woolfolk, 1998). Creating a classroom culture where students can learn and teachers can teach is an individual decision, yet the following specific organization and management decisions should always be made before students arrive:

1. How you will address the class and ask questions, will you require students to raise their hands before answering questions,
2. How you will hand out new music, and take up old music,
3. If the chairs, music stands, music, and other equipment will be in place before or after the students arrive,
4. How much student talk you will permit,
5. How you will avoid being confrontational with students during class,
6. How your students will be allowed to enter and exit the classroom,
7. What order you will present the music pieces to be rehearsed, and how you will mix announcements with the instruction,
8. How you will deal with unanticipated interruptions such as fire drills or administrative announcements.

Creating a well-managed classroom culture also means teaching students the classroom expectations. Good classroom organization and management not only contributes to a more effective teaching environment, but also teaches students the value of planning, having goals, and clearly understanding methods to reach those goals. Consequently, class organization and management requires:

1. Determining the physical arrangement of the room and the materials within the room; what will your room look like,
2. Finding out as much as you can about your students (background, previous experience) and the type of musical activities that have been previously presented,

3. Developing a list of short- and long-term instructional and learning objectives based on your students' ages and abilities; what you want your students to know at the end of the grading period or year,

4. Creating a list of rules and procedures for the class, routines that everyone will follow,

5. Trying to anticipate problems: students, parents, colleagues, administration, and of course your own, and how you will react to them,

6. Creating consequences, rewards, and contingencies that you will present to students to enhance the classroom experience,

7. Learning music scores and other materials to be presented in class BEFORE the rehearsal or class begins, and not with the students.

Summary

Can anyone be a teacher? Perhaps, but it does appear that not anyone can be an effective teacher unless certain traits and behaviors are learned and exhibited. Becoming a teacher requires commitment and dedication, with a dose of reality. It could be said that being a good teacher is a lifestyle, not a nine-to-five job. Indeed, it appears individuals considered effective teachers bring a personal approach to teaching that reflects their true personalities (Madsen & Kuhn, 1994). Effective teacher behaviors are complex, multidimensional, and demonstrate a commitment to helping students understand information and apply new knowledge and skills to varying situations.

Effective teachers are always looking for interactions that provide teachable moments. Opportunities to teach and learn can be brief or lengthy, contain many ideas or few, and can occur at any time, and anywhere. Teachable moments involve both subject matter and personal behavior. Effective music teachers create classroom cultures with interactions that foster learning (Adderly, Kennedy, & Berz, 2003; Morrison, 2001). They recognize learning involves teaching music and many other kinds of information and skills, some of which have little direct and immediate application to music.

Good music teachers recognize that learning is a constructive, not a receptive, process (Boardman, 2002; Wiggins, 2015). A constructive educational process is a student-centered, as students are the reasons schools exist and are the focus for what teachers do. A student-centered approach allows students to "construct" their knowledge of the world through a constantly evolving process of assimilation, accommodation, and adaptation (Piaget, 1950; Wiggins, 2015). In this manner, knowledge is developed in ways that are coherent and purposeful for the individual who is creating the meaning. Effective teachers seek opportunities for all students to experience music in a constructive, meaningful manner. This includes the most talented "all-state" student and the individual who appears to be least interested in music.

Finally, effective teachers understand the importance of teacher-student relationships. Studies have shown that students perform and attain greatest when they believe teachers care (Boswell, 1991; Hallinan, 2012). Effective teachers understand their students as individuals. They know the culture of their students. The best teachers are aware of the ever-changing nature of students and the interactions of cultures that influence development. Teachers recognize their impact on students will extend beyond the formal school days, well into adulthood. Subsequently, effective music teachers understand their influence and that the teacher-student relationship is the focus of any educational experience.

Becoming an effective teacher is a challenge. Striving to meet this challenge is what separates a professional music educator from a musician who is interested in teaching. Effective teachers enjoy the art of teaching, the school environment, and all of the students entering that environment. Teaching becomes not work, but a passion. Professional music educators are dedicated to achieving a high level of skills and knowledge they can present in an engaging style that reaches out to all students to provide a unique, meaningful experience.

Key Items

Effective Teacher Behaviors
Attribution Theory
Extrinsic motivation
Teacher praise
Social intelligence

Teacher Magnitude
Intrinsic motivation
Abraham Maslow
Self-actualization
Teacher Personality

Questions for Consideration

1. What are some characteristics of the best teacher you have experienced? How do your personal and professional characteristics reflect this person?
2. What are your concerns about teaching? What might you do to resolve these concerns?
3. What are your concerns in dealing with classroom management? What are specific techniques you might use to manage your music class?
4. What are intrinsic and extrinsic motivation ideas you would use to motivate students?
5. What are activities that music teachers might use to influence the musical preference and tastes of students?
6. What will your class environment be like? What will you do in the first ten minutes of your first class?
7. How might you develop characteristics of teacher magnitude and intensity?

Web Resources

Effective Teaching

About Education: http://teaching.about.com/od/pd/a/Qualities-Of-An-Effective-Teacher.htm
Edutopia: http://www.edutopia.org/discussion/11-habits-effective-teacher
Motivation: http://www.education.com/reference/article/motivation/
Music Teachers National Association: http://mtna.org/
National Association for Music Education: http://www.nafme.org/
Social Intelligence: http://www.aboutintelligence.co.uk/social-intelligence.html
Stanford University: https://teachingcommons.stanford.edu/resources/teaching/planning-your-approach/characteristics-effective-teachers
Teaching Music: http://teachingmusic.org/

Chapter 8

The Teaching Profession

Music education is a social experience!

—Clifford Madsen

From its beginnings in one-room schoolhouses, public education has emerged as a core institution in American society, with teachers at its center. As one of society's primary socialization agents, teachers serve as a bridge between community standards and educational benchmarks. The role of teachers directly reflects the reciprocal arrangement between education and society. Just as different cultures influence education, they seek to shape the role and function teachers perform in achieving education goals. From a sociological perspective, as society's expectations for education change, so do perceptions of how teachers function, how well their duties are performed, and the role in which they function both in and outside of schools. Chapter 8 will present educational components and issues that affect what and how teachers perform their duties and the teaching professional as a whole. The premise is that to be as professional teacher, an individual knows not only how to teach well, but is also knowledgeable of issues, people, and events that influence education. The novice teacher will soon recognize, as veteran teachers already do, that many components and issues are not directly associated with classroom activities and are often out of the control of most teachers.

Teaching and Society

The teaching profession is an ever-changing concept, largely due to societal expectations. As an interactive participant in educational systems, teachers are often influenced by their cultural backgrounds, including how they were enculturated into the teaching profession. Teachers differ in age, gender, educational background, and social class, each influencing how an individual will teach (Ballantine & Spade, 2012). Differences extend to music educators, as teaching identities, frequently intertwined with both performance and teaching behaviors, reflect how and why individuals teach. Despite their differences, teachers are the backbone of education and frequently the face of every educational approach. Understanding the role of the teacher is the key to understanding our educational system.

Perhaps no other society in the world demands more of education and its teachers than American society. Teachers in the United States are not only expected to distribute knowledge, but are also viewed as protectors of morality and character, gatekeepers between right and wrong, good and evil. Historically, society has asked teachers to promote patriotism, take loyalty oaths, help defeat communism, win technological races, solve poverty, improve race relations, and guide students into the global labor markets (Lortie, 2002; Thayer & Levit, 1966). Furthermore, should educators teach students to pass tests created by states and national reformers, or concentrate on preparing individuals to save the United States' position in the global economy? Ever-changing expectations make it easy to see that the role teachers have played, and presumably will continue to play, may be the most misunderstood position in our society.

The interpretations of "teacher" are frequently blurred between professional educator, parent, doctor, psychologist, and religious leader. Beginning with No Child Left Behind, all individuals seeking to teach must be "highly qualified" (No Child Left Behind, 2001). This requirement has directly affected the role, purpose, training, and certification of teachers (Spring, 2014). Music educators must also meet highly qualified requirements, and thus are also affected by the new legislation (Robinson, 2012). Consequently, society's expectations and changing concept of "teacher" extends to music educators. For example, should music teachers:

1. Transmit traditional music genres, skills, and values?
2. Serve both the community and school?
3. Teach to specific music competencies or to individual talents?
4. Concentrate on the "talented" or the masses?
5. Reflect contemporary tastes or present traditional music?
6. Justify music on musical elements or nonmusical aspects?

As a profession, music education has been called upon to meet society's needs, from the development of 17th-century singing schools for improving the quality of religious congregational singing to music improving the patriotism and overall academic achievement of young Americans (Birge, 1966; Keene, 1987). Similar to all teachers, contemporary music educators' roles have evolved to reflect public perceptions, yet they still approach teaching in much the same manner as they have historically(Labuta & Smith 1997). From the beginning of formal music instruction in this country, the emphasis on large performance group instruction has existed. Over time, our society has changed; education has subsequently changed, yet music education remains much the same by maintaining an emphasis on large group instruction punctuated with public performances. An emphasis on individual or small group experiences rarely occurs.

Despite varying expectations to which teachers are held accountable, every societal group in the United States appears to view teachers as links between the past, the present, and the future (Spring, 2006). For music teachers, this expectation involves building a bridge between the musical world and the education world, including expectations concerning education and schooling instructional concepts, process and product goals, different cultures, and both aesthetic and functional aspects of music.

Cultural expectations have always required teachers to prepare students to be successful in multiple manners. As society's concerns have moved from moral to global expectations, teaching approaches have evolved to meet these goals (Spring, 2014). The recognition of a more global pluralistic perspective requires teachers to rethink instructional approaches that have been based on pre-existing authority, strict content, or a narrow methodology. Increasing expectations of a global perspective demands expanding instructional approaches to include more focus on individual differences, curiosities, and interests. Relevancy has become a component of immediacy, as both impact the importance of information and experiences on individual lifestyle.

Demands of global perspectives apply to music education. The global information age, often gleaned through social media and networking, enables students to immediately access and share music they relate to and value. Exposure has led to students expecting more from their school music experiences. However, an individual focus is incompatible with many existing curricular structures, which often emphasize group instruction. The traditional American role of teacher frequently fails to make connections from the past to the present, and to the future. In a more global society, making musical connections requires a comprehensive evaluation of students' cultures, their influences, and development. This requires a genuine evaluation of the changes in the role and function of professional music teachers within our educational system.

Teaching as a Profession

The teaching profession is a challenging yet rewarding vocation. One challenge is understanding the reality of a daily classroom. Becoming aware of the issues and responsibilities affecting the music classroom is a necessary component of becoming a professional educator. While many in society believe teachers spend their entire day instructing students, the reality is that non-instructional responsibilities comprise a majority of every teacher's daily professional life. The reward is evident in a survey conducted by Goodlad (1984), which reported the primary reasons individuals gave for entering the teaching profession were "having a satisfying job" and "wanting to help children." Many people believe that teaching is more than a vocation; rather it is a lifestyle of enduring dedication. Teachers have their own language, jargon, dress, social and professional interactions, clubs and organizations. Whether viewed as a vocation, career, or lifestyle, teaching is a complicated task comprised of multiple components, challenges, and rewards.

Becoming a music teacher is also a complicated endeavor. Each year many college students declare their academic major as music education. However, do they *really* know what this means? Are young students aware of the challenges and commitment required to complete the education degree and become a successful teacher? Many students report they hope to become music teachers because they love music, want to share this love with others, and they enjoy school (Bergee, et. al, 2001; Madsen & Kelly, 2002). Some students state they had such a wonderful school experience that they want to be like their former music teacher, while others felt they had such bad experiences that they need to return to their former school and "right the wrong" with regards to perceived poor instruction. Still others report they thought music was fun or they believed they could not be successful in another field (Kelly, 2000a, 2000b; Madsen & Kelly, 2002).

Questions for Teachers

1. What factors, people, and/or events influenced your decision to become a music teacher?
2. How did your parents, teachers, and friends react to your decision to become a teacher?
3. When did you decide to become a music teacher?
4. What are characteristics you have that you believe will be useful as a teacher?
5. Do you believe that the qualifications to become a teacher are easily obtained?
6. Do you see yourself more as a musician-teacher or a teacher-musician?
7. What aspects of teaching do you think you will enjoy the most? What aspects might you enjoy the least?

Music teachers are shaped by a variety of factors, including our families, peers, and music experiences. Research studies have indicated students most frequently choose to become music teachers while in high school. However, some students decide to pursue music education as early as elementary school or as late as college (Bergee, et. al, 2001; Madsen & Kelly, 2002). Furthermore, students are usually influenced to become music teachers by their school music teacher. Interestingly, students indicate they are encouraged more by their teachers' actions than actual

Photo Figure 12 Becoming a professional music educator requires more than knowledge of the subject matter.

words. Many students report they made the decision to pursue music as a profession during a musical moment such as a performance or rehearsal. They indicate these experiences were so profound that they felt a "calling" to become a teacher (Madsen & Kelly, 2002) and become a role model for other students (Jones & Parkes, 2010). Often due to performing experiences, many music teachers perceive themselves first as performers (Cox, 1997, L'Roy, 1983; Roberts, 1991, 2000), frequently aspiring to be professional performing musicians. Their identity as musicians outweighs their identity as educators. However, as students move through the education curricula, exposure and interactions begin associating individuals more with teacher training. Initial field experiences provide opportunities to observe and interact in a teacher role. Consequently, students become more enculturated to the behaviors and expectations required to successfully enter the teaching profession (Froehlich, 2007; Isbell, 2008). The desire to become a teacher and the self-concept of teacher role identity can strengthen through involvement in teacher-like activities such as field experiences and student teaching (Jones & Parkes, 2010; Killian, Dye, & Wayman, 2011; Paul, Teachout, Sullivan, Kelly, Bauer, & Raiber, 2001; Raiber & Teachout, 2014).

Lortie (2002) found individuals make decisions to pursue teaching as a vocation based on attractors and facilitators. Attractors are variables that convince individuals to select teaching as a career rather than another vocation. Lortie stated that there are five attractors to teaching: (a) the interpersonal theme, which allows for extended interaction with young people, (b) the social theme, which perceives teachers as performing a special mission in our society, (c) the continuation theme, which indicates that teachers are individuals who liked school when they were students and continued to desire to be in school settings as adults, (d) the material benefits of steady, secure employment, adequate pay, regular time off, and a certain amount of prestige, and (e) the time compatibility, which acknowledges teachers are contracted to work considerably fewer days each year than the typical American worker. Lortie stated that facilitators are variables that help individuals enter the teaching profession. Accordingly, there are two facilitator variables: (a) a wide-decision range that allows individuals to become a teacher at any point in their life, and (b) subjective warrant variables that allows a wide degree of opinion regarding the qualifications for teachers.

Kelly (2005) surveyed preservice music teachers using Lortie's research to determine the extent that attractor and facilitator variables might influence undergraduate preservice teachers' decisions to pursue music education as an occupation. When comparing these results to Lortie's, the data revealed that: (a) most subjects decided to pursue music education as a vocation while they were in high school, (b) most wanted to initially teach high school, and (c) while many eventually wanted to teach at the college level, most subjects eventually wanted to teach high school. Overall, the subjects: (a) enjoyed working with children, (b) thought that teachers could improve society, and (c) enjoyed the school/learning environment. However, the subjects were undecided regarding issues related to teacher income and if teaching provided regular time-off opportunities. The variables regarding opportunities to decide to become teachers and ease of requirement to become teachers were not influential in decisions to become music teachers.

Lortie's and Kelly's research underscores the realization that to fully understand the scope of the teaching profession requires an acknowledgement that teaching is more than an instructional classroom experience. Individuals must be aware of an array of instructional and non-instructional variables affecting each individual teacher. This awareness is reflected in characteristics stated by the American Association of State Colleges and Universities (2006) for all professional educators to possess. These characteristics include knowledge of the:

1. Subject matter they are teaching.
2. Psychological and physical natures of students they plan to teach.
3. Political and social structures of institutions in which they will be teaching.
4. Methods by which people learn.
5. Best methods for teaching a particular subject matter.

Having knowledge and awareness of basic expectations extends to music teachers. The reality of teaching music is that while one may expect teachers to work with students, a tremendous amount of planning and organization must occur outside the instructional phase of the classroom to enable teachers to actually teach (Mark & Madura, 2010). Many teachers struggle with the "business side" of education and frequently underestimate the amount of time and effort required to stay organized and accountable (Mark & Madura, 2010). Non-instructional activities include score preparation, arranging for guest clinicians and private teachers, being attentive to budget issues, dealing with parent and administrative concerns, reserving buses for trips, maintaining inventory of instruments and music, participating in faculty meetings and committees, meeting music dealers, arranging and setting up rehearsal rooms, and repairing equipment.

From an instructional perspective, music teachers need to have knowledge of many different skills to effectively teach music. The organization responsible for accrediting university schools of music, the National Association of Schools of Music (NASM) (2014), requires music education majors to have skills and knowledge in areas of music theory, history, sight-singing and dictation, composition/arranging, technology, conducting, a variety of performance experiences, and various music methodologies. This knowledge must culminate in a student teaching experience where each student demonstrates the ability to bring each skill together in a comprehensive educational experience.

Specifically, NASM (2014) lists seven desirable attributes for prospective music teachers.

1. Personal commitment to the art of music.
2. The ability to lead students to an understanding of music as an art form.
3. The capability to inspire others and to excite the imagination of students.
4. The ability to articulate logical rationales for music as a basic component of general education.
5. The ability to work productively within specific education systems.
6. The ability to evaluate ideas, methods, and policies in the arts for their impact on the musical and cultural development of students.
7. The ability and desire to remain current with developments in the art of music and in teaching.

From these attributes it is easy to see that effectively teaching music requires both tremendous individual desire and a broad awareness of multiple issues. Many attributes require a strong social perspective and understanding. A student's background, family environment, peer relations, academic experiences, and overall health are just some cultural issues that affect a student's performance and must be acknowledged by the teacher. Providing a quality music education experience becomes more than conducting a rehearsal or performance. Music educators quickly find that rehearsing and performing music is not necessarily only teaching information and skills. Thus, being aware of the many attributes and issues affecting the teaching profession is part of being a professional music educator.

Another component of the teaching profession are teacher unions. It is estimated that over 90% of America's teachers belong to a professional association or union (Spring, 2006). Among many organizations representing educators in this country are two primary teacher unions: the National Education Association (NEA) and the American Federation of Teachers (AFT). Both are large and powerful forces in American society and are often political in their focus. Each participates in local, state, and national elections. Consequently, both unions are influential in shaping the direction of American education policy while advancing the interests of its members.

Both unions share many common issues while representing different segments of the education profession. While conflicts are common between the unions, both represent struggles teachers face and seek ways to improve educational conditions. Consequently, both unions participate in the constantly changing issues and trends in education.

Recognizing that teaching music is a constantly changing vocation involving many variables raises a series of questions affecting the future of music education. These questions include:

1.   Can anyone teach? Should there be a standard national requirement for individuals seeking to become teachers? Should every individual be required to be fully certified in order to teach?
2.   Who controls the content and distribution of knowledge within a school curriculum? To what extent does censorship affect the school music curriculum?
3.   What is the role of the professional music teacher? What components of school and society should professional teachers be accountable to?
4.   What factors lead to shortages of teachers, including music teachers?
5.   What is the role of teacher unions in the teaching profession?

Each question poses a difficult decision for the future success of the music education profession. The answers may lie in understanding the consequences of being labeled as a "professional" in our society.

Challenges to the Teaching Profession

What does the label "professional music educator" mean? What does being a "professional" signify? Professionalism has long been a source of hope and frustration for educators. From the early 20th century, teachers have sought a high level of professionalism in an attempt to acquire recognition for the complex, specialized nature of their work (Ingersoll & Merrill, 2012; Spring 2014; Thayer, & Levit, 1966). Yet within our society there is confusion and contention concerning the professionalization of teachers. At the center of the debate is the question of what constitutes professionalism. Is a professional an individual who has obtained advanced training and knowledge, or are individuals professionals when they hold a certain attitude about their work (Ingersoll & Merrill, 2012)?

The label of "professional" is frequently associated with an individual who is paid for working. Professionals are individuals considered by some in society as knowledgeable experts in a specific field or vocation. These individuals usually have acquired certain skills and behaviors unique to their profession that enable them to succeed in a chosen occupation or activity. Applied in this manner, there are many types of professionals in our society, including athletes, salespeople, artists, etc.

However, certain vocations are considered professional vocations due to established requirements necessary to obtain the label "professional." These vocations frequently carry a certain level of status in society. These professional vocations include doctors, lawyers, certified public accountants, certain engineers, and teachers. To successfully practice these vocations requires individuals to complete the following processes and skills:

1.   Acquire specialized knowledge and skills by obtaining a specific degree in the vocational area from a college or university (frequently advanced degrees are desired, if not required);
2.   Pass some type of certification exam, often at the state or national level, which leads to the attainment of credentials or licensing;
3.   Complete an internship or mentorship period;
4.   Stay abreast of changing current skills and information through constant professional development and re-certification while practicing their careers.

Individuals who obtain certified professional vocations are frequently among the highest compensated members of society and often imbued with high social stature.

It is interesting that teachers are considered in the same venue as other professional vocations by our society. Data from nationwide surveys continue to show that teaching is considered one of the most prestigious professions in our society (Ozimek, 2014). Teachers are frequently mentioned as parental figures and important influences in the lives of presidents and business CEOs (Spring, 1988). To obtain the label of "professional," teachers must meet the same standards required by other professional vocations, including attaining specialized degrees and obtaining current and continuous certification. Yet their status as professionals is frequently threatened.

Spring (2014) states that, while teaching as a profession has historically been debated, the federal guidelines of No Child Left Behind and Race to the Top have increased the debate, due to the requirement that every teacher must be a "highly qualified" teacher. Such requirements also apply to music teachers (Robinson, 2012). According to Spring (2014), and Ingersoll and Merrill (2012) this legislative provision changed the teaching profession is several manners:

1. Credentials: the requirements for licensing teachers has moved from the local and state levels to the federal level. However, qualifications vary, with some debating if teacher education courses are necessary as opposed to practical knowledge and previous job experience. Interestingly, Ingersoll and Merrill (2012) report that other traditional professions rarely lower their standards to recruit and retain members. For example, some organizations, such as Teach for America and El Sistema, require little if any specific training to become a teacher. Even among different types of schools there are big differences, as teachers at private schools often do not have the same credentials as teachers in public schools (Ingersoll & Merrill, 2012). Consequently, debates have occurred regarding the qualifications to become a teacher.

2. Specialization: No Child Left Behind requires that teachers only teach classes in their area of specialization. However, discrepancies exist as rural and urban schools, and schools with higher levels of low socioeconomic students, need teachers to teach in many areas outside their specialization. For example, science teachers teach biology, chemistry, natural science, and physics. Meeting this requirement can be further problematic with the shortage of teachers in many areas.

3. Teacher Autonomy: many new teachers believe they will determine the content of their instruction. However, through No Child Left Behind and the later Race to the Top legislation, many state and national education standards have altered what and how teachers teach. Benchmarks such as those set by the Common Core Standards, the National Standards for Arts Education, and state benchmarks require students pass various standardized tests in order to graduate and for teachers to be evaluated. Consequently, teachers often have little input in their classroom curriculum (Raiber & Teachout, 2014).

Challenges to the teaching profession have led to questions regarding the role of teachers. For example, are teachers considered technicians or professionals (Raiber & Teachout, 2014)? Teachers as technicians are driven by outside sources such as benchmarks or other outside curricular guides. Thus, classroom environments focus almost solely on classroom resources and stimuli (Raiber & Teachout, 2014). As professionals, teachers base decisions on an awareness and understanding of student needs. They adjust the presentation and informational flow to how students learn. Consequently, professional educators are influenced by individuality and recognize the large influence and role of the community in every student's education (Raiber & Teachout, 2014).

The debate over teaching as a profession is highlighted by the differences in education, especially differences between public and private schools (Ingersoll & Merrill, 2012). Many individuals act as if anyone can be a teacher, that life experiences alone can qualify a person for the classroom. This perception affects many aspects of the teaching profession. Subsequently, despite numerous federal and state mandates, many schools at both levels fail to meet many characteristics associated with other vocations considered professional. As such, teaching is often treating as a semi-professional vocation by many in society (Ingersoll & Merrill, 2012; Lortie, 2002).

Teacher Certification Issues

American society has long been concerned with the qualification of its teachers. Reports in the 1980s portrayed teachers as lacking in basic intellectual skills and competencies in e specific subject areas (Serow, Castelli, & Castelli, 2000; Spring, 2006). Due to changing societal perceptions of what constitutes a certified teacher and calls for higher standards for teachers (e.g., No Child Left Behind), the traditional processes of certifying teachers are changing. There are now multiple methods for achieving the label of certified teacher. Primarily, individuals seek teacher certification via (a) traditional statewide teacher certification processes, (b) national board certification, or (c) alternative state certification processes.

Common Types of Teacher Certification

Traditional—individuals follow a predetermined statewide process.

National Board Certification—identifies experienced master teachers capable of raising education standards.

Alternative certification—varies from state to state; typically, individuals do not intern or student teach while they are students, and do not complete advanced courses.

Lortie (2002) states that one attraction to becoming a teacher is the ease of the process. However, there is no single approach. Teacher certification requirements are unique among states, with each determining its own knowledge and skill requirements for certifying individuals to become teachers (Ingersoll & Merrill, 2012). Most states require individuals to pass a statewide exam or some form of national exam, such as the Praxis exam (2015). Because information required on teacher certification exams is usually determined by individual state agencies, the use of required examinations helps states to control the quality of teachers, and ultimately the quality of instruction within schools by controlling the content in teacher education programs. As teachers move from state to state, they must re-apply for a different license from each state by completing that state's certification process, which contains information the state believes each certified teacher should know. Once certified, teachers must maintain their certification at prescribed intervals, usually every 7–10 years, based on state requirements (Henry, 2005).

Despite certification process, teachers have long been criticized for being ill-prepared for the classroom (Lortie, 2002). Even the label of "certified" is being questioned within the teaching profession (Report of the National Commission on Teaching and America's Future, 1996; Spring 2006). Do individuals really need a teaching degree and certificate to become a teacher? Some believe that the process for gaining a teaching certification acts as a screening or "gatekeeper" and thus protects the quality of teachers in the profession. However, others seek the easing of restrictions as a way to allow individuals with special skills to more quickly become teachers and thus address teacher shortages (Ingersoll & Merrill, 2012). For instance, many private organizations such as Teach for America (2014) and the growing El Sistema music program (El Sistema USA, 2014) do not require teachers to be certified and require very little if any direct education training. Individuals who take these alternative routes into teaching frequently begin teaching immediately upon being hired.

It would appear few individuals entering the teaching profession expect long careers as teachers (Lortie, 2002). Many states are facing a shortage of certified teachers, especially in the areas of math and science (Ingersoll, 2001; Ingersoll & Perda, 2010; Merrow, 1999). One report states that approximately half of all teachers in the United States either move or leave the teaching profession each year (Seidel, 2014). Individuals leave the teaching profession for a number of reasons, including retirement, change careers, family issues, and professional concerns such as school safety and accountability standards (Boyd, Grossman, Ing, Lankford, Loeb, & Wyckoff, 2011; Dworkin & Tobe, 2012; Horng, 2009). The growing emphasis on standardized testing and resulting teacher evaluation processes such as value-added modeling have led many teachers to question their ability and willingness to teach. This concern has led many teachers to leave the profession (Darling-Hammond, 2010; Dworkin & Tobe, 2012). For example, a 1999 Education Weekly report estimated that 20% of all new teachers leave the classroom within the first three years of teaching, while 50% of all teachers quit within five years of teaching (Ingersoll, 2001; Merrow, 1999).

To meet demand for teachers, school districts are pursuing individuals who, while not completing specialized training in educational pedagogy, are completing alternative certification. While the method for obtaining alternative certification varies from state to state, typically individuals who obtain such certificates do not intern or student teach while they are students, and do not complete advanced courses providing information on topics such as classroom management, law, ethics, student motivation, developing teaching strategies, and school diversity. However, due to their background, these individuals usually have some amount of training in their area of interest (Berry, 2001; Henry 2005).

The issue of alternative certification or any certification for entry into teaching is highly debated in education, including music education. Many educators consider any form of alternative certification as demeaning and a lowering of professional standards (Cohen-Vogel & Smith, 2007). Proponents of alternative entry argue that job experience is all that is required for an effective teacher and that alternative entry helps ease teacher shortages (Ingersoll & Merrill, 2012). By implementing alternative certification procedures, or no certification requirements, many states are requiring less of individuals to be labeled "professional" teachers. This action may give society the perception that anyone can teach. Can anyone be a doctor, a lawyer, or an engineer? While desire is a powerful force in achieving any goal, the completion of strong requirements to obtain "professional" status separates those with true ability from those with only interest.

No one disputes that the existing teacher shortage will continue. The National Commission on Teaching and America's Future (1996) predicted that from 1996–2020 the biggest overhaul of the teaching force in American history would occur. The immediate intent of alternative certification methods to help ease an existing teacher shortage may be a well-intended "stopgap" measure. However, data suggest that alternatively certified teachers may be less qualified than more traditionally certified teachers (Cohen-Vogel & Smith, 2007). Learning "on the job" means that student progress may be hindered while the individual learns to teach. The students are in essence laboratory subjects in an experiment while the individual develops teaching skills. Thus, questions regarding preparation of alternatively certified individuals to enter the classroom remain:

1. Is alternative certification good for education, and specifically music education?
2. Are alternatively certified teachers fully prepared to teach effectively?

3. What are the effects on student learning? Do students, taught by teachers in their first year of teaching who are seeking alternative certification, achieve as well as students taught by traditionally trained teachers?
4. What does the issue of alternative certification do to the teaching profession?

Teacher Accountability

The term "accountability" denotes being responsible for actions and outcomes. In education, accountability specifies that teachers are responsible for what students learn. Due to the broad purposes of American education, a large, diverse segment of our population holds teachers accountable for student learning. Those most directly affected by educational outcomes have a particular interest in what and how well information is taught. These groups include parents, students, businesses, the military, religious organizations, and politicians. Each group has a vested interest in ensuring that teachers are accountable for teaching what they consider necessary for students to be successful.

Education accountability has increased in great part because of American taxpayers demanding more responsibility from politicians and school administrators for taxes they pay. In every state, a certain percentage of each individual's paycheck is deducted to support public education. As the public's perception of education changes, so does its desire for a better understanding of how their taxes are spent educating members of society. Typically, the public questions school administrators and politicians who control tax expenditures. Most recently, this has resulted in a dramatic increase in statewide testing to demonstrate not only how taxes are spent, but also the results of tax expenditures.

Most states have some form of statewide standardized testing intended to measure how much students have learned, and how well teachers have taught. The results of testing vary among states. Florida, for example, requires students to pass state-mandated tests at the fourth-, eighth-, and tenth-grade levels in order to advance to the next grade level, and ultimately graduate with a high school diploma (Florida Department of Education, 2006a). Schools must teach skills and knowledge required for students to pass these tests. Consequently, schools are held accountable for this instruction by receiving grades based on scores of their students. Each school's grade is publicized so parents and the public can see the effects of their tax dollars. Schools receiving continuous low grades can be shut down. Teachers and school administrators can lose jobs if students do not receive adequate scores.

Furthermore, some states are attempting to increase accountability and teacher assessment by proposing a "pay-for-performance" approach that connects the amount of teachers' pay to how well their students score on standardized testing (National School Boards Association, 2007). This type of accountability, known as value-added modeling (VAM), is a central component of the Race to the Top federal education program. VAM measures a teacher's contribution to each student's academic growth by comparing students' test scores each year to the scores of the previous year. The scores are then used to compare students across the same grade and to compare teachers to teachers, often resulting in a ranking of teachers. The rankings are then used to determine merit pay increases (Darling-Hammond, 2010; Marder, 2012).

Proponents of VAM believe the data gleaned from test score analyses are more objective and show the degree of direct impact on teacher effectiveness. However, teachers claim that test scores alone do not show the impact of a teacher on student growth. They point to the numerous variables influencing student growth that are not accounted for in VAM assessments. Furthermore, VAM does not account for differences in students, such as limited English speaking skills and disabilities (Darling-Hammond, 2010; Ravitch, 2010).

Teacher Salaries

Historically, teachers have been paid at or near the average wage for skilled workers, but below levels customarily received by most other certified professional occupations requiring equivalent levels of education, training, or expertise (Ingersoll & Merrill, 2012; Spring, 2006). Thus, teacher salaries are one reason for the existing teacher shortage (Lortie, 2002; Spring, 2006). It is interesting, however, that teaching is one profession in our society in which females are paid more equally to their male counterparts (Lortie, 2002).

Why teaching is not equally compensated with other professional vocations remains a question. One theory is that teaching is not a true profession; rather it is a service occupation that does not generate income or commerce (Lortie, 2002). Another theory is that many individuals believe anyone can teach because teaching does not really require expert knowledge, only common sense. Finally, many believe low teacher salaries are offset by an array of fringe benefits including job security, long vacations, and flexible hours (Lortie, 2002).

However, teacher salaries have followed the laws of supply and demand. During the 2011–2012 school year, the national average salary for public school teachers in the United States was $56, 643.00 (National Center for Education Statistics, 2014d). School districts experiencing severe teacher shortages are offering signing bonuses to attract new teachers. However, because school districts may be more interested in attracting new teachers than keeping experienced teachers, the steady salary increase has occurred only for beginning teachers, not experienced teachers. Evidence of this occurrence is that the average annual increase for experienced teachers was only 2.7% from 2001–2002, and from 1999 the average salary for experienced teachers rose just 1.6% (American Federation of Teachers, 2005).

There is a wide disparity in teacher salaries across the country (American Federation of Teachers, 2005). States in the New England, Mid-east and Far West regions of the country report higher teacher salaries. States in the Plains region report the lowest salaries. This disparity also exists within states. Since public school teachers are most often state employees, their salaries are based on taxes collected from citizens and businesses in that state. Most states pay teachers a base salary. States with larger populations typically pay higher teacher salaries due to a larger citizen tax base. In these states, funding for public education, including teacher salaries, comes from state individual income taxes. From that point, base salaries may be supplemented by the different local school districts. Funding for supplements usually comes from property taxes administered by individual communities. These taxes are frequently sales taxes on goods purchased at local stores and businesses. Thus, communities with a greater number of businesses and larger populations often pay higher supplemental salaries.

Salary differences also exist among types of schools and schools with differing socioeconomic levels (Kozol, 1991). Ingersoll & Merrill, 2012 report that, on average, individuals with a bachelor's degree and no teaching experience earn 25% more in a public school than a private school. Additionally, private schools frequently offer fewer benefits.

Salary increases have also remained small, and the process to receive an increase has changed in many states. Traditionally, teachers have been paid on a salary schedule that provides automatic salary increases with each year of teaching service and for added academic degrees (Spring, 2006). Under the traditional schedules, often known as the stepladder system, all beginning certified teachers are paid the same amount of starting base salary. For each year of teaching experience salaries increase at a fixed amount.

A major complaint regarding the stepladder system is that it does not reward teachers who demonstrate exceptional abilities and outstanding accomplishments, while providing job security for teachers not performing their responsibilities well (Spring, 2006). This issue is usually associated with the concept of tenure. Tenure is a contract between the teacher and the local school board after teachers have successfully completed their initial probationary period, usually the first three to five years of full-time teaching. Once a teacher receives a tenured contract, it is difficult to dismiss them unless an individual is proven incompetent or has committed a felony law infraction (Spring, 2006). Tenure is a controversial issue among many communities and schools. Many administrators feel once a teacher achieves tenure there is no motivation to continue to grow, stay updated on changing educational approaches and information, or become involved in the school environment. However, many teachers believe tenure offers them job security and protection from possible discrimination in handling student issues (Serow, Castelli, & Castelli, 2000; Spring 2014). However, many schools states have begun to eliminate tenure for new teachers (Dworkin & Tobe, 2012; Spring, 2014), citing the need to eliminate poor-performing teachers.

Responding to controversy surrounding tenure, many school districts have begun to offer extended contracts, or performance-based contracts, thus replacing tenure contracts (Spring, 2006, 2014). Similar to tenure contracts, extended contracts are offered to teachers who have successfully completed their initial probationary level. Instead of granting a permanent tenure contract, the teacher is offered an extended contract, usually lasting five to ten years. At the end of the extended contract, the school principal and consulting teachers review and evaluate the teacher's accomplishments and job performance. If assessed to be satisfactory, the teacher is offered another extended contract. This process repeats itself throughout the teacher's career.

Another salary method used to address differences in teacher ability and accomplishments is the merit pay system or performance-based pay. The intent of this system is to reward teachers based on their annual accomplishments and teaching (Spring, 2006, 2014). Thus, merit pay seeks to provide incentive for extra effort on the part of the teacher who in return receives salary increases for their work. Their school principal and usually a consulting teacher evaluate teachers in this system annually.

Under the merit system, teachers are not guaranteed annual salary increases or equal increase in compensation. Salary increases are based solely on the merit of each teacher. This practice has raised questions regarding what constitutes merit teaching and the qualifications of individuals to effectively evaluate teachers in all subject areas. Subjectivity may influence an individual's perception of teacher accomplishments, resulting in many school districts basing teacher accomplishment solely on student test standardized scores and teacher accountability (Spring, 2006). Yet these scores can be influenced by a variety of variables not under the control or influence of teachers. However, merit pay is a growing popular approach to rewarding teachers for job performance and accomplishments.

One method used to address this issue is the use of career ladders for teachers. In career ladders, beginning teachers usually start out as apprentice or probationary teachers. Typically, individuals have temporary teacher licenses and stay at the apprentice level for two to three years. While they stay at the beginning teacher salary, the school principal and consulting teachers evaluate their contracts and job performances on an annual basis. Following the successful completion of the novice level, teachers can advance to various additional levels based on annual evaluations of their accomplishments by the school principal and consulting teachers. Each level comes with additional pay and stature. Teachers at more advanced levels are considered lead teachers or master teachers and are frequently used to mentor apprentice- and novice-level teachers (Spring, 2006).

The fact remains that individuals who teach music do not necessarily teach for financial rewards. Music teachers frequently work long daily hours, including afternoon rehearsals, night concerts, and weekend trips (Scheib, 2003). Many activities contain additional supplemental pay from school districts. It is not unusual for music teachers to receive extra compensation for marching band, musicals, and other after school activities. Like many other educators, music teachers often spend summers seeking re-certification credits, planning fall marching band shows, and pursuing advanced degrees (Hamann, Daugherty, & Mills, 1987). Also, like many of their colleagues, music teachers supplement their own pay with outside jobs during the year. Many teach private lessons, direct church choirs, or perform in various ensembles (Madsen & Hancock, 2002). While some teachers regard this "moonlighting" as welcome diversion from teaching, for others it is a burden they trade for longer school hours and higher salaries (Hamann, Daugherty, & Mills, 1987).

Working Conditions

Every occupation has its own ideals, traditions, and ways to get things done. Teaching music is no exception, as it is a challenging profession. Historically, the training of teachers has focused more on learning methods and procedures than preparing students for the complexities of school environments (Froehlich, 2007). Teachers average a 45-hour work week that includes nights and weekends grading papers, preparing lessons, meeting parents, performing concerts, teaching individuals lessons, and conducting after school rehearsals. The National Center for Education Statistics (2014c) reported teachers encountered a 16 to 1 student-to-teacher ratio in the average public school classroom in 2010. Obviously, in large performing music ensembles this ratio increases dramatically, thereby increasing the stress on teacher time (Scheib, 2003). The demands on time often lead teachers to feel they must compromise ideals with the realities of teaching that may frequently rob students of learning opportunities (Task Force on Teaching as a Profession, 1986). Additionally, lost in the problem of adequate time is the time needed to stay updated on new knowledge by reading professional journals, learning new scores, and maintaining performance skills (Hamann, Daugherty, & Mills, 1987; Scheib, 2003).

The demands on teachers can also lead to considerable stress and possible burnout. Research has shown music teachers encounter a high degree of stress in their jobs. Sources of stress include a lack of commitment from students, a perceived lack of support from administrators, colleagues, and parents, performances at concerts and festival competitions, and budgetary constraints (Burrack, Payne, Bazan, & Hellman, 2014; Hamann, Daugherty, & Mills, 1987; Scheib, 2003). A survey by The Music Educators National Conference (2005) regarding teacher stress found 37% of music teachers spend 20% or more of their class time handling class management issues such as disruptions and student discipline problems. Other data from this survey showed that 31% of music teachers stated that their teaching contracts stipulate that teachers are expected to put in "overtime" in preparing lessons, performing concerts, and conducting rehearsals. Furthermore, 65% of music teachers reported they do not receive additional compensation for out-of-class time. Interestingly, research shows music teachers themselves frequently cause stress. Since music teachers are often the sole determiners of their own curriculum and expectations, stress often stems from personal pressure to succeed or trying to match their musical beliefs/values system to the school's and community's music beliefs/values system (Hamann, Daugherty, & Mills, 1987; Scheib, 2003).

School environments are complex organizations influenced by a variety of social, political, and educational agendas. It is the responsibility of professional educators to understand the culture of the educational setting in which they teach. For example, the value systems of students and parents may differ from those of the music teacher. Understanding the culture enables individuals to function within the organizational setting of school, the local school district, and the statewide school system in general. However, the goals of the individual teacher may not be the same as those in the organization. Frequently, teachers are subjected to bureaucratic authority and the consistent application of regulations over which they have little control. This feeling is especially true as the emphasis on mandated testing and evaluation continues to grow (Elpus, 2014; Gerrity, 2009, Spring 2014). As a result, teachers may feel restricted in implementing objectives

and experiences they feel are best for students. Furthermore, regulations often dictate responsibilities that teachers must follow to make the educational system function properly. Thus, in
addition to their teaching responsibilities, teachers (music teachers included) are required to
supervise bus duty, monitor lunch rooms, hallways, and bathrooms, chaperon dances and other
after school activities, meet parents, and attend other various functions that require school personnel to be present. While these functions frequently conflict with personal time and more
instructional activities (e.g., after school rehearsals), all teachers must contribute to the total
school environment. Meeting the needs of every student, not just the music students, should be a
goal of every music educator. This may involve participating in bureaucratic, non-music-related
functions within the school environment.

Despite the bureaucracy, music teachers have managed to retain substantial control over their
own classroom activities (Mark & Madura, 2010; Raiber & Teachout, 2014). For example, unlike
many teachers whose subject matter is controlled by required standardized tests or state mandates,
music teachers have considerable freedom to select music for their rehearsals and performances.
One reason for this is the physical layout of the school building (Serow, Castelli, & Castelli,
2000). School architecture has been labeled as "cellular," designed to separate groups of people
throughout the day. A complaint of many teachers is that, outside of lunchtime, they spend little
time with other adults. While this isolation creates a degree of autonomy, it unfortunately also
diminishes the possibility of cooperation with other teachers. Little time exists to discuss common problems, professional issues, and intellectual topics, or exchange ideas with other teachers
(Serow, Castelli, & Castelli, 2000).

Music teachers are not immune from cellular isolation. Research has shown that a feeling of
isolation is a fear of new music teachers as they enter the teaching profession, and contributes to
the burnout of experienced teachers (Hamann, Daugherty, & Mills, 1987; Krueger, 2000). Music
rooms are frequently separated from other more "academic" areas of the school. In larger schools,
it is not unusual to find music rooms in a separate building altogether. Furthermore, many elementary music teachers do not have a room at all, as they move from classroom to classroom,
transporting their materials on a cart. Physical isolation prevents many music teachers from col-
legial bonding with their fellow teachers and the overall school environment. Miscommunica-
tion and misinterpretation of activities may result in conflict, tension, and an under-appreciation
of the purpose of and accomplishments in the music classroom.

Music teachers appear to cope with isolation and stress associated with their jobs in many ways.
A study by Madsen and Hancock (2002) found music teachers frequently change schools in order
to stay fresh and motivated. Teachers in this study stated that attending professional conferences
helped them to cope with professional challenges. Professional conferences such as state and
National Association for Music Education (NAfME) meetings enable music teachers to stay current, meet other educators who share similar challenges, and exchange ideas. Furthermore, music
teachers are encouraged to actively participate in all areas of their school environment. This may
require actively seeking opportunities to work with non-music colleagues. Becoming involved in
the total school culture can have great results for students as well as teachers. Researchers have
demonstrated that professional dialogue and collegiality have a great impact on teacher morale
and retention by creating a therapeutic support system with other teachers (Hamann, Daugherty, & Mills, 1987; Scheib, 2003).

Common Legal Issues

Legal issues and many subsequent court decisions affect every aspect of the teaching profession.
Issues involve activities from student publications to searching students to the performance of

religious music by public school ensembles. One major legal issue is compulsory education. In 1922, the Compulsory Education Act was passed in Oregon, and later subsequently upheld by the U.S. Supreme Court. (Serow, Castelli, & Castelli, 2000). This law required every parent, guardian, or other person having control or charge over a child between the ages of eight and 16 years of age to send the child to a public school. Over the years the law has been amended to allow parents/guardians to send their children to schools other than public schools (e.g., private schools or home schooling), yet it still requires children attend a school or education setting.

Many legal issues affecting teachers involve the First and Fourteenth Amendments to the Constitution of the United States (Spring, 2006). The First Amendment addresses the issues of freedom of speech. For example, can public school teachers criticize the federal government? Can students conduct sit-ins on school property in protest of school regulations? Court decisions are frequently inconsistent, due to variance in situations. For example, while the courts recognize the importance of students and teachers having the right to express themselves, they also recognize the importance of maintaining order in schools and school boards retaining control.

Issues relating to the Fourteenth Amendment are no less difficult. The Fourteenth Amendment guarantees that states cannot take away any rights granted to an individual as a citizen of the United States, which includes schools violating students' basic rights as granted by the Constitution. Consider the possible ramification if a band director denies an individual who uses a wheelchair from marching in a parade or performing at a football game. Denying an individual in these situations could result in a claim of discrimination. Discrimination, defined as the unequal or different treatment of particular categories of people, is a major issue in education. An example is that schools cannot dismiss a student or teacher without due process. This has resulted in school districts having specified guidelines for the dismissal of students, as well as teachers.

Recognizing that every situation is different, courts frequently have not made absolute binding decisions regarding most school legal issues. Students have legal rights in schools that are guaranteed by the First and Fourteenth Amendments. However, actions by both students and teachers cannot cause a disruption in the educational process. It is the interpretation of what constitutes a "disruption" that often influences the direction of many court decisions.

A growing legal concern for all teachers is the use of various social media. While various forms of technology have enabled teachers to connect to other teachers (e.g., email), social media outlets such as Facebook, Instagram, YouTube, and MySpace have greatly expanded the ability to share information, pictures, and personal statements to anyone with access to a computer. While many of these cyberspace venues have excellent instructional and research applications (Giebelhausen, 2015; Whitaker, Orman, & Yarbrough, 2014), they are also a legal concern, as many teachers share personal views and images of themselves which are in conflict with community or school standards for teachers. Contacting and engaging students through social media can lead to inappropriate interactions and communications. According to the Harvard Institute of Politics (Institute of Politics, Harvard University, 2014), 84% of all teenagers in the United States used Facebook in 2014. Consequently, the possibility of connecting with a student, intentionally or not, is very likely. First Amendment rights to freedom of speech do not necessarily protect teachers whose postings may be considered as interrupting or distracting education processes, including moral and social expectations (Papandrea, 2012; Simpson, 2010). Education and legal officials are struggling with the legal ramifications of and their authority in determining the extent teachers can use social media in their personal lives (Papandrea, 2012; Simpson, 2010). Subsequently, all teachers should be mindful of community and school expectations, and any contact with students via cyberspace venues.

Legally, teachers are responsible for protecting the rights of their students. The extent of legality extends to holding teachers increasingly liable for harm that may come to students because of teacher actions, discrimination, or negligence. Such actions could include students injured as a result of tripping over chairs in an unorganized music class, students being stung by a bee on the marching band field and no action taken if an allergic reaction occurs, or students experiencing dehydration or physical harm as a result of activities initiated by the teacher. In each case, the resulting consequences can be viewed as the teacher's fault and thus can be used against the teacher. Furthermore, liable actions could include not reporting possible child abuse cases, including mental and physical harm, sexual abuse, and other maltreatment.

Federal and state laws have been increasingly used to protect teachers. Still, the U.S. Supreme Court has not clearly defined if activities in a teacher's private life can be used as a basis for dismissal from a school system (Spring 2014). While the personal lives of teachers may still be private, it is important they meet the community expectations and views of professional conduct. It is common for teachers to be held to a higher standard than publicly elected officials, including senators, governors, and even the President of the United States! Given the public nature of music teachers' lives, it is possible that certain private behaviors are themselves likely to violate certain community standards and therefore distract from a teacher's effectiveness in dealing with students and parents. Teachers must remember that it is unlikely they will be protected by the courts for engaging in certain felony behaviors, including inappropriate student contact and communications, drug use, theft, human physical harm, excessive drinking, or academic cheating.

Music teachers are affected by many of the same legal issues as other educators. However, like many other teachers, they are frequently unaware of their legal responsibilities. For example, the issue of copyright infringement is a repeated violation of the law by many music educators. Modern technologies have made information and materials increasingly accessible and easily copied, thus making misuse of documents, including music, more common (Liske, 1999). Infringements include redistribution of printed media, sound recordings, television tapings, digital materials, and Internet content, and photocopying music (Liske, 1999; Woody, 1994). Many teachers may believe they have the legal right to photocopy or record music for educational purpose, however, the Copyright Act of 1976 and its subsequent amendments have placed strict guidelines on all individuals, including music educators, as to the extent all media materials can be used. This law is very specific regarding legal ramifications for both individuals and school districts if copyrights are infringed upon (Woody, 1994).

Another legal issue of great concern to music teachers is the use of sacred music. While the extent of religion in public schools has long been a debatable issue, musical activities have historically been part of many music performances. Scared music of some religious perspective is part of every culture and thus is difficult to avoid in music of any culture. Yet, the Establishment Clause of the First Amendment prohibits public schools from endorsing religion or holding religious exercises during the school day (U.S. Constitution, First Amendment, 1791). The issue is the separation of church and state, and there have been many challenges throughout American history to this issue. After reviewing several federal decisions concerning the use of scared music in public schools, Cranmore and Fossey (2014) concluded, "The performance or rehearsal of religious music in a public school setting is not in itself a violation of the Establishment Clause, as long as that music is used for secular purposes" (p. 34). However, because the use of scared music creates the involvement of religion in public schools and is still greatly debated, music educators should be prudent when planning programs; always be mindful of community expectations.

The table below contains many common legal issues of which music educators should be aware. As a good rule of thumb, when in doubt, music educators should check with their school principal for any question of legality.

Examples of Common Legal Issues Facing Music Teachers

Issues	Examples of Teacher Concerns
1. Copyright	Fair use of music, recordings, videos, DVDs
2. Inappropriate Contact/Conduct	Body contact/touching, language, outside meetings
3. Negligence	Student care, unreasonable risk/carelessness, student injury
4. Liability	Parent release for activities, medical attention, required approval from school board
5. Use of Volunteers & Private Instructors	Information and activities found through background checks and fingerprinting
6. Religion in schools	Class prayer, performance of religious music, performance during religious holidays
7. Parent Rights	Parental conduct, accessibility
8. Student property on School property	Searching student lockers or instrument cases
9. Finances	Collecting/handling student fees or fund raising monies
10. Teacher Rights	Tenure, academic freedom, personal lives, liability

Historically, court decisions have had great impact on how, what, and who can teach children in American society (Serow, Castelli, & Castelli, 2000). It is safe to assume the impact on school decisions by the American legal system will continue. Because public schools attempt to educate a large segment of our diverse population, there is always a danger that someone's rights will be forgotten or lost within the educational system. It is important professional music educators keep vigilance on the protection of their students and themselves by being aware of possible legal issues and protecting students and their own rights regarding education.

The Rewards of Teaching

Teaching is often negatively portrayed in our society. Why do people become teachers if the pay is so poor, the work environment so negative, and they are so often under-supported? However, the rewards outnumber the challenges. Research has shown that teachers, including music teachers, find their greatest reward in the interactions with students (Lortie, 2002; Madsen, & Hancock, 2002; Scheib, 2003; Spring 2014; Waller, 1965). Teachers enjoy working with students of all ages and find great satisfaction in helping students learn (Goodlad, 1984). They feel a great sense of intrinsic satisfaction in seeing faces light up when a student finally understands something new. Many teachers report they enjoy making a difference in people's lives. In fact, research has shown teachers gain a greater sense of satisfaction from intrinsic rewards (helping students) than extrinsic rewards (e.g., salary level)! This is especially true of music teachers, who enjoy sharing their love and enthusiasm of music with others (Raiber & Teachout, 2014). This chance to influence the musical development of younger individuals provides a great sense of achievement and satisfaction (Hamann, Daugherty, & Mills, 1987; Madsen, & Hancock, 2002; Scheib, 2003).

Photo Figure 13 Teaching music is a challenging, but rewarding, experience.

Few people think of becoming a teacher to become financially rich. Teaching appears to be a viewed as a "calling" rather than simply a job. Many teachers, including music teachers, describe teaching as a tradition of honor or service to society (Lortie, 2002; Madsen & Kelly, 2002; Waller, 1965). The tradition of teaching makes people who seek money, prestige, or power appear somewhat suspect! However, one reward of teaching is the pay structure. When individuals go into teaching they frequently know how much they will earn in salary each year due to established school district pay scales. This structure enables individuals to plan for financial goals. Additionally, the fact that females are paid more equally to their male counterparts is something often uncommon in the business world (Lortie, 2002; Waller, 1965).

Another reward enjoyed by teachers is the relative autonomy of their classrooms (Lortie, 2002; Waller, 1965). There is nothing routine about teaching, as educators are often free to make quick decisions regarding students and activities. The best-organized lesson plans can quickly be tossed out due to an unexpected event such as a fire drill, weather event, or the anticipation of the high school prom. It has been estimated that teachers make over two hundred decisions daily regarding their instruction and class activities (Ballantine, 2001). Thus, achieving a sense of accomplishment by making decisions from which the effects can be directly observed is a reward valued by teachers. This sense further supports the "honored tradition" of teaching and providing a needed service to society.

Other attractors for teaching include extended vacations, job security, and regular holidays (Lortie, 2002). Most school systems also permit great variance in teacher individualism, or the amount of involvement in school functions. Some teachers become very active in a wide variety of school activities in addition to teaching their classes, while others are content to teach their classes and attend only required extra duties or responsibilities.

Finally, perhaps a unique aspect for music teachers is that they can continue to actively participate in something they love—making music. Opportunities to continue actively engaged in practicing the subject matter they teach provide many music educators with a continued connection to their love of performance. This can include teaching private lessons, participation in performing ensembles, or sharing the enjoyment of music with others, including their students. Many music teachers became teachers due to their love of music and desire to share this love with others. Being music teachers enables them to accomplish this desire. Thus, many music teachers are active musicians in their communities and schools, further contributing to their credibility as role models for their students.

Summary

Few professions in the United States have such a profound effect on society as teaching. Though not as well-funded or financially rewarding as many other professions, professional teachers are highly regarded individuals who have tremendous impact on our society. This respect and influence extends to music educators, as they are frequently intertwined with their communities. Thus, teaching is a profession that is reputable to, even honored by, many in our society.

Teaching requires commitment to the subject matter, as well as the diversity of interactions encountered every day. Being a professional educator can be a challenge, and harsh. For many new teachers, encountering culture shock in their first year of teaching is very common (Krueger, 2000; Madsen & Hancock, 2002). Many new teachers expect their classrooms to be like the schools they grew up in and enjoyed. They often model themselves based on the teachers who inspired them to become teachers. While this idealism is good to a point, reality demands an acceptance that students and situations change quickly and therefore are not the same as when the teachers were students. What works for teachers one year does not work the next year. Reality in the teacher profession requires individuals to be open and flexible, knowledgeable and aware, personable yet firm. Reality includes understanding not only subject content, but also non-instructional, even non-educational, factors affecting teachers every day.

From a sociological perspective, teaching is an interaction of people from different cultures, each with different norms and folkways, including different musical values (Ballantine, 2001; Ballantine & Spade, 2012; Macionis, 1997). The socialization process should not be dictatorial, but rather a stimulating interaction of ideas leading toward the general goals of education. The interaction in a classroom illustrates the highly personalized nature of teaching. Due to the constant demands on a teacher's judgments and human relation skills, the profession requires that individuals have an enormous amount of energy and enthusiasm in the classroom.

Music educators are not exempt from the challenges and demands of the teaching profession. Perhaps our biggest challenge is being accepted by other education groups as contributing to the overall education of all students. Music educators must promote the educational value of music instruction while maintaining the intrinsic value of music itself. Perhaps the very nature of training received by many music education majors contributes to this challenge. Music teachers are well-trained as musicians, but not necessarily as educators. We confuse the act of conducting with teaching. We often assume that because our students participate in our ensembles, they automatically learn. We confuse the performance of music with music education. We often are uncomfortable with the business side of education and unaware of many legal issues in our profession. Music teachers are frequently criticized as being elitists who want to teach only those with talent and only "classical" music. Subsequently, music teachers are often thought to be out of touch with mainstream music values in our society. Thus, we have difficulty justifying what we teach and what our students learn with other educational views. The challenges for music educators are the same as for all educators: remember why you entered the profession, keep the focus on students, create wonderful, beautiful music, and teach everyone from the most talented to the most challenging.

Key Items

Teaching Professional

National Board Certification

National Education Association

Master Teachers/Lead Teachers

Tenure

Stepladder Pay Scale

Career Ladders

Legal Issues

Compulsory Education

Alternative Certification

American Federation of Teachers

Teach for America

El Sistema

Extended Contracts

Merit Pay

Value-added Modeling

First and Fourteenth Amendments

Social Media

Questions for Consideration

1. How can teacher training be improved to better reflect classroom realities?
2. If music education becomes more focused on individual needs, how will this affect traditional large performing ensembles?
3. What are pros and cons of having the different salary systems for teachers? How will evaluators with no music background accurately assess music teachers and how might this affect their salary with the merit system?
4. How might various teacher assessments affect the quality of teaching and the teaching profession as a whole?
5. How can tenure affect teacher performance?
6. How flexible may the music curriculum need to be in order to reach out to every student?
7. What are examples of situations involving various legal issues that music teachers may encounter?

Web Resources

Professional Organizations

American Bandmasters Association: http://americanbandmasters.org/

American Choral Directors Association: http://acda.org/

American School Band Directors Association: http://asbda.com/

American String Teachers Association: http://www.astaweb.com/

El Sistema: http://www.elsistemausa.org/

National Association of Schools of Music: http://nasm.arts-accredit.org/

National Band Association: https://www.nationalbandassociation.org/

National Board Certification: http://www.nbpts.org/national-board-certification

National Music Foundation: http://www.musiciansnetwork.com/network/Education/Organizations/National_Music_Foundation-info60571.html

Teach for America: https://www.teachforamerica.org/

U.S. Department of Education: http://www.ed.gov/

Social Media

Digital Learning: http://toponlineuniversityreviews.com/2009/25-excellent-social-media-sites-for-teachers/
Edutopia: http://www.edutopia.org/blog/social-media-resources-educators-matt-davis
Scholastic: http://www.scholastic.com/teachers/article/social-media-teachers

Teacher Unions

American Federation of Teachers: http://www.aft.org/
National Education Association: http://www.nea.org/

References

Abeles, H. (1980). Responses to music. In D. A. Hodges (Ed.), *Handbook of music psychology* (pp. 105–140). Lawrence, KS: National Association for Music Therapy.

Abeles, H. (2004). The effect of three orchestra/school partnerships on students' interest in instrumental music instruction. *Journal of Research in Music Education, 52*(3), 248–263. doi:10.2307/3345858

Abeles, H. F., & Porter, S. Y. (1978). The sex-stereotyping of music instruments. *Journal of Research in Music Education, 26*, 65–75. doi:10.2307/3344880

Abril, C. R. (2011, February). *A view of school band from the perspective of hardcore band kids.* Paper presented at the 19th International Symposium for Research in Music Behavior, Barcelona, Spain.

Abril, C. R. (2013). Toward a more culturally responsive general music classroom. *General Music Today, 27*(1) 6–11. doi:10.1177/1048371313478946

Abril, C. R., & Bannerman, J. K. (2013, March). *A sociological view of the perceived factors impacting school music programs.* Paper presented at the 20th International Symposium for Research in Music Behavior, Seattle, WA.

Abril, C. R., & Gault, B. (2008). The state of music in the secondary schools: The principal's perspective. *Journal of Research in Music Education, 56*(1), 6–20. doi:10.1177/0022429408317516

Adamek, M. S., & Darrow, A. A. (2005). *Music in special education.* Silver Spring, MD: American Music Therapy Association.

Adderly, C., Kennedy, M., & Berz, W. (2003). "A home away from home": The world of the high school music classroom. *Journal of Research in Music Education, 51*(3), 190–205. doi:10.2307/3345373

Adorno, T. (1976). *Introduction to the sociology of music* (E. B. Ashton, Trans.). New York, NY: Seabury Press. (Original work published 1962).

Albert, D. J. (2006). Socioeconomic status and instrumental music: What does the research say about the relationship and its implications? *Update: Applications of Research in Music Education, 25*(1), 39–45. doi: 10.1177/87551233060250010104

Allsup, R. E., & Shieh, E. (2012). Social justice and music education: The call for a public pedagogy. *Music Educators Journal, 98*(4), 47–51. doi:10.1177/0027432112442969

Alwin, D., & Thornton, A. (1984). Family origins and school processes: Early versus late influence of parental characteristics. *American Sociological Review, 49*, 784–802.

American Association of State Colleges and Universities. (2006). *Delivering America's promise.* Retrieved from http://www.aascu.org/

American Educational Research Association. (2013). *Prevention of bullying in schools, colleges, and universities.* Washington, DC: Author.

American Federation of Teachers. (2005). *2003 survey & analysis of teacher salary trends.* Retrieved from http://www.aft.org/salary/index.htm

American Federation of Teachers. (2007). *A union of professionals.* Retrieved from http://www.aft.org/

American Music Conference. (1997). *American attitudes toward music, 1997.* Available from the National Association of Music Merchants.

American Psychological Association. (2010). *Publication manual of the American Psychological Association* (6th ed.). Washington, DC: Author.

Arum, R., & Beattie, I. R. (2000). *The structure of schooling: Readings in the sociology of education.* Boston, MA: McGraw-Hill.

Asmus, E. P. (1985). Sixth graders' achievement motivation: Their views of success and failure in music. *Bulletin of the Council for Research in Music Education, 85*, 1–13.

Asmus, E. P. (1986). Student beliefs about the causes of success and failure in music: A study of achievement motivation. *Journal of Research in Music Education, 34*(4), 262–278. doi:10.2307/3345260

Austin, J. R. (1997a). Conceptions of musical ability in American society: The influence of competition and other sociocultural factors. In R. Rideout (Ed.), *On the sociology of music education* (pp. 154–165). Norman: School of Music, University of Oklahoma.

Austin, J. R. (1997b, April). *The privatization of public education: Implications for school music programs and music teacher education.* Paper presented at the Innovations in Music Teacher Education Symposium, University of Oklahoma, Norman.

Austin, J. R. (1997c). The relationship of music self-esteem to degree of participation in school and out-of-school music activities among upper-elementary students. *Contributions to Music Education, 17*, 20–31.

Ayn Rand Institute. (2014). *Introduction to objectivism.* Retrieved from http://www.aynrand.org/ideas/overview

Bakan, M. B. (2012). *World music: Traditions and transformations* (2nd ed.). New York, NY: McGraw-Hill.

Ballantine, J. H. (2001). *The sociology of education* (5th ed.). Upper Saddle River, NJ: Prentice Hall.

Ballantine, J. H., & Spade, J. Z. (2012). *Schools and society: A sociological approach to education* (4th ed.). Los Angeles, CA: SAGE.

Bandura, A. (1976). *Social learning theory.* Englewood Cliffs, NJ: Prentice-Hall.

Bandura, A. (1993). Perceived self-efficacy in cognitive development and functioning. *Educational Psychologist, 28*, 117–148.

Banks, J. A. (2001). Multicultural education: Characteristics and goals. In J. A. Banks & C.A.M. Banks (Eds.), *Multicultural education: Issues and perspectives* (4th ed., pp. 3–30). New York, NY: John Wiley and Sons.

Banks, J. A., & Banks, C.A.M. (2001). *Multicultural education: Issues and perspectives* (4th ed.). New York, NY: John Wiley and Sons.

Bell-Robertson, C. G. (2014). "Staying on our feet": Novice music teachers' sharing of emotions and experiences within an online community. *Journal of Research in Music Education, 61*(4), 431–451. doi:10.1177/0022429413508410

Bergee, M. J., Coffman, D. D., Demorest, S. M., Humphreys, J. T., & Thorton, L.P. (2001). *Influences on collegiate students' decision to become a music educator.* Summary available on the NAfME Web site at http://www.menc.org/networks/rnc/Bergee-Report.html

Bergee, M. J., & Grashel, J. W. (1995). Psychosocial profiles of music education undergraduates based on Erickson's principles and epigenetic development. *Quarterly Journal of Music Teaching and Learning, 6*(1), 5–15.

Berger, P., & Luckmann, T. (1966). *The social construction of reality: A treatise in the sociology of knowledge.* New York, NY: Doubleday.

Berry, B. (2001). No shortcuts to preparing good teachers. *Educational Leadership, 58*(8), 32–36.

Berstein, B. (1971). *Class, codes, and control. Volume I: Theoretical studies towards a sociology of language.* London: Routledge & Kegan Paul.

Birge, E. B. (1966). *History of public school music in the United States.* Music Educators National Conference: Washington, DC.

Blacking, J. (1973). *How musical is man?* Seattle: University of Washington Press.

Blocher, L., Greenwood, R., & Shellahamer, B. (1997). Teaching behaviors of middle school and high school band directors in the rehearsal setting. *Journal of Research in Music Education, 45*(3), 457–469. doi:10.2307/3345539

Bloom, B. S. (1956). *Taxonomy of educational objectives.* New York, NY: Longmans.

Boardman, E. (Ed.). (2002). *Dimensions of musical learning and thinking.* Reston, VA: Music Educators National Conference.

Boswell, J. (1991). Comparisons of attitudinal assessments in middle and junior high school general music. *Bulletin of the Council for Research in Music Education, 108*, 49–58.

Bourdieu, P. (2000). Cultural reproduction and social reproduction. In R. Arum & I. R. Beattie (Eds.), *The structure of schooling: Readings in the sociology of education* (pp. 56–68). Boston, MA: McGraw-Hill.

Bower, G. H., & Hilgard, E. R. (1981). *Theories of learning* (5th ed.). Englewood Cliffs, NJ: Prentice-Hall.

Bowles, C. L. (1991). Self-expressed adult music education interests and music experiences. *Journal of Research in Music Education, 39*, 191–205. doi:10.2307/3344719

Bowles, S., & Gintis, H. (1976). *Schooling in capitalist America*. New York, NY: Basic Books.

Boyd, D., Grossman, P., Ing, M., Lankford, H., Loeb, S., & Wyckoff, J. (2011). The influence of school administrators on teacher retention decisions. *American Educational Research Journal, 48*(2), 303–333. doi:10.3102/0002831210380788

Brand, M. (1986). Relationships between home music environment and selected musical attributes of second-grade children. *Journal of Research in Music Education, 34*(2), 11–120. doi:10.2307/3344739

Brittin, R. V. (2000). Children's preference for sequenced accompaniments: The influence of style and perceived tempo. *Journal of Research in Music Education, 48*(3), 237–248. doi:10.2307/3345396

Bruner, J. (1977). *The process of education*. Cambridge, MA: Harvard University Press.

Burnett, G. (1995). *Alternatives to ability grouping: Still unanswered questions*. New York, NY: Clearinghouse on Urban Education, Number 111.

Burrack, F. W., Payne, P., Bazan, D. E., & Hellman, D. S. (2014). The impact of budget cutbacks on music teaching positions and district funding in three Midwestern states. *Update: Applications of Research in Music Education, 33*(1), 36–41. doi:10.1177/8755123314521039

Bushaw, W. J., & Calderon, V. J. (2014). *The 46th annual Phi Delta Kappa/Gallup Poll of the public's attitudes toward the public schools*. Retrieved from http://pdkintl.org/noindex/PDKGallupPoll_Oct2014.pdf

Byo, J. L. (1990). Recognition of intensity contrasts in gestures of beginning conductors. *Journal of Research in Music Education, 38*, 157–163. doi:10.2307/3345179

Cahill, R. (2008). Media literacy in K–12: Using media to advance critical thinking. In J. Ensign, E. Hargrave, & R. Lasso (Eds.). *Masters in teaching program 2006–2008: Teaching the child in front of you in a changing world* (pp. 37–44). Olympia, WA: Evergreen State College.

Caine, R. N., & Caine, G. (1997). *Education on the edge of possibility*. Alexandria, VA: Association for Supervision and Curriculum Development.

Calhoun, C. (1995). *Critical social theory*. Cambridge, MA: Blackwell.

Callaghan, J. (2007). *Theodor Adorno*. Retrieved from http://english.emory.edu/Bahri/Adorno.html

Campbell, D. (2006, February 22). Education, chutzpah and the GOP. *USA Today*, p. 13A.

Campbell, P. S. (2004). *Teaching music globally*. New York, NY: Oxford University Press.

Campbell, P. S., Connell, C., & Beegle, A. (2007). Adolescents' expressed meanings of music in and out of schools. *Journal of Research in Music Education, 55*(3), 220–236. doi:10.1177/002242940705500304

Carey, K. (2004). *The funding gap 2004: Many states still shortchange low-income and minority students*. Washington, DC: Education Trust.

Cartledge, G. (1996). *Cultural diversity and social skills instruction*. Champaign, IL: Research Press.

Cauley, K., & Tyler, B. (1989). The relationship of self-concept to prosocial behavior in children. *Early Childhood Research Quarterly, 4*, 51–60.

Center for Disease Control and Prevention. (2011). *FastStats: Marriage and divorce*. Retrieved from http://www.cdc.gov/nchs/fastats/marriage-divorce.htm

Chipman, S. R. (2004). *A survey of perceptions of at-risk students by Florida secondary school band directors* (Unpublished doctoral dissertation). Florida State University, Tallahassee.

Choate, R. A. (Ed.). (1968). *Documentary report of the Tanglewood Symposium*. Washington, DC: Music Educators National Conference.

Ciskszentmihalyi, M., & Nakamura, J. (1989). The dynamic of intrinsic motivation: A study of adolescents. In C. Ames & R. Ames (Eds.). *Research on motivation in education* (Vol. 3, pp. 45–71). San Diego, CA: Academic Press.

Clifford, M. M., & Walster, E. (1973). Research note: The effect of physical attractiveness on teacher expectations. *Sociology of Education, 46*, 248–258.

Cofer, R. S. (1998). Effects of conducting-gesture instruction on seventh-grade band students' performance response to conducting emblems. *Journal of Research in Music Education, 46*, 360–373. doi:10.2307/3345548

Coffman, D. D., & Adamek, M. S. (2001). Perceived social support of New Horizons Band participants. *Contributions to Music Education, 28*(1), 27–40.

Cohen-Vogel, L., & Smith, T. M. (2007). Qualifications and assignments of alternatively certified teachers: Testing core assumptions. *American Educational Research Journal, 44*(3), 732–753. doi:10.3102/0002831207306752

Coleman, J. S. (1990). *Equality and achievement in education*. Boulder, CO: Westview Press.

Coleman, J., & Hoffer, T. (2000). Schools, families, and communities. In R. Arum & I. R. Beattie (Eds.). *The structure of schooling: Readings in the sociology of education* (pp. 69–77). Boston, MA: McGraw-Hill.

Common Core State Standards Initiative. (2014). *Preparing America's students for success.* Retrieved from http://www.corestandards.org/

Conway, C. M. (2003). An examination of district-sponsored beginning music teacher mentor practices. *Journal of Research in Music Education, 51*(1), 6–23. doi:10.2307/3345645

Conway, C. M. (2012). Ten years later: Teachers reflect on "perceptions of beginning teachers, their mentors, and administrator regarding preservice music teacher preparation." *Journal of Research in Music Education, 60*(3), 324–338. doi:10.1177/0022429412453601

Conway, C. M. (2015). Beginning music teacher mentor practices: Reflections on the past and suggestions for the future. *Journal of Music Teacher Education, 24,* 1–15. doi:10.1177/1057083713512837

Cook, G, A, (1993). *George Herbert Mead: The making of a social pragmatist.* Urbana: University of Illinois Press.

Cooley, C. H. (1902). *Human nature and the social order.* New York, NY: Schocken Books.

Cooper, H., & Conswella, J. M. (1995). Teenage motherhood, mother-only households, and teacher expectations. *Journal of Experimental Education, 63*(3), 231–248.

Cox, P. (1997). The professional socialization of music teachers as musicians and educators. In R. Rideout (Ed.). *On the sociology of music education* (pp. 112–120). Norman: University of Oklahoma.

Cranmore, J., & Fossey, R. (2014). Religious music, the public schools, and the establishment clause: A review of federal case law. *Update: Application of Research in Music Education, 33*(1), 31–35. doi:10.1177/8755123314540663

Cremin, L. A. (1957). *The republic and the school: Horace Mann on the education of free men.* New York, NY: Teachers College Press.

Custodero, L. A., & Johnson-Green, E. A. (2003). Passing the cultural torch: Musical experience and musical parenting of infants. *Journal of Research in Music Education, 51*(2), 102–114. doi:10.2307/3345844

Darling-Hammond, L. (2010). *The flat world and education: How America's commitment to equity will determine our future.* New York, NY: Teachers College Press.

Darrow, A. A. (1993). The role of music in deaf culture: Implications for music educators. *Journal of Research in Music Education, 41*(2), 93–110. doi:10.2307/3345402

Darrow, A. A. (2014). Taking the special out of special learners in music education. *Florida Music Director, 68*(4), 36–40.

Darrow, A. A., & Johnson, C. M. (1994). Junior and senior high school students' attitudes toward individuals with a disability. *Journal of Music Therapy, 31,* 266–279.

Deisler, A. M. (2011). *A comparison of common characteristics of successful high school band programs in low socioeconomic schools and high socioeconomic schools.* Unpublished doctoral dissertation, Florida State University, Tallahassee, FL.

DeLorenzo, L. C. (1992). The perceived problems of beginning music teachers. *Bulletin of the Council for Research in Music Education, 113,* 9–26.

Delzell, J. K., & Leppla, D. A. (1992). Gender association of music instruments and preferences of fourth-grade students for selected instruments. *Journal of Research in Music Education, 40*(2), 93–103. doi:10.2307/3345559

Demorest, S. M., & Schultz, S. J. M. (2004). Children's preference for authentic versus arranged versions of world music recordings. *Journal of Research in Music Education, 52*(4), 300–313. doi:10.1177/002242940405200403

Dewey, J. (1900). *The school and society.* Chicago, IL: University of Chicago Press.

Dewey, J. (1915). *Democracy and education.* New York, NY: Free Press.

Dillon, S. (2006, August 27). In schools across the U.S., the melting pot overflows. *New York Times,* pp. A7, A16.

Diperna, P. (2014). *2014 schooling in America survey: Perspectives on school choice, common Core, and standardized testing.* Friedman Foundation for Educational Choice. Retrieved from http://www.edchoice.org/Research/Reports/2014-Schooling-in-America-Survey—Perspectives-on-School-Choice—Common-Core—and-Standardized-Testing.aspx

Draves, T. J. (2013). Transition from student to teacher–student teaching: The capstone experience. *Journal of Music Teacher Education, 23*(1), 50–62. doi:10.1177/1057083712474935

Droe, K.L. (2012). Effect of verbal praise on achievement goal orientation, motivation, and performance attribution. *Journal of Music Teacher Education, 23*(1), 63–78. doi:10.1177/1057083712458592

Duke, R.A., Flowers, P.J., & Wolfe, D.E. (1997). Children who study piano with excellent teachers in the United States. *Bulletin for the Council for Research in Music Education, 132*, 51–84.

Durkheim, E. (1893). *The division of labor in society.* New York, NY: Free Press.

Dworkin, A.G., & Tobe, P.F. (2012). Teacher burnout in light of school safety, student misbehavior, and changing accountability standards. In J.H. Ballantine & J.Z. Spade (Eds.), *Schools and society: A sociological approach to education* (4th ed., pp. 199–211). Thousand Oaks, CA: SAGE.

Ebie, B. (1998). Can music help? A qualitative investigation of two music educators' views on the role of music in the lives of at-risk students. *Contributions to Music Education, 25*(2), 63–78.

Education of All Handicapped Children Act. (1975). Retrieved from http://scn.org/~bk269/94–142.html

Education Week. (2011). *Achievement gap.* Retrieved from http://www.edweek.org/ew/issues/achievement-gap/

Elliott, D.J. (1995). *Music matters: A new philosophy of music education.* New York, NY: Oxford University Press.

Elliott, D.J., & Silverman, M. (2014). *Music matters: A new philosophy of music education* (2nd ed.). New York, NY: Oxford University Press.

Elpus, K. (2014). Evaluating the effect of No Child Left Behind on U.S. music course enrollments. *Journal of Research in Music Education, 62*(3), 215–233. doi:10.1177/0022429414530759

Elpus, K., & Abril, C.R. (2011). High school music ensemble students in the United States: A demographic profile. *Journal of Research in Music Education, 59*(2), 128–154. doi:10.1177/0022429411405207

El Sistema USA. (2014). *Home page.* Retrieved from https://elsistemausa.org/

Erickson, F. (2001). Culture in society and in educational practices. In J.A. Banks & C.A.M. Banks (Eds.), *Multicultural education: Issues and perspectives* (4th ed., pp. 31–58). New York, NY: John Wiley and Sons.

Erikson, E. (1963). *Childhood and society* (2nd ed.). New York, NY: Norton.

Erikson, E. (1980). *Identity and the life-cycle.* New York, NY: Norton.

Estrich, S. (1994, September 15). Single-sex education deserves a real chance. *USA Today*, p. A11.

Etzkorn, K.P. (Ed.). (1989). Preface. In P. Honigsheim, *Sociologists and music: An introduction to the study of music and society through the latter works of Paul Honigsheim* (pp. xiii–xvi). New Brunswick, NJ: Transaction.

Feinber, W., & Soltis, J.F. (1998). *School and society.* New York, NY: Teachers College Press.

Feller, B. (2005, April 21). NEA, schools sue over No Child Left Behind. *Tallahassee Democrat*, p. 4A.

Fennell, F. (n.d.). *Time and the winds.* Kenosha, WI: G. Leblanc.

Figlio, D.N. (2006). Testing, crime and punishment. *Journal of Public Economics, 90*, 837–851.

Fitzpatrick, K.R. (2006). The effect of instrumental music participation and socioeconomic status on Ohio fourth-, sixth-, and ninth-grade proficiency test performance. *Journal of Research in Music Education, 54*(1), 73–84. doi:10.1177/002242940605400106

Florida Department of Education. (2006a). *Florida comprehensive assessment test.* Retrieved from http://www.firn.edu/doe/sas/fcat.htm

Florida Department of Education. (2006b). *Memorandum: New high school graduation requirements, "It's a major opportunity."* Retrieved from http://www.fldoe.org/APlusPlus/

Froehlich, H.C. (2007). *Sociology for music teachers.* Upper Saddle River, NJ: Prentice Hall.

Froehlich, H.C., & L'Roy, D. (1985). An investigation of occupational identity in undergraduate music education majors. *Bulletin of the Council for Research in Music Education, 85*, 65–75.

Fulcher, J., & Scott, J. (2011). *Sociology* (4th ed.). New York, NY: Oxford University Press.

Fung, C.V. (1994). Undergraduate non-music majors' world music preference and multicultural attitudes. *Journal of Research in Music Education, 42*(1), 45–57. doi:10.2307/3345336

Fung, C.V. (1995). Rationales for teaching world music. *Music Educators Journal, 82*(1), 36–40. doi:10.2307/3398884

Gallup Organization. (2003a). *American attitudes toward making music.* Princeton, NJ: Author.

Gallup Organization. (2003b). *Americans overwhelmingly want music education in schools.* New York, NY: Author.

Gallup Organization. (2014). *Education: Historical trends.* New York, NY: Author.

Gardner, H. (1985). *Frames of Mind: The theory of multiple intelligences.* New York, NY: Basic Books.

Gardner, H. (1993). *Multiple intelligences: The theory in practice*. New York, NY: Basic Books.

Gardner, H. (1999). *Intelligence reframed: Multiple intelligences for the 21st century*. New York, NY: Basic Books.

Geertz, C. (1965). The impact of the concept of culture on the concept of man. In J. R. Platt (Ed.), *New Views of the Nature of Man*. Chicago, IL: University of Chicago Press.

Gerrity, K. W. (2009). No Child Left Behind: Determining the impact of policy on music education in Ohio. *Bulletin of the Council for Research in Music Education, 179*, 79–93.

Gerrity, K. W., Hourigan, R. M., & Horton, P. W. (2013). Conditions that facilitate music learning among students with special needs: A mixed-methods inquiry. *Journal of Research in Music Education, 61*(2), 144–159. doi:10.1177/0022429413485428

Gfeller, K., Darrow, A. A., & Hedden, S. K. (1990). Perceived effectiveness of mainstreaming in Iowa and Kansas schools. *Journal of Research in Music Education, 38*(2), 90–101. doi:10.2307/3344929

Giebelhausen, R. (2015). What the tech is going on? Social media and your music classroom. *General Music Today, 28*(2), 39–46. doi:10.1177/1048371314552523

Goleman, D. (2006). *Social intelligence*. New York, NY: Bantam Dell.

Gollnick, D. A., & Chinn, P. C. (1994). *Multicultural education in a pluralistic society* (4th ed.). New York, NY: Merrill.

Gollnick, D. M., & Chinn, P. C. (2002). *Multicultural education in a pluralistic society* (6th ed.). Upper Saddle River, NJ: Prentice Hall.

Goodenough, W. (1987). Multi-culturalism as the normal human experience. In E. M. Eddy & W. L. Partridge (Eds.), *Applied anthropology in America* (2nd ed.). New York, NY: Columbia University Press.

Goodlad, J. (1984). *A place called school*. New York, NY: McGraw-Hill.

Goolsby, T. W. (1996). Time use in instrumental rehearsals: A comparison of experienced, novice, and student teachers. *Journal of Research in Music Education, 44*, 286–303. doi:10.2307/3345442

Goolsby, T. W. (1997). Verbal instruction in instrumental rehearsals: A comparison of three career levels and preservice teachers. *Journal of Research in Music Education, 45*(1), 21–40. doi:10.2307/3345463

Goolsby, T. W. (1999). A comparison of expert and novice music teachers' preparing identical band compositions: An operational replication. *Journal of Research in Music Education, 47*(2), 174–187. doi:10.2307/3345722

Gordon, D. G., & Hamann, D. L. (2001). Effective qualities of arts educators: A survey of fine arts deans, department chairs, and fine arts professors. *Contributions to Music Education, 28*, 65–80.

Gordon, E. E. (1967). *A three-year study of the musical aptitude profile*. Iowa City: University of Iowa.

Gordon, E. E. (1968). A study of the efficacy of general intelligence and musical aptitude tests in predicting achievement in music. *Bulletin of the Council for Research in Music Education, 13*, 40–45.

Gordon, E. E. (1971). *The psychology of music teaching*. Englewood Cliffs, NJ: Prentice Hall.

Gordon, E. E. (1979). *Primary measures of music audiation*. Chicago, IL: GIA.

Gracey, H. L. (2012). Learning the student role: Kindergarten as academic boot camp. In J. H. Ballantine & J. Z. Spade (Eds.), *Schools and society: A sociological approach to education* (4th ed., pp. 149–153). Thousand Oaks, CA: SAGE.

Green, L. (2008). *Music, informal learning and the school: A new classroom pedagogy*. London: Ashgate.

Grout, D. J., & Palisca, C. V. (1988). *A history of western music* (4th ed.). New York, NY: Norton Music.

Guerrini, S. C. (2005). An investigation of the association between the music aptitude of elementary students and their biological parents. *Update: Applications of Research in Music Education, 1*, 27–33. doi:10.1177/87551233050240010104

Gunderson, I. N., Jones, R., & Scanland, K. (2004). *The jobs revolution: Changing how America works*. Austin, TX: Copywriters.

Haack, P. (1997). Toward a socio/functional music education. In R. Rideout (Ed.), *On the sociology of music education* (pp. 85–94). Norman: University of Oklahoma School of Music.

Hallinan, M. T. (1990). The effects of ability grouping in secondary schools: A response to Slavin's best-evidence synthesis. *Review of Educational Research, 1*(3), 501–504.

Hallinan, M. T. (2012). Teacher influences on students' attachment to school. In J. H. Ballantine & J. Z. Spade (Eds.), *Schools and society: A sociological approach to education* (4th ed., pp. 212–215). Thousand Oaks, CA: SAGE.

Hamann, D. L., Daugherty, E., & Mills, C. R. (1987). An investigation of burnout assessment and potential job related variables among public school music educators, *Psychology of Music, 15*(2), 128–140.

Hamilton, L., & Stecher, B. (2004, April). Responding effectively to test-based accountability. *Phi Delta Kappan,* 578–583.

Hanna, J. (2005, May 6). Kansas board of education starts evolution hearings. *Tallahassee Democrat,* p. A2.

Hardman, M. L., Drew, C. J., & Egan, M. W. (2002). *Human exceptionality* (7th ed.). Boston, MA: Allyn and Bacon.

Harrington, M. (1962). *The other America: Poverty in the United States.* New York, NY: Collier Books.

Haston, W., & Russell, J. A. (2012, January). Turning into teachers: Influences of authentic context learning experiences on occupational identity development of preservice music teachers. *Journal of Research in Music Education, 59*(4), 369–392. doi:10.1177/0022429411414716

Hedden, S. K. (1982). Prediction of music achievement in the elementary school. *Journal of Research in Music Education, 30*(1), 61–68. doi:10.2307/3344867

Hendel, C. (1995). Behavioral characteristics and instructional patterns of selected music teachers. *Journal of Research in Music Education, 43*(3), 182–203. doi:10.2307/3345635

Henry, M. (2005). An analysis of certification practices for music educators in the fifty states. *Journal of Music Teacher Education, 14*(2), 47–61. doi:10.1177/10570837050140020108

Herrnstein, R. J., & Murray, C. (1994). *The bell curve.* New York, NY: Free Press.

Hinsdale, B. A. (2010). *Horace Mann and the common school revival in the United States.* New York, NY: Qontro Legacy.

Hoffman, A. R. (2012). Performing our world: Affirming cultural diversity through music education. *Music Educators Journal, 98*(4), 61–65. doi:10.1177/0027432112443262

Horng, E. L. (2009). Teacher tradeoffs: Disentangling teachers' preferences for working conditions and student demographics. *American Educational Research Journal, 46*(3), 690–717. doi:10.3102/0002831208329599

Hornyak, R. R. (1966). An analysis of student attitudes toward contemporary American music. *Council for Research in Music Education, 8,* 1–14.

Hruska, B. J. (2011). Using mastery goals in music to increase student motivation. *Update: Applications of Research in Music Education, 30*(1), 3–9. doi:0.1177/8755123311418477

Hughes, J. A., Sharrock, W. W., & Martin, P. J. (2003). *Understanding classical sociology* (2nd ed.). London: SAGE.

Hunt, D. E., & Sullivan, E. V. (1974). *Between psychology and education.* Hinsdale, IL: Dryden.

Ingersoll, R. M. (2001). Teacher turnover and teacher shortages: An organizational analysis. *American Educational Research Journal, 38,* 499–534.

Ingersoll, R. M., & Merrill, E. (2012). The status of teaching as a profession. In J. H. Ballantine & J. Z. Spade (Eds.), *Schools and society: A sociological approach to education* (4th ed., pp. 185–198). Thousand Oaks, CA: SAGE.

Ingersoll, R. M., & Perda, D. (2010). Is the supply of mathematics and science teachers sufficient? *American Educational Research Journal, 47*(3), 563–594. doi:10.3102/0002831210370711

Institute of Politics, Harvard University. (2014). *Survey of young Americans' attitudes toward politics and public service* (25th ed.). Cambridge, MA: Author. Retrieved from http://www.iop.harvard.edu/sites/default/files_new/Harvard_ExecSummarySpring2014.pdf

Isbell, D. (2007, Fall/Winter). Popular music and the public school music curriculum. *Update: Applications of Research in Music Education, 26*(1), 53–63. doi:10.1177/87551233070260010106

Isbell, D. (2008). Musicians and teachers: The socialization and occupational identity of preservice music teachers. *Journal of Research in Music Education, 56,* 162–178. doi:10.1177/0022429408322853

Jellison, J. A. (2000). How can all people continue to be involved in meaningful music participation? In C. K. Madsen (Ed.), *Vision 2020: The Housewright symposium on the future of music education* (pp. 109–138). Reston, VA: Music Educators National Conference.

Johnson, C. M., & Darrow, A. A. (1997). The effect of positive models of inclusion on band students' attitudinal statements regarding the integration of students with disabilities. *Journal of Research in Music Education, 45*(2), 173–184. doi:10.2307/3345578

Johnson, C. M., Fredrickson, W. E., Achey, C. A., & Gentry, G. (2000). *The effect of nonverbal elements of conducting on the overall evaluation of student and professional conductors.* Poster session presented at the National Biennial In-Service Conference of MENC: National Association for Music Education, Washington, DC.

Johnson, G. T. (1985). Learning from music. In G. T. Johnson (Ed.), *Becoming human through music* (pp. 53–68). Reston, VA: Music Educators National Conference.

Johnson, V. V. (2014). Preservice music teachers' social skills: Are they really prepared? *Update: Applications of Research to Music Education, 32*(2), 18–25. doi:10.1177/8755123314521035

Jones, B. D., & Parkes, K. A. (2010). The motivation of undergraduate music students: The impact of identification and talent beliefs on choosing a career in music education. *Journal of Music Teacher Education, 19*(2), 41–56. doi:10.1177/1057083709351816

Jones, S. M., & Dindia, K. (2004). A meta-analytic perspective on sex equity in the classroom. *Review of Educational Research, 74*(4), 443–471.

Jorgensen, E. R. (2003). *Transforming music education.* Bloomington: Indiana University Press.

Jorgensen, E. R. (2006). Reflections of futures for music education. *Philosophy of Music Education Review, 14*(1), 15–22.

Juchniewicz, J. (2008). *The influence of social intelligence on effective music teaching* (Unpublished doctoral dissertation). Florida State University, Tallahassee.

Juchniewicz, J. (2014). An examination of social intelligence development in preservice music teachers. *Journal of Music Teacher Education, 23*(1), 21–32. doi:10.1177/1057083713475628

Juchniewicz, J., Kelly, S. N., & Acklin, A. (2014). Rehearsal characteristics of superior band directors. *Update: Applications of Research in Music Education, 32*(2), 35–43. doi:10.1177/8755123314 521221

Kantorski, V. J. (2004). Music education majors' perceptions of their "best" K–12 teacher. *Contributions to Music Education, 31*(1), 25–47.

Kaplan, M. (1990). *The arts: A social perspective.* Cranbury, NJ: Associated University Presses.

Keene, J. A. (1987). *A history of music education in the United States.* Hanover, NH: University Press of New England.

Kelly, S. N. (1997a). An investigation of the influence of timbre on gender and instrument association. *Contributions to Music Education, 24*(1), 43–56.

Kelly, S. N. (1997b). Effects of conducting instruction on the musical performance of beginning band students. *Journal of Research in Music Education, 45*(2), 295–307. doi:10.2307/3345588

Kelly, S. N. (2000a). Sociological and musical influences of prospective undergraduate music teacher candidates. In R. R. Rideout & S. J. Paul (Eds.), *On the sociology of music education II* (pp. 121–130). Amherst: University of Massachusetts.

Kelly, S. N. (2000b). Preservice music education student fears of the internship and initial inservice teaching experiences. *Contributions to Music Education, 27*(1), 41–49.

Kelly, S. N. (2002). A sociological basis for music education. *International Journal of Music Education, 39,* 40–49.

Kelly, S. N. (2005, September). *An investigation of attractor and facilitator variables' influence on preservice teachers' decisions to teach music.* Paper presented at the 2005 Symposium on Music Teacher Education, Greensboro, NC.

Kelly, S. N. (2009). *2007–2008 twelfth grade cohort and fine arts enrollment comparison.* Retrieved from http:// flmusiced.org/dnn/Advocacy/12GradeCohortFineArtsEnrollmentComparison.aspx

Kelly, S. N. (2010). Public school supervising teachers' perceptions of skills and behaviors necessary in the development of effective music student teachers. *Bulletin of the Council for Research in Music Education, 185,* 21–32.

Kelly, S. N. (2012). John Dewey and James Mursell: Progressive educators for contemporary music education. *Visions of Research in Music Education, 21.* Retrieved from http://users.rider.edu/~vrme/

Kelly, S. N., & Heath, J. (in press). A comparison of nationally ranked high schools and their music curricula. *Update: Applications of Research in Music Education.*

Kelly, S. N., & VanWeelden, K. (2004). Connecting meaningful music experiences in a multiculutural-multimusical classroom. *Music Educators Journal, 90*(3), 35–39. doi:10.2307/3399953

Kelly-McHale, J. (2013). The influence of music teacher beliefs and practices on the expression of musical identity in an elementary general music classroom. *Journal of Research in Music Education, 61*(2), 195–216. doi:10.1177/0022429413485439

Khadaroo, S. T. (2014). As testing outcry grows, education leaders pull back on standardized tests. *Christian Science Monitor*. Retrieved from http://www.csmonitor.com/USA/Education/2014/1016/As-overtesting-outcry-grows-education-leaders-pull-back-on-standardized-tests

Killian, J. N. (1990). Effect of model characteristics on musical preference of junior high students. *Journal of Research in Music Education, 38*(2), 115–123. doi:10.2307/3344931

Killian, J. N., Dye, K. G., & Wayman, J. B. (2011, February). *Transformation of music student teachers: Five years of pre-student teaching concerns and post-student teaching perceptions.* Paper presented at the 19th International Symposium for Research in Music Behavior, Barcelona, Spain.

Kinney, D. W. (2008). Selected demographic variables, school music participation and achievement test scores of urban middle school students. *Journal of Research in Music Education, 56*(2), 145–161. doi:10.1177/0022429408322530

Kinney, D. W. (2010). Selected nonmusic predictors of urban students' decisions to enroll and persist in middle school band programs. *Journal of Research in Music Education, 56*(4), 145–161. doi:10.1177/0022429409350086

Koza, J. E. (1994). Females in 1988 middle school textbooks: An analysis of illustrations. *Journal of Research in Music Education, 42*, 145–171. doi:10.2307/3345498

Kozol, J. (1991). *Savage inequalities: Children in America's schools.* New York, NY: Crown.

Kozol, J. (2005a). Confections of apartheid: A stick-and-carrot pedagogy for the children of our inner-city poor. *Phi Delta Kappan, 87*(4), 264–275.

Kozol, J. (2005b). *The shame of the nation.* New York, NY: Three Rivers Press.

Krueger, P. J. (2000). Beginning music teachers: Will they leave the profession? *Update: Applications of Research in Music Education, 19*(1), 22–26. doi:10.1177/875512330001900105

Kuntz, T. L. (2011). High school students' participation in music activities beyond the school day. *Update: Applications of Research in Music Education, 30*(1), 23–31. doi:10.1177/8755123311418478

Labuta, J. A., & Smith, D. A. (1997). *Music education: Historical contexts and perspectives.* Upper Saddle River, NJ: Prentice Hall.

Law & Higher Education. (2010). *Equal Educational Opportunities Act (EEOA).* Retrieved from http://lawhighereducation.org/52-equal-educational-opportunities-act-eeoa.html

LeBlanc, A. (1981). Effects of style, tempo, and performing medium on children's music preference. *Journal of Research in Music Education, 29*(2), 143–156. doi:10.2307/3345023

LeBlanc, A. (1982). An interactive theory of musical preference. *Journal of Music Therapy, 19*, 28–45.

LeBlanc, A., & McCrary, J. (1983). Effect of tempo on children's music preference. *Journal of Research in Music Education, 31*(4), 283–294. doi:10.2307/3344631

LeBlanc, A., & Sherrill, C. (1986). Effect of vocal vibrato and performer's sex on children's music preference. *Journal of Research in Music Education, 34*(4), 222–237. doi:10.2307/3345258

Lee, B. (2013). *The U.S. immigration debate.* Council on Foreign Relations. Retrieved from http://www.cfr.org/immigration/us-immigration-debate/p11149

Lee, J. (2014, August 6). Schools brace for up to 50,000 migrant kids. *USA Today.* Retrieved from http://www.usatoday.com/story/news/nation-now/2014/08/06/public-schools-immigrant-children/13661353/

Legette, R. M. (1998). Casual beliefs of public school students about success and failure in music. *Journal of Research in Music Education, 46*(1), 102–111. doi:10.2307/3345763

Lentsch, M. A. (2000). *An examination of curricular and social factors influencing participation in public high school music programs* (Unpublished master's thesis). Florida State University, Tallahassee.

Levine, D. U., & Levine, R. F. (1996). *Society and education.* Boston, MA: Allyn and Bacon.

Lind, V. R. (1999). Classroom environment and Hispanic enrollment in secondary choral music programs. *Contributions to Music Education, 26*(2), 64–77.

Liske, K. L. (1999, Fall/Winter). Intellectual property rights: Guideline for fair use of electronic music in music education. *Update: Applications of Research in Music Education, 21*–25. doi:10.1177/875512339901800104

Lorah, J. A., Sanders, E. A., & Morrison, S. J. (2014). The relationship between English language learner status and music ensemble participation. *Journal of Research in Music Education, 62*(3), 234–244. doi:10.1177/0022429414542301

Lortie, D. C. (2002). *Schoolteacher* (2nd ed.). Chicago, IL: University of Chicago Press.

L'Roy, D. (1983). The development of occupational identity in undergraduate music majors. (Doctoral dissertation, North Texas State University). *Dissertation Abstracts International, 52*, 4502-A.

Lubienski, S. T., & Lubienski, C. (2005, May). A new look at public and private schools: Student background and mathematics achievement. *Phi Delta Kappan*, 696–699.

Macionis, J. J. (1997). *Sociology* (6th ed.). Upper Saddle River, NJ: Prentice Hall.

MacLeod, R. B., & Napoles, J. (2012). Preservice teachers' perceptions of teaching effectiveness during teaching episodes with positive and negative feedback. *Journal of Music Teacher Education*, *22*, 91–102. doi:10.1177/1057083711429851

Madsen, C. K. (Ed.). (2000). *Vision 2020: The Housewright symposium on the future of music education*. Reston, VA: Music Educators National Conference.

Madsen, C. K., & Duke, R. A. (1993). Selection and development of prospective music teachers. *Journal of Music Teacher Education*, *3*(1), 5–11. doi:10.1177/105708379300300103

Madsen, C. K., & Hancock, C. B. (2002). Support for music education: A case study of issues concerning teacher retention and attrition. *Journal of Research in Music Education*, *50*(1), 6–19. doi:10.2307/3345689

Madsen, C. K., & Kaiser, K. A. (1999). Pre-internship fears of student teachers, *Update: Applications of Research in Music Education*, *17*(2), 27–32.

Madsen, C. K., & Kelly, S. N. (2002). First remembrances of wanting to become a music teacher. *Journal of Research in Music Education*, *50*(4), 323–332. doi:10.2307/3345358

Madsen, C. K., & Kuhn, T. L. (1994). *Contemporary music education* (2nd ed.). Raleigh, NC: Contemporary.

Madsen, C. K., & Madsen, C. H. (1981). *Teaching/discipline: A positive approach for educational development* (4th ed.). Raleigh, NC: Contemporary.

Madsen, C. K., Stanley, J. M., Byo, J. L., & Cassidy, J. W. (1989). Assessment of effective teaching by instrumental music student teachers and experts. *Update: Applications of Research in Music Education*, *10*, 20–24. doi:10.1177/875512339201000206

Madsen, C. K., Stanley, J. M., & Cassidy, J. W. (1989). Demonstration and recognition of high/low contrasts in teacher intensity. *Journal of Research in Music Education*, *37*(2), 85–92. doi:10.2307/3344700

Madsen, K. (2003). The effect of accuracy of instruction, teacher delivery, and student attentiveness on musicians' evaluation of teacher effectiveness. *Journal of Research in Music Education*, *51*(1), 38–50. doi:10.2307/3345647

Maehr, M. L., Pintrich, P. R., & Linnenbrink, E. A. (2002). Motivation and achievement. In R. Colwell & C. Richardson (Eds.), *New handbook of research on music teaching and learning* (pp. 348–372). New York, NY: Oxford University Press.

Marder, M. (2012). Measuring teacher quality with value-added modeling. *Kappa Delta Pi Record*, *48*(4), 156–161.

Mark, M. L. (1996). *Contemporary music education* (3rd ed.). New York, NY: Schirmer Books.

Mark, M. L. (2008). *Music education: Source readings from ancient Greece to today* (3rd ed.). New York, NY: Routledge.

Mark, M. L., & Madura, P. (2010). *Music education in your hands: An introduction for future teachers*. New York, NY: Routledge.

Marsh, H. W. (1990). Influences of internal and external frames of reference on the formation of math and English self-concepts. *Journal of Educational Psychology*, *82*, 107–116.

Marx, K., & Engels, F. (1845). Manifesto of the communist party. In R. C. Tucker (Ed.), *The Marx-Engels reader* (pp. 331–362). New York, NY: Norton.

Marzano, R. J. (2003). *What works in schools: Translating research into action*. Alexandria, VA: Association for Supervision and Curriculum Development.

Maslow, A. H. (1968). *Toward a psychology of being* (2nd ed.). New York, NY: Van Nostrand.

Maslow, A. H. (1970). *Motivation and personality* (2nd ed.). New York, NY: Harper and Row.

McCarthy, M. (2002). Social and cultural contexts of music teaching and learning: An introduction. In R. Colwell & C. Richardson (Eds.), *The new handbook of research on music teaching and learning* (pp. 563–565). New York, NY: Oxford University Press.

McCormick, T. M. (1994). *Creating the nonsexist classroom: A multicultural approach*. New York, NY: Teachers College Press.

McKoy, C. L. (2013). Effects of selected demographic variables on music student teachers' self-reported cross-cultural competence. *Journal of Research in Music Education*, *60*(4), 375–394. doi:10.1177/0022429412463398

McWhirter, J. J., McWhirter, B. T., McWhirter, A. M., & McWhirter, E. H. (1998). *At-risk youth: A comprehensive response* (2nd ed.). Albany, NY: Brooks/Cole.

Mead, G. H. (1934). *Mind, self, and society*. Chicago, IL: University of Chicago Press.

Mehr, S. A. (2014). Music in the home: New evidence for an intergenerational link. *Journal of Research in Music Education, 62*(1), 78–88. doi:10.1177/0022429413520008

Meier, K. J., Stewart, J., & England, R. E. (1989). *Race, class, and education: The politics of second generation discrimination*. Madison: University of Wisconsin Press.

Merriam, A. P. (1964). *The anthropology of music*. Chicago, IL: Northwestern University Press.

Merrow, J. (1999). The teacher shortage: Wrong diagnosis, phony cures. *Education Weekly, 19*(6).

Miksza, P., & Gault, B. M. (2014). Classroom music experiences of the U.S. elementary school children: An analysis of the Early Childhood Longitudinal Study of 1998–1999. *Journal of Research in Music Education, 62*(1), 4–17. doi:10.1177/0022429413519822

Minear, C. (1999). [*Demographics and diversity*]. Unpublished raw data.

Morrison, K. (1995). *Marx, Durkheim, Weber: Formation of modern social thought*. London: SAGE.

Morrison, S. J. (1998). A comparison of preference responses of white and African-American students to musical versus musical/visual stimuli. *Journal of Research in Music Education, 46*(2), 208–222. doi:10.2307/3345624

Morrison, S. J. (2001). The school ensemble: A culture of our own. *Music Educators Journal, 88*(2), 24–28. doi:10.2307/3399738

Morrow, R. D. (1991). The challenge of Southeast Asian parental involvement. *Principal, 70*(3), 20.

Mueller, J. H. (1958). Music and education: A sociological approach. In N. B. Henry (Ed.), *Basic concepts in music education* (pp. 88–122). Chicago, IL: University of Chicago Press.

Muller, C. (1998). Gender differences in parental involvement and adolescents' mathematical achievement. *Sociology of Education, 71*(4), 336–356.

Mursell, J. L. (1934). *Human values in music education*. San Francisco, CA: Silver Burdett.

Mursell, J. L. (1943). *Music in American schools*. New York, NY: Silver Burdett.

Mursell, J. L. (1948). *Education for music growth*. New York, NY: Ginn.

Music Educators National Conference. (1994). *National standards for arts education*. Reston, VA: Author.

Music Educators National Conference. (2005). *Membership survey*. Retrieved from http://www.menc.org/

Music Educators National Conference. (2006). Principals say music programs affect graduation. *Music Educators Journal, 14*(2), 16.

Napoles, J., & MacLeod, R. B. (2013). The influences of teacher delivery and student progress on preservice teachers' perceptions of teaching effectiveness. *Journal of Research in Music Education, 61*(3), 249–261. doi:10.1177/0022429413497234

National Assessment of Educational Progress. (2008). *Arts: Music & Visual Arts*. Retrieved from http://nces.ed.gov/nationsreportcard/pdf/main2008/2009488_1.pdf

National Assessment of Education Progress. (2011). *Achievement gaps: How Hispanic and White students in public schools perform in mathematics and reading on the National Assessment of Educational Progress*. Retrieved from http://nces.ed.gov/nationsreportcard/pdf/studies/2011459.pdf

National Association for Music Education. (2014a). *National core arts standards*. Retrieved from http://www.nafme.org/the-new-national-core-music-standards-are-out-and-heres-nafme-wants-you-to-know/

National Association for Music Education. (2014b). *National core arts standards: A conceptual framework for arts learning*. Retrieved from http://www.nationalartsstandards.org/sites/default/files/NCCAS%20%20Conceptual%20Framework_2.pdf

National Association for Music Education. (2014c). *Take action*. Retrieved from http://www.nafme.org/take-action/

National Association for Music Education. (2014d). *The value and quality of arts education*. Retrieved from http://www.nafme.org/about/position-statements/the-value-and-quality-of-arts-education-position-statement/the-value-and-quality-of-arts-education/

National Association of Music Merchants. (2009). *New Gallup survey by NAMM reflects majority of Americans agree with many benefits of playing musical instruments*. Retrieved from http://www.namm.org/news/press-releases/new-gallup-survey-namm-reflects-majority-americans

National Association of Schools of Music. (2014). *Standards/handbook*. Retrieved from http://nasm.arts-accredit.org/index.jsp?page=Standards-Handbook

National Association of Social Workers. (2015). *Social justice*. Retrieved from https://www.socialworkers. org/pressroom/features/issue/peace.asp

National Center for Education Statistics. (1999). *The conditions of education*. Washington, DC: U.S. Department of Education.

National Center for Education Statistics. (2001). *Educational achievement and black-white inequality*. Washington, DC: U.S. Department of Education.

National Center for Education Statistics. (2003a). *CCD Quick Facts*. Retrieved from http://nces.ed.gov/ccd/quickfacts.html

National Center for Education Statistics. (2003b). *Trends in the use of school choice, 1993–1999*. Washington, DC: U.S. Department of Education.

National Center for Education Statistics. (2006). *Comparing private schools and public schools using hierarchical linear modeling*. Washington, DC: U.S. Department of Education.

National Center for Education Statistics. (2008). *1.5 million homeschooled students in the United States in 2007*. Washington, DC: U.S. Department of Education.

National Center for Education Statistics. (2012). *Arts education in the public schools, 1999–2000 and 2009–10*. Retrieved from nces.ed.gov/pubs2012/2012014_2.pdf

National Center for Education Statistics. (2013a). *Fast facts: Students with disabilities*. Retrieved from http://nces.ed.gov/fastfacts/display.asp?id=64

National Center for Education Statistics. (2013b). *Fast facts: Educational institutions*. Retrieved from http://nces.ed.gov/fastfacts/display.asp?id=84

National Center for Education Statistics. (2013c). *The condition of education*. Retrieved from http://nces.ed.gov/programs/coe/indicator_cgc.asp

National Center for Education Statistics. (2014a). *The conditions of education*. Washington, DC: U.S. Department of Education.

National Center for Education Statistics. (2014b). *Fast facts: Dropout rates*. Retrieved from http://nces.ed.gov/fastfacts/display.asp?id=16

National Center for Education Statistics. (2014c). *Fast facts: Pupil/teacher ratio*. Retrieved from http://nces.ed.gov/fastfacts/display.asp?id=28

National Center for Education Statistics. (2014d): *Fast facts: Salary*. Retrieved from http://nces.ed.gov/fastfacts/display.asp?id=28

National Commission on Teaching and America's Future. (1996). *What matters most: Teaching for America's future*. Washington, DC: U.S. Department of Education.

National Conference for Community and Justice. (1994). *Taking America's pulse: A summary report of the National Conference Survey on Intergroup Relations*. New York, NY: Author.

National Conference for Community and Justice. (2008). *Taking America's pulse III*. Retrieved from http://www.nccj.org/nccj/nccj.nsf/articleall/4537?opendocument&1#874

National Conference for Community and Justice. (2011). *The "yes" campaign*. Retrieved from https://www.nccj.org/sites/default/files/uploaded_documents/yes_conference_report_2012.pdf

National Dropout Prevention Center/Network. (2014). *Why students drop out*. Retrieved from http://www.dropoutprevention.org/statistics/quick-facts/why-students-drop-out

National Education Association. (2007). *Great public schools for every child*. Retrieved from http://www.nea.org/index.html

National Education Commission on Time and Learning. (1994). *Prisoners of time*. Washington, DC: U.S. Government Printing Office.

National Forum on Educational Statistics. (2006). *Forum guide to elementary/secondary virtual education*. Retrieved from http://nces.ed.gov/pubs2006/2006803.pdf

National School Boards Association. (2007). *Florida's pay-for-performance program will tie teacher pay directly to student performance on standardized tests*. Retrieved from http://www.nsba.org/site/doc_cosa.asp?TRACKID=&CID=445&DID=38249

National Standards for Arts Education. (1994). Reston, VA: Music Educators National Conference.

Nettl, B. (1956). *Music in primitive cultures*. Cambridge, MA: Harvard University Press.

Nierman, G.E., & Veak, M.H. (1997). Effect of selected recruiting strategies on beginning instrumentalists' participation decisions. *Journal of Research in Music Education*, *45*(3), 380–389. doi:10.2307/3345533

No Child Left Behind Act. (2001). Pub. L. No. 107–110. Washington, DC: U.S. Government Printing Office.

Oakes, J., & Lipton, M. (1999). *Teaching to change the world.* Boston, MA: McGraw-Hill College.

Olsen, L. (1997). *Made in America: Immigrant students in our public schools.* New York, NY: New Press.

Ozimek, A. (2014). The data shows teachers are still highly respected. *Forbes.* Retrieved from http://www.forbes.com/sites/modeledbehavior/2014/06/14/teachers-highly-respected/

Paige, R. (2004). *Federal education grants aimed at making children healthier decreasing childhood obesity.* Retrieved from http://www.ed.gov/news/pressreleases/2004/09/09282004.html

Papandrea, M.R. (2012). Social media, public school teachers, and the first amendment. *North Carolina Law Review, 90,* 1597–1642.

Paul, S., Teachout, D., Sullivan, J., Kelly, S., Bauer, W., & Raiber, M. (2001). Authentic context learning activities in instrumental music teacher education. *Journal of Research in Music Education, 49,* 136–146. doi:10.2307/3345865

Paul, S.J., Teachout, D.J., Kelly, S.N., Bauer, W.I., & Raiber, M.A. (2002). Role development activities and initial teaching performance. *Contributions to Music Education, 29*(1), 85–95.

Peikof, L. (1993). *Objectivism: The philosophy of Ayn Rand.* New York, NY: Meridian.

Pemberton, C.A. (1985). *Lowell Mason: His life and work.* Ann Arbor: University of Michigan Research Press.

Pew Research. (2014a). *Emerging and developing economies much more optimistic than rich countries about the future.* Retrieved from http://www.pewglobal.org/2014/10/09/emerging-and-developing-economies-much-more-optimistic-than-rich-countries-about-the-future/

Pew Research. (2014b). *Public sees religion's influence waning.* Retrieved from http://www.pewforum.org/2014/09/22/public-sees-religions-influence-waning-2/

Pflederer, M. (1967). Conservation laws applied to the development of musical intelligence. *Journal of Research in Music Education, 5*(3), 215–223. doi:10.2307/3343862

Piaget, J. (1950). *The psychology of intelligence.* New York, NY: Routledge.

Pintrich, P.R., & Schunk, D.H. (1996). *Motivation in education: Theory, research, and applications.* Columbus, OH: Merrill.

Plato. (1995). *Plato's Republic, Book I.* Commentary by G.R. Rose. Bryn Mawr, PA: Bryn Mawr College.

Phillips, D., & Zimmerman, M. (1990). The developmental course of perceived competence and incompetence among competent children. In R. Sternberg & J. Kolligian (Eds.), *Competence Considered* (pp. 41–66). New Haven, CT: Yale University Press.

Pole, J.R. (1993). *The pursuit of equality in American history* (2nd ed.). Berkeley: University of California Press.

Praxis. (2015). *Home page.* Retrieved from http://www.ets.org/praxis/

Price, H.E. (1983). The effect of conductor academic task presentation, conductor reinforcement, and ensemble practice on performers' musical achievement, attentiveness, and attitude. *Journal of Research in Music Education, 31*(4), 245–257. doi:10.2307/3344628

Radocy, R.E., & Boyle, J.D. (2003). *Psychological foundations of musical behavior* (4th ed.). Springfield, IL: Charles C. Thomas.

Raiber, M., & Teachout, D. (2014). *The journey from music student to teacher: A professional approach.* New York, NY: Routledge.

Rand, A. (1996). *Atlas shrugged.* New York, NY: Signet Books. (Reprinted from original publication by the author, 1943)

Rand, A. (2005). *The fountainhead.* New York, NY: Penguin Books. (Reprinted from original publication by Bobbs-Merrill, 1943)

Ravitch, D. (2010). *The death and life of the great American school system: How testing and choice are undermining education.* New York, NY: Basic Books.

Raywid, M.A. (1989). Separate classes for the gifted? A skeptical look. *Educational Perspectives, 26*(1), 41–48.

Regelski, T.A. (2007). *Critical theory as a foundation for critical thinking in music education.* Retrieved from http://www-usr.rider.edu/~vrme/v6n1/vision/regelski_2005.htm

Reimer, B. (2003). *A philosophy of music education* (3rd ed.). Englewood Cliffs, NJ: Prentice Hall.

Renzetti, C., & Curran, D. (2000). *Social problems: Society in crisis* (5th ed.). Boston, MA: Allyn and Bacon.

Report of the National Commission on Teaching and America's Future. (1996). *What matters most: Teaching for America's future.* New York, NY: Author.

Riley, P. E. (2006). Including composition in middle school band: Effects on achievement, performance, and attitude. *Update: Applications of Research in Music Education, 25*(1), 28–38. doi:10.1177/875512330 60250010104

Roberts, B. A. (1991). Music teacher education as identity construction. *International Journal of Music Education, 18*, 30–39.

Roberts, B. (2000). The sociologist's snare: Identity construction and socialization in music. *International Journal of Music Education, 35*, 54–58. doi:10.1177/025576140003500116

Robinson, M. (2014). *What is social justice?* Retrieved from http://gjs.appstate.edu/social-justice-and-human-rights/what-social-justice

Robinson, C. R. (2000, June). *Choral students' assessments of novice choral conductors.* Poster session presented at the National Biennial In-Service Conference of MENC: The National Association for Music Education, Washington, DC.

Robinson, N. R. (2000). *The "at-risk" student: Music teachers' perceptions, attitudes, and effective teaching strategies* (Unpublished doctoral dissertation). Florida State University, Tallahassee.

Robinson, N. R. (2012). Preservice music teachers' employment preferences: Consideration factors. *Journal of Research in Music Education, 60*(3), 294–309. doi:10.1177/0022429412454723

Rohwer, D., & Henry, W. (2004). University teachers' perceptions of requisite skills and characteristics of effective music teachers. *Journal of Music Teacher Education, 13*(2), 18–26. doi:10.1177/1057083704013 0020104

Ross, J., & Bell, P. (2014). School is over for the summer. So is the era of majority white U.S. public schools. *National Journal.* Retrieved from http://www.nationaljournal.com/next-america/education/school-is-over-for-the-summer-so-is-the-era-of-majority-white-u-s-public-schools-20140701

Rueda, R., & Stillman, J. (2012). The 21st century teacher: A cultural perspective. *Journal of Teacher Education, 63*(4), 245–253. doi:10.1177/0022487104263977

Russell, J. (2012). The occupational identity of in-service secondary music educators: Formative interpersonal interactions and activities. *Journal of Research in Music Education, 60*, 145–165. doi:10.1177/0022429412445208

Sadker, M., & Sadker, D. (1995). *Failing at fairness: How America's schools cheat girls.* New York, NY: Scribner.

Salvador, K. (2013). Inclusion of people with special needs in choral settings: A review of applicable research and professional literature. *Update: Applications of Research in Music Education, 31*, 37–44. doi:10.1177/8755123312473760

Scheib, J. W. (2003). Role stress in the professional life of the school music teacher: A collective case study. *Journal of Research in Music Education, 51*(2), 124–136. doi:10.2307/3345846

Schmidt, C. P. (2005). Relations among motivation, performance achievement, and music experience variables in secondary instrumental music students. *Journal of Research in Music Education, 53*(2), 134–147. doi:10.1177/002242940505300204

Schultz, T. W. (2000). Investment in human capital. In R. Arum & I. R. Beattie (Eds.), *The structure of schooling: Readings in the sociology of education* (pp. 46–55). Boston, MA: McGraw-Hill.

Schwadron, A. A. (1967). *Aesthetics: Dimensions for music education.* Washington, DC: Music Educators National Conference.

Schwandt, T. (1998). Constructivists, interpretivist approaches to human inquiry. In N. Denzin & Y. Lincoln (Eds.), *The landscape of qualitative research: Theories and issues* (pp. 221–259). Thousand Oaks, CA: SAGE.

Seidel, A. (2014). The teacher dropout crisis. *NPREd.* Retrieved from http://www.npr.org/blogs/ed/2014/07/18/332343240/the-teacher-dropout-crisis?utm_source=facebook.com&utm_medium=social&utm_campaign=npr&utm_term=nprnews&utm_content=20140719#mainContent

Serow, R., Castelli, P., & Castelli, V. (2000). *Social foundations of American education* (2nd ed.). Durham, NC: Carolina Academic Press.

Shaw, J. (2012). The skin that we sing: Culturally responsive choral music education. *Music Educators Journal, 98*(4), 75–81. doi:10.1177/0027432112443561

Shulman, L.S. (1987). Knowledge and teaching: Foundations of the new reform. *Harvard Educational Review, 19*(2), 4–14.

Siebenaler, D.J. (1999). Student song preference in the elementary music class. *Journal of Research in Music Education, 47*(3), 213–233. doi:10.2307/3345780

Silveira, J.M. (2014). The perception of pacing in a music appreciation class and its relationship to teacher effectiveness and teacher intensity. *Journal of Research in Music Education, 62*(3), 302–318. doi:10.1177/0022429414542978

Simpson, M. (2010). *Social networking nightmares.* National Education Association. Retrieved from http://www.nea.org/home/38324.htm

Sims, W. (1992). Effects of attending an in-school opera performance of attitudes of fourth-, fifth-, and sixth-grade students. *Council for Research in Music Education, 114,* 47–58.

Skadsem, J.A. (1997). Effect of conductor verbalization, dynamic markings, conductor gesture, and choir dynamic level on singers' dynamic responses. *Journal of Research in Music Education, 45*(4), 509–520. doi:10.2307/3345419

Skinner, B.F. (1974). *About behaviorism.* New York, NY: Vintage Books.

Sloboda, J.A. (1985). *The musical mind.* New York, NY: Oxford Press.

Small, C. (1997). Musicking: A ritual in social space. In R. Rideout (Ed.), *On the sociology of music education* (pp. 1–12). Norman: University of Oklahoma School of Music.

Smith, T.M., & Ingersoll, R.M. (2004). What are the effects of induction and mentoring on beginning teacher turnover? *American Educational Research Journal, 41*(3), 681–714. doi:10.3102/00028312041003681

Spearman, C.E. (2000). How will societal and technological changes affect the teaching of music? In C.K. Madsen (Ed.), *Vision 2020: The Housewright symposium on the future of music education* (pp. 153–184). Reston, VA: Music Educators National Conference.

Spring, J. (1988). *Conflict of interest.* New York, NY: Longman.

Spring, J. (1990). *The American school: 1642–1992* (2nd ed.). New York, NY: Longman.

Spring, J. (2002). *American education* (10th ed.). New York, NY: McGraw-Hill.

Spring, J. (2006). *American education* (12th ed.). New York, NY: McGraw-Hill.

Spring, J. (2014). *American education* (16th ed.). New York, NY: McGraw-Hill.

STEAM. (2010). *Science, technology, engineering, arts, mathematics.* Retrieved from http://steam-notstem.com/

Stewart, C. (1991). *Who takes music? Investigating access to high school music as a function of social and school factors* (Doctoral dissertation). Available from ProQuest Dissertations and Theses database.

Swift, D.W. (1976). *American education: A sociological view.* Boston, MA: Houghton Mifflin.

Tallahassee Democrat. (2006, December 1). Stay in school, win a car. p. 7A.

Task Force on Teaching as a Profession. (1986). *A nation prepared: Teachers for the 21st century.* New York, NY: Carnegie Corporation of New York.

Teach for America. (2014). *Home page.* Retrieved from https://www.teachforamerica.org/

Teachout, D.J. (1997). Preservice and experienced teachers' opinions of skills and behaviors important to successful music teaching. *Journal of Research in Music Education, 45*(1), 41–50. doi:10.2307/3345464

Teachout, D.J. (2001). The relationship between personality and the teaching effectiveness of music student teachers. *Psychology of Music, 29,* 179–192.

Thayer, V.T., & Levit, M. (1966). *The role of the school in American society* (2nd ed.). New York, NY: Dodd, Mead.

Thorndike, E.L. (1903/2007). *Educational psychology.* New York, NY: Thorndike Press.

Toppo, G., Amos, D., Gillum, J., & Upton, J. (2011, March 7). When scores seem too good to be true. *USA Today,* pp. A1, A6–A7.

Toppo, G., & Overberg, P. (2014, November 26). Anger, resentment over school diversity. *USA Today,* pp. B1–B2.

Tyack, D., & Hansot, E. (1982). *Managers of virtue: Public school leadership in America, 1820–1980.* New York, NY: Basic Books.

USA Today. (2006). Dropouts say their schools expected too little of them. Retrieved from http://www.usatoday.com/news/education/2006–03–01-dropouts-expectations_x.htm

U.S. Census Bureau. (2012). *U.S. religions census 2010: Summary findings*. Retrieved from http://www.rcms2010.org/press_release/ACP%2020120501.pdf

U.S. Census Bureau. (2013). *International migration is projected to become primary driver of U.S. population growth for first time in nearly two centuries*. Retrieved from http://www.census.gov/newsroom/releases/archives/population/cb13–89.html

U.S. Constitution, Amendment I. (1791).

U.S. Department of Agriculture. (2010). *Schools meals: Healthy hunger-free kids act*. Retrieved from http://www.fns.usda.gov/school-meals/healthy-hunger-free-kids-act

U.S. Department of Education. (1997). *History: Twenty-five years of progress in educating children with disabilities through IDEA*. Retrieved from http://www.ed.gov/policy/speced/leg/idea/history.pdf

U.S. Department of Education. (2000). *The state of charter schools: Fourth year report*. Washington, DC: Office of Educational Research and Improvement.

U.S. Department of Education. (2002a). *National board for professional teaching standards*. Arlington, VA.

U.S. Department of Education. (2002b). *Twenty-fourth annual report to Congress on the implementation of the Individuals with Disabilities Education Act*. Washington, DC: U.S. Government Printing Office.

U.S. Department of Education. (2009). *Race to the top: Executive summary*. Retrieved from https://www2.ed.gov/programs/racetothetop/executive-summary.pdf

U.S. Department of Education. (2014a). *Department of Education projects public schools will be "majority-minority" this fall*. Retrieved from http://www.pewresearch.org/fact-tank/2014/08/18/u-s-public-schools-expected-to-be-majority-minority-starting-this-fall/

U.S. Department of Education. (2014b). *Science, technology, engineering and math: Education for global leadership*. Retrieved from http://www.ed.gov/stem

U.S. Department of Health and Human Services. (2001). *The surgeon general's call to action to prevent and decrease overweight and obesity 2001*. Washington, DC: Office of the Surgeon General.

U.S. Department of Labor. (2012). *Number of jobs held, labor market activity, and earnings growth among the youngest baby-boomers: Results from a longitudinal study*. Washington, DC: Bureau of Labor Statistics. Retrieved from http://www.bls.gov/news.release/pdf/nlsoy.pdf

U.S. Department of Labor. (2014). *Earnings and unemployment by educational attainment*. Washington, DC: Bureau of Labor Statistics. Retrieved from http://www.bls.gov/emp/ep_chart_001.htm

Valsiner, J. (1989). *Human development and culture: The social nature of personality and its study*. Lexington, MA: Lexington Books.

VanWeelden, K. (2002). Relationship between perceptions of conducting effectiveness and ensemble performance. *Journal of Research in Music Education, 50*(2), 165–176. doi:10.2307/3345820

VanWeelden, K., & Whipple, J. (2014). Music educators' perceived effectiveness of inclusion. *Journal of Research in Music Education, 62*(2), 148–160. doi:10.1177/0022429414530563

Varian, H., & Lyman, P. (2003). *How much information?* UC Berkeley School of Information Management & Services. Retrieved from http://www2.sims.berkeley.edu/research/projects/how-much-info/

Vat-Chromy, J. V. (2010). *Safety, identity, transmission, and enculturation: An investigation of four formative aspects of choral cultures on music majors in undergraduate audition and non-audition collegiate choirs* (Unpublished doctoral dissertation). Florida State University, Tallahassee.

Veenman, S. (1984). Perceived problems of beginning teachers. *Review of Educational Research, 54*(2), 143–178.

Vygotsky, L. S. (1978). *Mind and society: The development of higher mental processes*. Cambridge, MA: Harvard University Press.

Walker, L. M., & Hamann, D. L. (1995). Minority recruitment: The relationship between high school students' perceptions about music participation and recruitment strategies. *Council for Research in Music Education, 124*, 24–38.

Waller, W. (1965). *The sociology of teaching*. New York, NY: John Wiley and Sons.

Wallin, N. L., Merker, B., & Brown, S. (Eds.). (2000). *The origins of music*. Cambridge, MA: MIT Press.

Wayman, V. E. (2005). The meaning of music education experience to middle school general music students. *Dissertation Abstracts International, 66*(7), 2526.

Weber, M. (1918). Science as a vocation. In H. H. Gerth & C. Wright Mills (Eds.), *Max Weber: Essays on sociology* (pp. 129–156). New York, NY: Oxford Press.

Weber, M. (2000). The "rationalization" of education and training. In R. Arum & I. R. Beattie (Eds.), *The structure of schooling: Readings in the sociology of education* (pp. 16–18). Boston, MA: McGraw-Hill.

Weiner B. (1974). *Achievement motivation.* Morristown, NJ: General Learning Press.

Weiner, B. (1979). A theory of motivation for some classroom experiences. *Journal of Educational Psychology, 71*, 3–25.

Weiner, B. (1992). *Human motivation: Metaphors, theories, and research.* Newbury Park, CA: SAGE.

West, C. (2012). Teaching music in an era of high-stakes testing and budget reductions. *Arts Education Policy Review, 113*, 75–79.

Whitaker, J. A., Orman, E. K., & Yarbrough, C. (2014). Characteristics of "music education" videos posted on YouTube. *Update: Application of Research in Music Education, 33*(1), 49–56. doi:10.1177/8755123314540662

Wiggins, J. (2015). *Teaching for musical understanding* (3rd ed.). New York, NY: Oxford University Press.

Wilson, S. J., & Wales, R. J. (1995). An exploration of children's musical compositions. *Journal of Research in Music Education, 43*(2), 94–111. doi:10.2307/3345672

Woodford, P. G. (1997). Transfer in music as social and reconstructive inquiry. In R. Rideout (Ed.), *On the sociology of music education* (pp. 43–54). Norman: University of Oklahoma School of Music.

Woodford, P. G. (2005). *Democracy and music education.* Bloomington: Indiana University Press.

Woody, R. H. (1994). Copyright law and sound recordings. *Music Educators Journal, 80*(6), 29–32. doi:10.2307/3398708

Woolfolk, A. E. (1998). *Educational psychology* (7th ed.). Boston, MA: Allyn and Bacon.

Yarbrough, C. (1975). Effects of magnitude of conductor behavior on students in selected mixed choruses. *Journal of Research in Music Education, 23*(2), 134–146. doi:10.2307/3345286

Zdzinski, S. F. (1992). Relationships among parental involvement, musical aptitude, and musical achievement of instrumental music students. *Journal of Research in Music Education, 40*(2), 114–125. doi:10.2307/3345561

Zdzinski, S. F. (1996). Parental involvement, selected student attributes, and learning outcomes in instrumental music. *Journal of Research in Music Education, 44*(1), 34–48. doi:10.2307/3345412

Zernike, K. (2002, August 23). Georgia school board requires balance of evolution and Bible. *New York Times.* Retrieved from http://www.nytimes.com/2002/08/23/education/23EVOL.html

Zuckerman, M. B. (2011, September 27). Why math and science education means more jobs. *US News & World Report.* Retrieved from http://www.usnews.com/opinion/articles/2011/09/27/why-math-and-science-education-means-more-jobs

Index

Abeles, Harold 76, 78, 99, 103
Abril, Carlos 9, 51, 81, 83, 103, 104
Achey, Carol 111
achievement gap 68, 82–3
Acklin, Amy 111, 114
Adamek, Mary 69, 76, 79, 106
Adderley, Cecil 36, 80, 103, 104, 116
Adorno, Theodor 24
aesthetics 22; theory 22, 23, 39
Albert, Daniel 104
Allsup, Randall 83
Alwin, Duane 65, 66, 67, 71
American Association of State Colleges and
    Universities 122
American Educational Research Association 83
American Federation of Teachers 123, 129
American Music Conference 58
American Psychological Association 69
Amos, Dennis 51
Arum, Richard 33
Asmus, Edward 80, 108
Atlas Shrugged 21
at-risk students 79
attribution theory 107–8
Austin, James 81, 82, 97, 98, 103
Ayn Rand Institute 21, 22

Bakan, Michael 10
Ballantine, Jeanne 3, 11, 15, 16, 17, 19, 20, 21, 30,
    63, 64, 65, 66, 68, 69, 70, 71, 104, 105, 114, 118,
    136, 137
Bandura, Albert 88, 106
Banks, Cherry 7, 8, 9, 10
Banks, James 7, 8, 9, 10, 62
Bannerman, Julie 51
Bauer, William 112, 122
Bay Psalm Book 47
Bazan, Dale 131
Beattie, Irene 33
Beegle, Amy 103
Bell, Peter 7
The Bell Curve 68
Bell-Robertson, Catherine 112
Bergee, Martin 96, 120
Berger, Peter 19

Berlyne, David 22
Bernstein, Basil 10, 32
Berry, Barnett 127
Berz, William 36, 80, 103, 104, 116
Birge, Edward 47, 48, 49, 50, 119
Blacking, John 60, 76
Blocher, Larry 37
Bloom, Benjamin 92, 93, 94
Boardman, Eunice 86, 87, 116
Boswell, J. 103, 105, 116
Bourdieu, Pierre 32, 33
Bower, Gordon 87
Bowles, Chelcy 77
Bowles, Samuel 33
Boyd, Donald 127
Boyle, David 51, 52, 53, 54, 57, 77, 87, 97, 98, 99,
    100
Brand, Manny 75, 76, 77, 99
Brittin, Ruth 100
Brown, Steven 52, 53, 54, 55
Bruner, Jerome 91, 92
bullying 83
Burnett, Gary 64
Burrack, Frederick 131
Bushaw, William 28, 42
Byo, James 108, 111

Cahill, R. 83
Caine, Geoffrey 91
Caine, Renate 91
Calderon, Valerie 28, 42
Calhoun, Craig 23
Callaghan, Jennifer 24
Campbell, D. 74
Campbell, Patricia 10, 103
Carey, K. 68, 71, 72, 81
Cartledge, Gwendolyn 10, 104
Cassidy, Jane 108, 110, 111
Castelli, Perry 46, 63, 73, 126, 130, 132, 133, 135
Castelli, Vivian 46, 63, 73, 126, 130, 132, 133, 135
Cauley, K. 96
Center for Disease Control and Prevention 31
Chinn, Philip 4, 5, 7, 8, 9, 12, 65, 68
Chipman, Shelby 78, 80
Choate, Robert 50

Ciskszentmihalyi, M. 106
Civil Rights Act 66
classroom 112; characteristics of 113–15;
    management of 115–16
Clifford, M. M. 110, 111
Cofer, Shane 111
Coffman, Don 106, 120
Cohen-Vogel, L. 127
Coleman, James 33, 64, 68, 71, 71, 84
common core 51, 63, 125
common schools 48
common school model 74, 75
Compulsory Education Act 133
conflict theory 18, 19, 32
Connell, Claire 103
conservation 90
constructivism 19, 90
Conswella, J. 66
Conway, Colleen 112, 113
Cook, Gary 20
Cooley, Charles 20, 96
Cooper, H. 66
Copyright Act of 1976, 134
Council on Foreign Relations 7
Cox Patricia 122
Cranmore, Jeff 134
Cremin, Lawrence 48
critical theory 23, 24
culture 3, 7, 8, 9, 10, 11, 40, 53, 54, 67, 76, 79,
    100, 103, 104, 114, 115, 119;
    characteristics of 8, 11, 12, 114; symbols
    of 3, 20
Curan, Daniel 64, 65, 66, 67, 73
Custodero, Lori 76, 77, 97, 99

Darling-Hammond, Linda 29, 63, 64, 68, 71, 71,
    83, 127, 128
Darrow, Alice-Ann 69, 70, 76, 79
Daugherty, Elza 131, 132, 135
Deisler, Anne 80
DeLorenzo, Lisa 112, 113
Delzell, Judith 76, 78
Demorest, Steven 100, 120
Dewey, John 15, 20, 22, 38, 63, 109
Dillon, Sam 7
Dindia, Kathryn 66, 67, 71
DiPerna, Paul 42
discrimination 65, 133
diverse learners 69–70
Draves, Tami 112
Drew, Clifford 69, 70
Droe, Kevin 109
dropout rates 51
Duke, Robert 37, 77, 112
Durkeim, Emile 17, 18
Dworkin, Anthony 127, 130
Dye, Kevin 110, 122

Ebie, Brian 76, 78, 80
education 3, 4, 5, 17, 18, 20, 21, 22, 30, 31,
    40; definition 30–2; equality of opportunity
    62, 70, 78, 83, 84; models of equality 62–4;
    instructional concept 38, 39; process-orientated
    38–9; product-oriented 28, 32, 33, 34, 35, 36,
    37, 38–9
Education for All Handicapped Children Act 70,
    79, 83
Education Week 83
Egan, Winston 69, 70
Einstein, Albert 28
Elementary and Secondary Education Act 83
Elliott, David 24, 25, 39
Elpus, Kenneth 81, 83, 103, 104, 131
El Sistema USA, 82, 125, 127
enculturation 10–12, 13, 54
England, Robert 63, 65, 66, 68
Engles, Friedrich 18, 19
Equal Education Opportunities Act 63
Erickson, Frederick 8
Erikson, Erik 94, 95, 96
Estrich, Susan 67
ethnicity 67–9, 76, 78–9, 98, 99, 100, 103
Etzkorn, Peter 12

family 65, 76; influence of 65–6, 76–7
Feinberg, Walter 11, 12, 63
Feller, Brian 74
Fennell, Frederick 50
Figlio, David 41
First Amendment 133
Fitzpatrick, Kate 76, 80, 104
Florida Department of Education 35, 128
Flowers, Patricia 77
folkway 8
Fossey, Richard 134
The Fountainhead 21
Fourteenth Amendment 133
Fredrickson, William 111
Friedman Foundation for Educational Choice 42
Froehlich, Hildegard 1, 12, 36, 110, 122, 131
Fulcher, James 7, 8, 16, 17, 18, 66
functionalist theory 17, 32
*The Funding Gap 2004: Many States Still
    Shortchange Low-income and Minority Students* 68
Fung, Victor 10, 100

Gallup Poll 28, 43, 51, 56
Gardner, Howard 30, 96, 97, 98
Gates, Terry 24, 62
Gault, Brent 51, 81, 83, 104
Geertz, Clifford 10, 13
gender 2, 64, 66, 67, 76, 78, 83, 84, 97, 99, 100,
    104
Gentry, Greg 111
Gerrity, Kevin 79, 83, 131

Gfeller, Kate 79
Giebelhausen, Robin 133
gifted students 70, 76, 79
Gillum, Jack 51
Gilmore, Patrick S. 50
Ginitis, Herbert 33
Goleman, Daniel 110
Gollnick, Donna 4, 5, 7, 8, 9, 12,
    65, 68
Goodenough, W. 7, 8, 9
Goodlad, John 120, 135
Goolsby, Thomas 37, 75, 107, 111
Gordon, Deborah 110
Gordon, Edward 5, 76, 77
Gracey, Harry 104
Grashel, John 96
Green, Lucy 51, 86
Greenwood, Richard 37
Grossman, Pam 127
Grout, Donald 2
Guerrini, Susan 75, 76, 77
Gunderson, I. N. 29

Haack, Paul 45, 56
Hallinan, Maureen 41, 64, 84, 105, 116
Hamann, Donald 68, 76, 78, 80, 110, 131,
    132, 135
Hamilton, Linda 74
Hancock, Carl 113, 131, 132, 135, 137
Hanna Jim 29
Hansot, Elisabeth 48
Hardman, Michael 69, 70
Harrington, Michael 66, 72
Harvard Institute of Politics 133
Haston, Warren 110, 112
Healthy Hunger-Free Kids Act 34
Heath, Julia 13, 51, 81, 114
Hedden, Steve 75, 79, 80
Hellman, Daniel 131
Hendel, Catherine 111
Henry, Michelle 2, 110, 126, 127
Herrnstein, Richard 68
high-stakes testing 40, 41, 42, 72, 74,
    81, 84
Hilgard, Ernest 87
Hinsdale, Burke 34
Hoffer, Thomas 33
Hoffman, Adria 10
Horng, Eileen 127
Hornyak, R. R. 100
Horton, Patrick 79
Hourigan, Ryan 79
Housewright, Wiley 50
Hruska, Bradley 106
Hughes, John 10, 11, 15, 17, 18, 19
Humphreys, Jere 120
Hunt, David 87

immigration 7
Individuals with Disabilities Education Act
    (IDEA), 1, 70, 79
Ing, Marsha 127
Ingersoll, Richard 113, 124, 125, 126, 127, 128,
    129
intelligence 97, 100
interaction theory 19, 20, 21, 32
Isbell, Daniel 51, 110, 112, 122

Jellison, Judith 56, 74, 79, 84
Johnson, Christopher 70, 76, 79, 111
Johnson, G. T. 54, 55
Johnson, Vicky 110
Johnson-Green, Elissa 76, 77, 97, 99
Jones, Brent 121, 122
Jones, R. 29
Jones, Susanne 66, 67, 71
Jorgensen, Estelle 24, 25
Juchniewicz, Jay 110, 111, 114

Kaiser, Keith 112
Kantorski, Victor 80
Kaplan, Max 54, 55, 56
Kaplan's social functions of art 55–6
Keene, James 47, 48, 49, 62, 119
Kelly, Steven 1, 10, 13, 22, 37, 51, 78, 81, 103,
    110, 111, 112, 113, 114, 120, 121, 122, 136
Kelly-McHale, Jacqueline 10
Kennedy, Mary 36, 80, 103, 104, 116
Khadaroo, Stacy 41, 42
Killian, Jan 100, 110, 122
Kinney, Daryl 51, 76, 77, 80, 104
Koza, Julia 98
Kozol, Jonathan 63, 66, 68, 69, 71, 72, 84, 129
Krueger, Patti 112, 113, 132, 137
Kuhn, Terry 30, 109, 116
Kuntz, Tammy 10

Labuta, Joseph 37, 42, 46, 47, 48, 49, 50, 119
Langer, Suzanne 22
Lankford, Hamilton 127
Law & Higher Education 63
learning 86, 87, 88, 100
learning theories 86–8; behavioral 88; of cognitive
    development 89, 91; psychosocial theory of
    development 94, 95; social 88; sociocultural 90;
    stage theory 89; taxonomy of learning 92–4;
    Theory of Multiple Intelligences 96
LeBlanc, Albert 5, 76, 77, 99, 100
Lee, Brianna 7
Lee, Jolie 7, 67
Legette, Roy 80, 108
Lentsch, Mark 59
Leonhard, Charles 22
Leppla, David 76, 78
Levin, Daniel 62, 66, 68, 71, 72

Levin, Rayna 62, 66, 68, 71, 72
Levit, Martin 28, 30, 31, 33, 38, 42, 46, 63, 118
Lind, Vicki 76, 80
Linnenbrink, Elizabeth 106
Lipton, Martin 7, 10, 12, 62, 64, 65, 67, 68, 78
Liske, Kenneth 134
Loeb, Susanna 127
Looking-Glass Self 20
Lorah, Julie 83
Lortie, Dan 2, 46, 48, 113, 118, 122, 126, 127, 129, 135, 136
L'Roy, DiAnn 1, 122
Lubienski, Christopher 73
Lubienski, Sarah 73
Luckmann, Thomas 19
Lyman, Peter 31

Macionis, John 6, 7, 8, 10, 31, 53, 66, 67, 70, 71, 110, 137
McCarthy, Marie 3, 4
McCormick, Theresa 67, 78
McCrary, Jan 99, 100
McKoy, Constance 9
MacLeod, Rebecca 109
McWhirter, Benedict 79
McWhirter, Ellen 79
McWhirter, Jeffries 79
McWhirter, Robert 79
Madsen, Charles 107, 109, 115
Madsen, Clifford 1, 22, 30, 36, 37, 51, 56, 58, 79, 103, 107, 108, 109, 110, 111, 112, 113, 115, 116, 118, 120, 121, 131, 132, 135, 136, 137
Madura, Patrice 110, 111, 112, 123, 132
Maehr, Martin 106
Mandela, Nelson 86
Mann, Horace 38, 48, 62, 63
Marder, Michael 128
Mark, Michael 2, 36, 49, 50, 110, 111, 112, 123, 132
Marsh, Herbert 67, 96
Martin, Peter 10, 11, 15, 17, 18, 19
Marx, Karl 18, 19
Marzano, Robert 41, 68, 72
Maslow, Abraham 108
Maslow's hierarchy of needs 108
Mason, Lowell 22, 48, 57
MayDay Group 25
Mead, George 19, 20, 96
Mehr, Samuel 76, 77
Meir, Kenneth 63, 65, 66, 68
Merker, Bjorn 52, 53, 54, 55
Merriam, Alan 54, 55, 60
Merriam's functions of music 55
Merrill, Elizabeth 124, 125, 126, 127, 129
Merrow, Robert 128
Miksza, Peter 81, 83, 104
Mills, Charlotte 131, 132, 135
Minear, Carolyn 104

Morrison, Kenneth 18
Morrision, Steven 80, 83, 100, 104, 114, 116
Morrow, R. D. 69
motivation 76, 91, 105–8, 112; extrinsic 106; instrinsic 106
Mueller, John 22
Muller, C. 67, 73
multicultural education 9, 10
multiculturalism 8, 9, 13; characteristics of 8, 9; controversial aspects 10; definition of 8
Murray, Charles 68
Mursell, James 22
music 51, 52, 54; ability 76, 77, 97, 98; aptitude 76, 97; development 77, 87, 98, 99; definition 52–4; functions 53, 54, 55, 56; preference 97, 98, 100; role in society 51–2; talent 97; taste 97; theories of origin 52–3
music education 1, 2, 5, 13, 30, 60; equality of opportunity 74; multicultural 9, 13; purposes and roles 5, 36–7; process-orientated 39–40; product-oriented 39–40; re-defining 41, 43, 57–9; role of 56–7
Music Educators National Conference 2, 49, 79, 105, 131
Music Supervisors National Conference 49
musicking 57

Nakamura, J. 106
Napoles, Jessica 109
National Assessment of Education Progress 83
National Association for Music Education 2, 37, 49, 62, 109, 132
National Association of Music Merchants 43, 51
National Association of Schools of Music 123
National Association of Social Workers 83
National Center for Educational Statistics 11, 13, 66, 68, 69, 72, 73, 74, 81, 105, 129, 131
National Coalition for Core Arts Standards 109
National Commission on Teaching and America's Future 127
National Conference for Community and Justice 10
National Core Arts Standards 2
National Dropout Prevention Center/Network 105
National Education Association 123
National Education Commission on Time and Learning 75
National Forum on Educational Statistics 72
National School Boards Association 128
National Standards for Arts Education 2, 109, 125
Nettl, Bruno 45, 52, 53, 54, 55, 60
Nierman, Glen 103, 104
No Child Left Behind 28, 34, 35, 41, 63, 72, 73, 81, 82, 83, 118, 125, 126
norm 4, 8, 11

Oakes, Jeannie 7, 10, 12, 62, 64, 65, 67, 68, 78
Obama, Michelle 34

objectivism 21, 32
Olsen, Laurie 10
operant conditioning 88
Orman, Evelyn 133
Overberg, Paul 7
Ozimek, Adam 125

Palisca, Claude 2
parental influences 65, 76, 77, 82, 99, 104
Perda, David 129
Papandrea, Mary-Rose 133
Parkes, Kelly 121, 122
Paul, Stephen 112, 122
Payne, Phillip 131
Peikof, Leonard 21, 22
Pemberton, Carol 22, 49
Pew Research Poll 31, 62
Pflederer, Marilyn 90
Phi Delta Kappa 28
Phillips, D. 66
Piaget, Jean 89, 90, 91, 94, 96, 98, 116
Pintrich, Paul 106, 107
Plato 2
Pole 63, 66
Porter, Susan 76, 78
Praxis exam 126
prejudice 65
Price, Harry 111
Progressive Era 49

race 2, 67–9, 76, 78–9, 83, 84, 98, 99, 100, 103, 104
Race to the Top 1, 28, 34, 41, 72, 82, 83, 125, 128
Radocy, Rudolf 51, 52, 53, 54, 57, 77, 87, 97, 98, 99, 100
Raiber, Michael 110, 112, 114, 122, 125, 132, 135
Rand, Ayn 21
Ravitch, Diane 41, 42, 63, 72, 128
Raywid, Mary Anne 70
Regan, Ronald 2
Regelski, Thomas 23, 25
Reimer, Bennett 22, 25, 102
relativism 22
Renzetti, Claire 64, 65, 66, 67, 73
Report of the National Commission on Teaching and America's Future 126
Riley, Patricia 75
Rohwer, Deborah 110
Roberts, Brian 1, 110, 122
Robinson, Charles 78, 113
Robinson, Matthew 83
Robinson, Nicole 63, 65, 78, 80, 113, 119, 125
Ross, Janell 7
Rueda, Robert 110, 111
Russell, Joshua 110, 112

Sadker, David 66, 67
Sadker, Myra 66, 67

Salvador, K. 79
Sanders, Elizabeth 83
Scanland, K. 29
Scheib, Joe 130, 131, 132, 135
Schmidt, Charles 108
school choice 72, 73, 81, 82
schooling instructional concept 38, 39
school reform 41, 72, 83
schools 31, 32, 71, 72; charter 72, 81, 82; homeschools 72, 73, 82; inequality within 71–4; magnet 72, 81, 82; relation to society 4; parochial schools 72; private 72, 73, 74, 82; virtual schools 72; vouchers 73, 74
Scott, John 7, 8, 16, 17, 18, 66
Schultz, Sara 33, 100
Schunk, Dale 107
Schwadron, Abraham 22
Schwandt, T. A. 19
Seidel, Aly 128
self-fulfilling prophecy 71, 105
Serow, Robert 46, 63, 73, 126, 130, 132, 133, 135
Sharrock, Wes 10, 11, 15, 17, 18, 19
Shaw, Julia 10
Shellahamer, Bentley 37
Sherrill, Carolyn 99, 100
Shieh, Eric 83
Shulman, Lee 109
Siebenaler, Dennis 100
Silveira, Jason 109
Silverman, Marissa 25, 39
Simpson, Michael 133
Sims, Wendy 100
singing schools 47
Skadsem, Julie 111
Skinner, B. F. 88
Sloboda, John 77, 98, 99, 106
Small, Christopher 54, 57
Smith, Deborah 37, 42, 46, 47, 48, 49, 50, 119
Smith, Thomas 113, 127
social behaviorism 20
social intelligence 110
socialization 10, 11, 12, 13, 66, 78; agents of 11, 71, 118
social justice 10, 83
social media 133
social reproduction 19
social theories 15–16
society 3, 5–8, 9, 10, 12, 13, 16, 17, 18, 19, 20, 25, 94, 97; diversity 7, 9, 12; melting pot concept 7, 8, 9, 10; pluralistic concept 7, 8, 9, 10
socioeconomics 2, 11, 62, 66, 68, 73, 76, 80, 82, 83, 84, 104
sociological theories 15
sociology 1, 2, 3, 5, 6, 7, 12, 15
Soltis, Jonas 11, 12, 63
sorting machine model 63, 74, 75, 76
Sousa, John Philip 50
Spade, Joan 3, 15, 17, 20, 118, 137

Spearman, Carlesta 104
spiral curriculum 91
Spring, Joel 2, 29, 30, 31, 33, 34, 35, 41, 42, 48, 51,
    62, 64, 66, 67, 72, 74, 81, 82, 111, 112, 119, 123,
    125, 126, 129, 130, 131, 133, 134, 135
Sputnik 50
Standley, Jane 108, 110, 111
status attainment 33; cultural capital 33; human
    capital 33; social capital 33
STEAM 38, 43
Stecher, Brian 74
STEM 38
stereotypes 65, 78, 98
Stewart, C. 103, 104
Stewart, Joseph 63, 65, 66, 68
Stillman, Jamy 110, 111
students,103, 104; characteristics of 103; dropout
    rates of 66, 105; motivating 105–8, 112; with
    disabilities 69–70, 79–80, 83
Sullivan, Edmund 87
Sullivan, Jill 112, 122
Swift, David 5, 63, 64

Tallahassee Democrat 105
Tanglewood Declaration and the Goals and
    Objectives (GO) Project 50
Tanglewood Symposium 45, 50
Task Force on Teaching as a Profession 131
teacher 13, 70, 71, 86, 136, 137, 138;
    accountability 128; concept of 119, 123;
    effective characteristics of 102, 108–12, 116–17;
    expectations 90, 91, 92, 94, 97, 100, 118–19;
    extended contracts 130; identity 121, 122;
    influences 70–1, 75, 76, 80; roles 104, 120; stress
    131–2; tenure contracts 129–30; unions 123
teacher certification 126–8; alternative 126, 127;
    national board 126; traditional 126
teacher salaries 129–31, 136; career ladder/
    stepladder 129, 130; merit pay 128, 130;
    performance-based 130
Teach for America 125, 128
teaching profession 120; challenges to 124–6; legal
    issues 132–5
Teachout, David 110, 112, 114, 122, 125, 132, 135
Thayer, Victor 28, 30, 31, 33, 38, 42, 46, 63, 118
theory 15
Theory of Multiple Intelligences 96
Thorndike, Edward 88
Thornton, Arland 65, 66, 67, 71
Thorton, Linda 120
Title IX, 66
Tobe, Pamela 127, 130
Toppo, Greg 7, 51
tracking 19, 76

transfer 92
Tyack, David 48
Tyler, B. 96

Upton, Jodi 51
USA Today 105
U.S. Census 7, 31, 67
U.S. Department of Education 35, 36, 38, 41, 67,
    69, 70, 72, 73, 81, 82
U.S. Department of Health and Human Services
    34
U.S. Department of Labor 29, 32
utilitarian theory 23, 39

Valsiner, Jaan 4, 6, 8
value-added modeling 128
VanWeelden, Kimberly 10, 79, 110
Varian, Hal 31
Vat-Chromy, Jo-Anne 11
Veak, Michael 103, 104
Veenman, Simon 112
Vision 2020: The Housewright Symposium
    on Music Education 22, 45, 50, 56,
    79, 109
Vygotsky, Lev 90, 91

Wales, Roger 77
Walker, Linda 68, 76, 78, 80
Waller, Willard 1, 2, 135, 136
Wallin, Nils 52, 53, 54, 55
Walster, E. 110, 111
Wayman, John 110, 122
Wayman, V. E. 103
Weber, Max 18, 19, 32
Weiner, Bernard 107
West, Chad 83
Whipple, Jennifer 79
Whitaker, Jennifer 133
Wiggins, Jackie 86, 88, 116
Wilson, Sarah 77
Wolfe, David 77
Woodford, Paul 2, 36, 37, 58, 63, 81
Woody, Robert 134
Woolfolk, Anita 66, 67, 69, 70, 88, 90,
    91, 95, 97, 98, 105, 106, 107, 109, 112, 115
Wyckoff, James 127

Yarbrough, Cornelia 110, 111, 133

Zdzinski, Stephen 75, 76, 77, 99
Zernike, Kate 29
Zimmerman, M. 66
Zone of Proximal Development 90
Zukerman, Mortiman 38